Excel 2000
An Introductory Course for Students

Excel 2000
An Introductory Course for Students

Jim Muir

Senior Lecturer in Business Computing

Bournemouth University

Learning Matters

Windows 98™ and Excel™ © Microsoft Corporation, all rights reserved. Screen displays from Excel 2000 and Windows 98 reprinted with permission from Microsoft Corporation.

First published in 2001 by Learning Matters Ltd.

All rights reserved. No part of this publication may be reproduced, stored in a retrieval system, or transmitted in any form or by any means, electronic, mechanical, photocopying, recording, or otherwise, without prior permission in writing of Learning Matters.

© Jim Muir

British Library Cataloguing in Publication Data
A CIP record for this book is available from the British Library.

ISBN 1 903300 16 9

Cover and text design by Code 5 Design Associates Ltd
Project management by Deer Park Productions
Typeset by PDQ Typesetting
Printed and bound in Great Britain by The Baskerville Press Ltd, Salisbury, Wiltshire.

Learning Matters Ltd
58 Wonford Road
Exeter EX2 4LQ
Telephone 01392 215560
Email: info@learningmatters.co.uk
www.learningmatters.co.uk

Contents

Learning with this book		vii
Topic 1.	Finding Your Way Around Excel	1
Topic 2.	Creating Your First Worksheet	19
Topic 3.	Printing, Formatting and Copying your Worksheet	35
Topic 4.	Further Worksheet Activities	48
Topic 5.	Excel Charts	55
Topic 6.	Formatting, Copying and Naming Charts	65
Topic 7.	Further Chart Skills	75
Topic 8.	Excel Databases	88
Topic 9.	Using Linked Worksheets	100
Topic 10.	Linking and Copying Workbooks	109
Topic 11.	Using Tables and Goal Seek	114
Topic 12.	Using Functions	123
Topic 13.	Introduction to Macros	131
Topic 14.	Excel on the Web	140
Appendices		147
Index		151

Titles in this series

This is one of a series of course books for students, covering the three major components of the Microsoft Office 2000 suite of software.

Access 2000
An Introductory Course for Students
Sue Coles and Jenny Rowley
ISBN 1 903300 14 2

Access 2000
An Advanced Course for Students
Sue Coles and Jenny Rowley
ISBN 1 903300 15 0

Excel 2000
An Introductory Course for Students
Jim Muir
ISBN 1 903300 16 9

Excel 2000
An Advanced Course for Students
Jim Muir
ISBN 1 903300 17 7

Word 2000
An Introductory Course for Students
Sue Coles and Jenny Rowley
ISBN 1 903300 18 5

Word 2000
An Advanced Course for Students
Sue Coles and Jenny Rowley
ISBN 1 903300 19 3

To order, please contact our distributors:
Plymbridge Distributors, Estover Road, Plymouth, PL6 7PY.
Tel: 01752 202301   Fax: 01752 202333   Email: orders@plymbridge.com

Learning with this book

This book introduces Excel 2000, the latest version of Microsoft's Excel spreadsheet software. Excel is a component of the Office 2000 suite of application software, which also includes Access, Word and PowerPoint. Data can be easily transferred between these different applications.

The book is designed for anyone who wants to learn how to use Excel. This includes students in further, higher and adult education, as well as employees of an organisation. Students who might benefit from this book are likely to be learning spreadsheets as part of an accounting, business studies, social sciences, information systems, management studies, or marketing course. It has been written for people who have little or no previous knowledge of Excel and makes no assumptions about learners' previous experience of either computing, business or accounting. Both the Excel skills and the examples used are explained in simple terms, and the author has avoided examples where specialised skill or knowledge are required.

If you have completed this book and need to extend your Excel skills you may like to try the companion volume *Excel 2000 – An Advanced Course for Students*.

Approach

The underlying philosophy of this book is concerned with learning by doing. It focuses on tasks and activities, and in every Topic the commands, mouse movements and key strokes are thoroughly explained and illustrated with screen shots. You are recommended to work through the topics in sequence, especially the earlier introductory ones, as activities build on skills gained in earlier topics and in some cases use workbooks created previously.

The book is divided into 14 Topics, each one taking up to an hour to complete. Each Topic is based around one or two straightforward examples; the Excel screen shots provided will help you check your learning at key stages. Each Topic concludes with a summary of commands and functions used, and there are also a number of independent tasks for you to check your progress through the units. These could provide the basis for assessment and solutions are provided, where appropriate, as appendices.

Features in the text

The following features have been used throughout the book to make the practical instructions clear:

1. Bold capitals indicate a feature from the screen, for example **BUTTON** or **DIALOG BOX NAME**.
   Menu instructions are also presented this way: **EDIT-COPY** means choose **COPY** from the **EDIT** menu.

2. White bold capitals in a panel indicate the names of keys on the keyboard, for example **ESC** or **F1**.

3. Bold text in upper and lower case indicates names of **Fields**, **Tables**, **Queries**, **Forms** and **Reports**.

4. Italic text on a shaded background indicates *Text to be keyed in*.

Online Copies of the Workbooks

The Excel workbooks created in this book can be obtained free of charge from the publisher's website **www.learningmatters.co.uk**

TOPIC 1

Finding your way around Excel

Introduction

In this topic we will cover the basics of starting up Excel, identifying the various parts of the worksheet, working with windows and the mouse, selecting cell ranges and using the Help features. If you have never used Excel before, go through these preliminaries very carefully. Don't be afraid to try things out and make mistakes, you will learn how to correct them for yourself.

Topic objectives

- To start up and exit Excel.
- To identify the components of the Excel window.
- To change the size of the Excel window.
- To learn mouse actions.
- To select cell ranges and menu options.
- To use Excel Help and Office Assistant.

Starting up Excel

Most Excel 2000 users are still using the Windows 98 operating system at the moment, but by the time you use this book Windows 2000 – the latest version – may well be installed on your PC. Don't worry as this will make little, if any, difference to the start-up instructions that follow.

There are different ways to start up Excel, depending on how it has been installed on your PC. These instructions will cover most setups.

 The Windows Desktop. If your PC is turned on then Windows will start up automatically. This screen will resemble Figure 1.1 below.

This is the Windows desktop – the starting screen from which you carry out all Windows activities. Your desktop will look different to this, depending on which programs, options, shortcuts etc have been installed. All of these features are represented as *icons* – small pictures of the items.

At the bottom of the desktop is the *Taskbar*; as well as holding a number of small icons it always shows the *Start button* on the left and the current time on the right. It is called the Taskbar because it also shows any tasks that are currently running, eg programs or open files. We will use this feature later.

Topic 1 · Finding your way around Excel

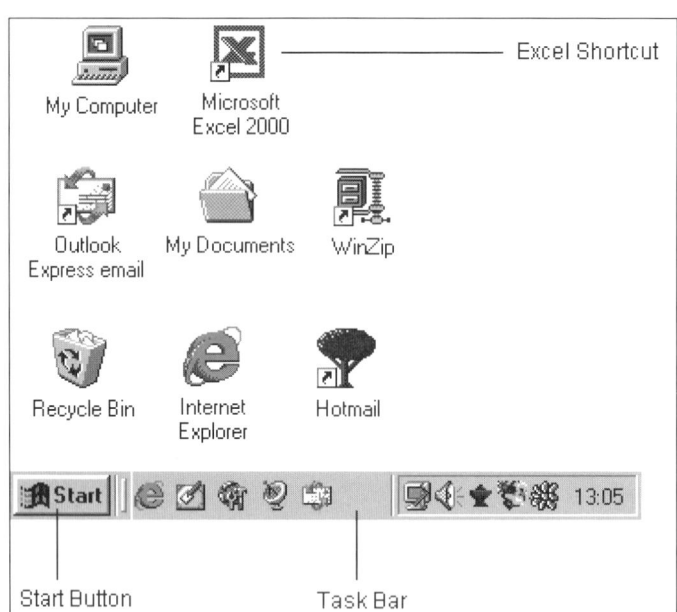

FIGURE 1.1

When you move the mouse on your desk an arrow-shaped pointer moves around the desktop; this is the *screen pointer* or *cursor*.

② **Using an Excel Shortcut**. First look for an Excel icon on the desktop labelled 'Microsoft Excel 2000', 'Office 2000', 'Shortcut to Excel' etc, as in Figure 1.1 above.

Move the mouse so that the screen pointer moves on top of the Excel icon, then click the *left* mouse button twice in quick succession. Excel should now start to load up – if so go to section 3d. If not try clicking the left mouse button more quickly!

③ **Using the Start Menu**.

a. Move the mouse so that the screen pointer is located on top of the **START** button. Click the left mouse button once.

b. A *pop-up menu* opens, displaying a number of options. Choosing menu options can be tricky at first, so if you make a mistake and select the wrong option simply start again. To cancel menus use the mouse to move the screen pointer off the menu and click the left mouse button once – the menu closes.

If you select the wrong option and a window opens then cancel it by clicking the **Close** button, marked with a cross, at the top right of the window – see Figure 1.3.

c. Move the screen pointer onto the menu option **PROGRAMS** – a further menu opens – it will resemble Figure 1.2, but the specific options will depend on how your PC has been set up.

d. The next options that you choose will depend on whether you have all the Microsoft Office 2000 set of programs installed, or just Excel 2000.

Office 2000 Users: Move the screen pointer onto the menu option **MICROSOFT OFFICE**. A further menu window will open, move the screen pointer onto **MICROSOFT EXCEL** and click the left mouse button.

Topic I · Finding your way around Excel

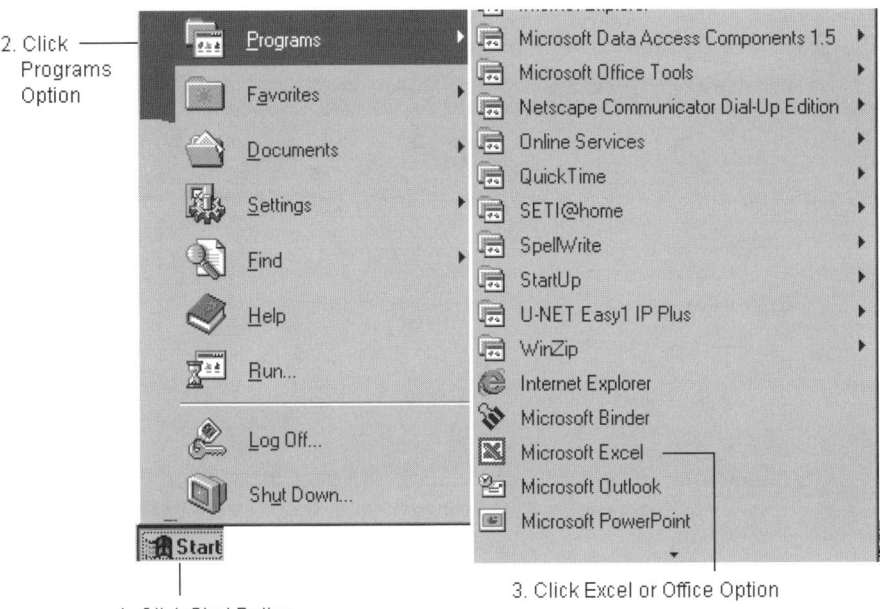

FIGURE 1.2

2. Click Programs Option
1. Click Start Button
3. Click Excel or Office Option

Excel 2000 Users: Move the screen pointer onto the menu option **MICROSOFT EXCEL 2000** and click the left mouse button.

e. Excel will begin to load up and the screen pointer changes to an hour-glass symbol. While loading takes place the version of Excel and licensing details are displayed, so if in doubt check you have Excel 2000 installed.

When loading is complete a blank Excel worksheet screen is displayed.

The Excel window

① Overview

An Excel worksheet is like a large sheet of paper, divided into vertical columns and horizontal rows. Where columns and rows intersect they form *cells* where you can enter data. A *workbook* contains a number of *worksheets* like the pages in a book – Sheet1, Sheet2 etc. If you look at the Excel window shown below in Figure 1.3 it consists of two windows:

The *Application Window* is round the outside and holds all the Excel commands, menus, toolbars etc.

The *Document Window* is inside the Application window and contains the worksheet columns and rows and other features, eg sheet numbers and scroll bars.

② Before we begin let's take a few minutes to identify the following Excel features, as shown in Figure 1.3. We will not be using the mouse or keyboard at this stage.

The Excel window on your PC may well look slightly different but you should still be able to identify these elements:

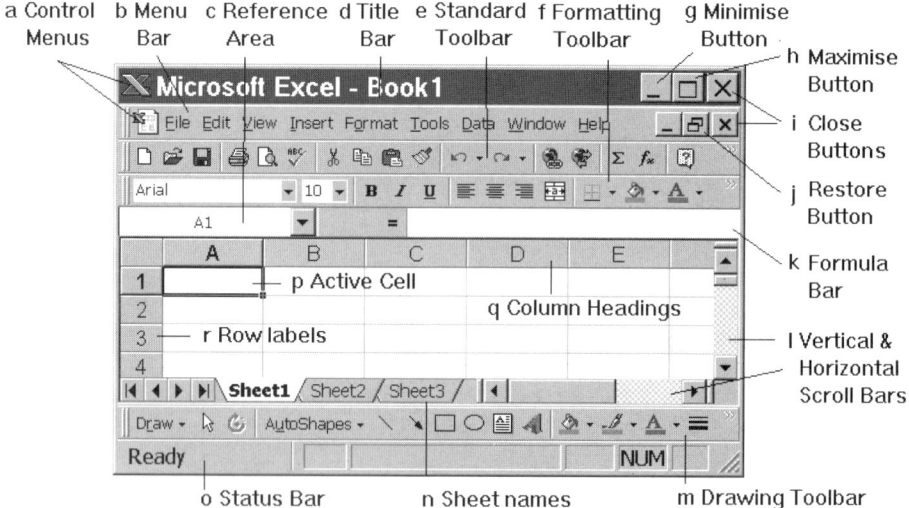

FIGURE 1.3

a. **Control Menus** offer options to move, close and re-size windows.

b. **Menu Bar**. The Menu Bar is at the top of the window and offers a number of options – File, Edit, View etc. As we will see all the major Excel commands can be selected from these menus.

c. **Reference Area**. Gives the row and column reference of the cell that is currently selected. In Figure 1.3 it is cell A1 – see section p below.

d. **Title Bar**. When you start Excel it will automatically open a new workbook with a temporary or default name Book1. If you open another workbook during the same session it is named Book2 etc. This name is changed when you save the workbook under a permanent name.

e. & f. **Toolbars**. Immediately below the menu bar are two toolbars displaying various buttons. When you click a button you can carry out a particular task, eg opening and saving files, copying, printing, formatting etc. Often buttons offer alternative ways of issuing commands to the Menu Bar. Excel offers a large number of toolbars, but the two normally displayed are the **Standard** toolbar and the **Formatting** toolbar. A labelled diagram of the buttons on these toolbars is included at the end of this topic. This book tends to concentrate on menu commands rather than their button equivalent.

Buttons g – j control the size of the window and are features of all Windows applications. You may see two sets, one to control the inner worksheet document, and one for the overall application.

g. **The Minimise Button** (shown as a line) shrinks the window to a button on the Taskbar.

h. **The Maximise Button** (shown as a square) enlarges the window to fill the whole screen.

i. **The Close Button** (shown as an 'X') closes either the workbook if you click the lower of the two **CLOSE** buttons, or the whole Excel application if you click the upper of the two **CLOSE** buttons. If you click this button by

Topic 1 · Finding your way around Excel

mistake then you will need to re-open the workbook or the Excel application.

j. **The Restore Button** (shown as overlapping squares) restores the window to its original size, eg the size it was before it was maximised.

k. **The Formula Bar** will display the contents of whatever cell is currently selected – the 'active' cell – see section p below. Figure 3.1 shows a new workbook so all the cells are blank.

l. **Vertical and Horizontal Scroll Bars** are features of all windows and allow you to move to parts of the worksheet currently not in view. As a worksheet can consist of thousands of cells the window can only show a small proportion of them.

m. **The Drawing Toolbar** may be displayed. You can use it to add standard shapes to your worksheet, as well as altering text style and colour effects.

n. **Sheet Names**. A workbook holds a number of worksheets; each one has a default name – Sheet1, Sheet2 etc. These temporary names can be changed, as we will see later. To identify it each sheet has a name *tab* – the name of the sheet currently being used – or 'active' is shown in bold.

o. **The Status Bar** shows the progress of any commands, operations etc currently being executed; it displays a 'Ready' message when no commands are executing.

p. **The Active Cell** is the cell currently in use, identified by a heavy border; in Figure 3.1 this is cell A1.

q. **Column Headings and** r, **Row Headings**. Columns are identified by letters and rows by numbers. The cell reference or address, eg A1, D5, is given in the Reference Area – see section c above.

④ The rest of this topic gives you practice in trying out some of these basic Excel features – refer to Figure 1.3 if necessary.

⑤ **Minimising a Window**. As mentioned previously the Excel window really consists of two windows, each of which can be re-sized independently of the other. We will experiment with minimising and restoring the window size.

a. Using the mouse, place the screen pointer on the topmost **MINIMISE** button (marked with a single line) at the top right of the window and click the left mouse button. Excel shrinks to a button on the Windows Taskbar. This button shows that Excel is still running as a 'task' – see Figure 1.4.

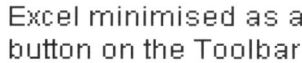

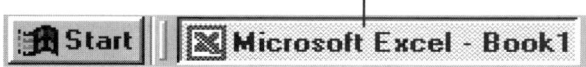

FIGURE 1.4

b. To restore the Excel window to its previous size, place the screen pointer on the **EXCEL** button on the Taskbar and click the left mouse button once. The Excel window is displayed again.

(6) ***Troubleshooting***: If you are ever in the situation where you can't see the Excel button on the Taskbar do the following:

   a. Press the **ALT** key bottom left of the keyboard.

   b. Press the **TAB** key – on the left of the keyboard, marked with two opposite-facing arrows. A window opens showing the various tasks that are currently running.

   c. Still holding down the **ALT** key press the **TAB** key again until Excel is selected.

   d. Release the **TAB** then the **ALT** key and Excel is re-displayed.

(7) Maximising and Restoring the Excel Application Window.

   a. First check whether the Excel window is displaying two sets of Maximise, Minimise and Close buttons – see Figure 1.5. The top set of buttons control the Application Window and the lower set the Document Window (this is explained in section 1 above).

   b. If the topmost set of buttons contains a **MAXIMISE** button then use the mouse to move the screen pointer onto it and click the left mouse button – the Excel window enlarges to the whole screen.

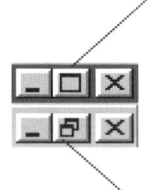

FIGURE 1.5

Maximise button shows that outer window can be maximised

Restore button shows that inner window is maximised already

   c. If the topmost set of buttons contains a **RESTORE** button then click it with the left mouse button (see Figure 1.5) – the window is 'restored' to a smaller size. Exactly what this size is will depend on what you (or a previous user) have previously set it to – see section 9 below. Maximise the window before proceeding with the next section.

(8) Maximising and Restoring the Excel Document Window. Let's try out the lower set of buttons which control the size of the workbook rather than the whole Excel application.

   a. If the lower set of buttons contains a **RESTORE** button then click it with the left mouse button (see Figure 1.5) – the document window is 'restored' to a smaller size. The Restore button on the document window now becomes a Maximise button.

   b. Try this out again until you get the idea, remembering that if the **RESTORE** button is displayed then the window must already be maximised and can only be 'restored' to its previous size. Conversely if the **MAXIMISE** button is displayed the window is at its smaller 'restored' size and can be maximised.

c. Now click the **MINIMISE** button on the lower of the two sets of buttons – the document window shrinks so that only the Title Bar is visible, leaving the outer document window unaffected – see Figure 1.6.

Click the **RESTORE** button on the minimised window to restore it.

FIGURE 1.6

9 **Re-sizing Windows**. You can adjust a window to any size by '**dragging**' the sides.

a. Use the mouse to move the screen pointer until it is located on the bottom right-hand edge of the inner **document** window – see Figure 1.7. The screen pointer will change to a double-headed arrow shape when you have correctly placed it on the corner.

b. *Note*: If you cannot see the edge of the document window then click the **RESTORE** button on the document window (ie on the lower of the 2 sets of buttons).

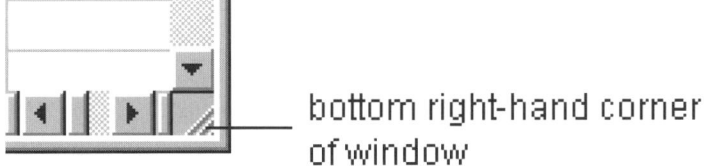

bottom right-hand corner of window

FIGURE 1.7

c. Now hold down the left mouse button.

d. Keeping the mouse button pressed down, drag the edge of the worksheet diagonally up towards the top left of the window.

e. When you reach cell **D8** let go of the mouse button. Check that the document window is like Figure 1.8.

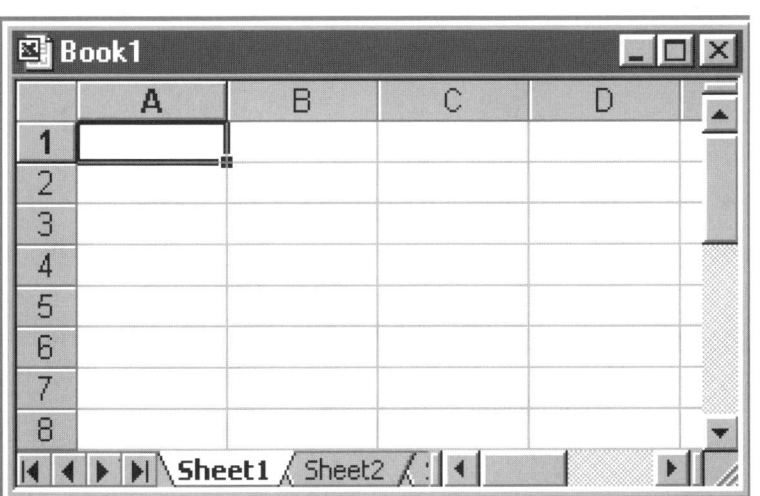

FIGURE 1.8

f. Now use the same dragging technique to re-size the outer **application** window so that it fits around the document window – see Figure 1.9. You may need to click the **RESTORE** button on the topmost set of buttons first.

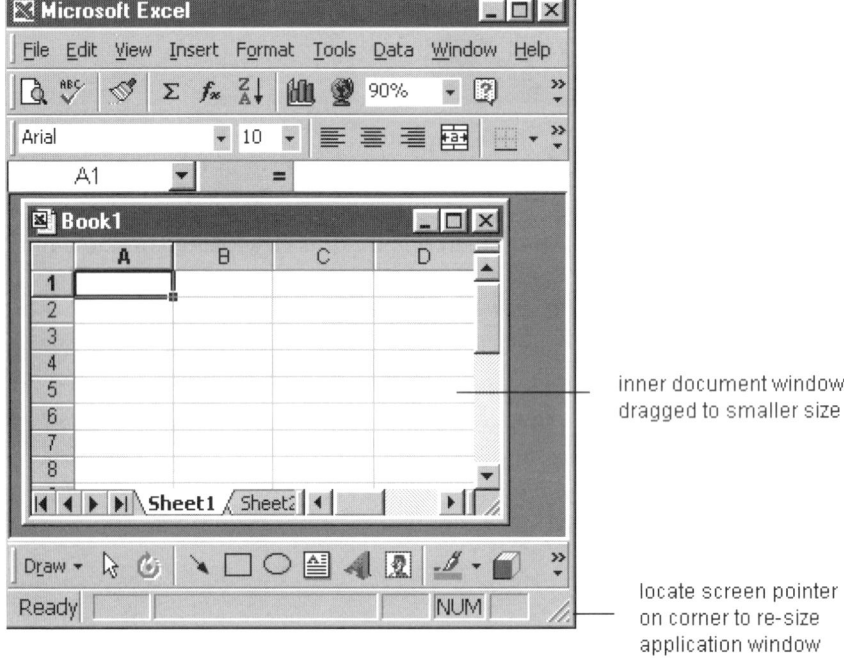

FIGURE 1.9

inner document window dragged to smaller size

locate screen pointer on corner to re-size application window

g. Now enlarge the both the windows by dragging the right hand corners outwards.

h. Experiment with dragging the sides of the windows as well as the corners; you can adjust the horizontal and vertical size independently.

10 **Moving Windows**. You cannot move a window if it is maximised, so first ensure that both the application window and the document window are in 'restored' size – click the **RESTORE** buttons if not.

a. Use the mouse to move the screen pointer onto the Title Bar of the *outer* Application Window, it is normally dark blue and should have the title 'Microsoft Excel'.

b. Holding down the left mouse button drag the mouse and the whole window can be moved to a new position on the desktop.

c. Use the same technique to move the inner document window too.

11 **Mouse Actions**. You have now learnt two of the standard mouse actions:

a. **(left) clicking** – use the mouse to locate the screen pointer, then press the left mouse button once. Usually this is simply referred to as clicking.

b. **dragging** – use the mouse to locate the screen pointer, then hold down the left button while moving the mouse.

Later in this topic we will be learning the two other standard mouse actions:

Topic I · Finding your way around Excel

c. **double clicking** – locate the screen pointer and quickly press the mouse button twice.

d. **right clicking** – locate the screen pointer and press the right mouse button once.

From now on I shall be using these four terms to refer to these standard mouse actions.

12 **Scrolling Around the Excel Window**. There are a number of ways you can move to different parts of the worksheet; we will briefly review all of them, using Figure 1.10 as a reference guide to the vertical scroll bar:

a. Maximise the inner and outer windows. Move the screen pointer onto the **VERTICAL SCROLL BAR** and click the **DOWN ARROW** button once. The worksheet scrolls up a row at a time and the row numbers on the left of the window change to reflect this.

b. Keep the screen pointer on the **DOWN ARROW** button and this time keep the left mouse button pressed down – the rows scroll up continuously.

c. Reverse the scrolling using the **UP ARROW** button – eventually row 1 will appear again at the top of the worksheet window.

d. The rectangular box on the vertical scroll bar is called the *scroll box* – see Figure 1.10. Use the screen pointer to drag this box and the worksheet cells scroll up or down more quickly. A scroll *tip* box shows the row that will appear at the top of the window when you release the mouse button.

e. Now move the screen pointer on a blank part of the vertical toolbar and click. Depending whether you click above or below the scroll box the rows will scroll up or down, a screenful at a time.

f. Now try out operations a to e using the **HORIZONTAL** scroll bar which controls the scrolling of worksheet columns.

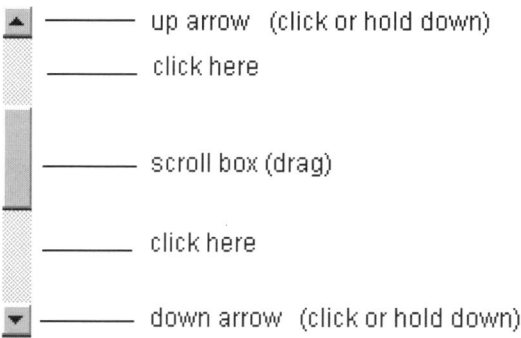

FIGURE 1.10

13 **Scrolling Using the Keyboard**. You can also change the position of columns and rows by holding down the **CTRL** key on the keyboard and various other keys. Try the following; in the operations that follow I use, eg, the convention **CTRL – HOME** to indicate that the Ctrl key should be held down while the second key is pressed.

a. Press the **CTRL – HOME** keys – this will always return you to the top of the worksheet and make A1 the active cell.

Topic I · Finding your way around Excel

b. Press the **CTRL** key then the **DOWN ARROW** key and the last row of the worksheet is displayed. If any of the lower rows contained data then this row would be displayed.

c. Press **CTRL – RIGHT ARROW** and the last column of the worksheet is displayed.

d. Now try **CTRL – LEFT ARROW** followed by **CTRL – UP ARROW** and the top of the worksheet is re-displayed. The **PAGE UP** and **PAGE DOWN** keys can also be used without the **CTRL** key.

Note: These keys are very useful, especially when you are first learning Excel and the data that you have entered seems to have disappeared. Often you have accidentally used one of the scroll bars and the data has scrolled out of view.

14 **Selecting Individual Cells.** Make sure that the worksheet window is maximised and then press **CTRL – HOME**. Cell A1 is now the selected or 'active' cell.

a. Click cell **B3** – it is now selected as the active cell and its reference is confirmed in the reference box – check this.

b. Now select cells **G10**, **C17** and **H13**.

c. Now using the scrolling controls, select the following cells currently not in view – **N91**, **BQ141** and **M304**.

15 **Selecting Cell Ranges.** Now let's try selecting groups or *ranges* of cells:

a. Place the screen pointer on cell **B2** and, using the left mouse button, drag down and across to cell **D8**. When you release the mouse button 21 cells should be selected – see Figure 1.11. This is a fairly precise mouse movement and may require some practice.

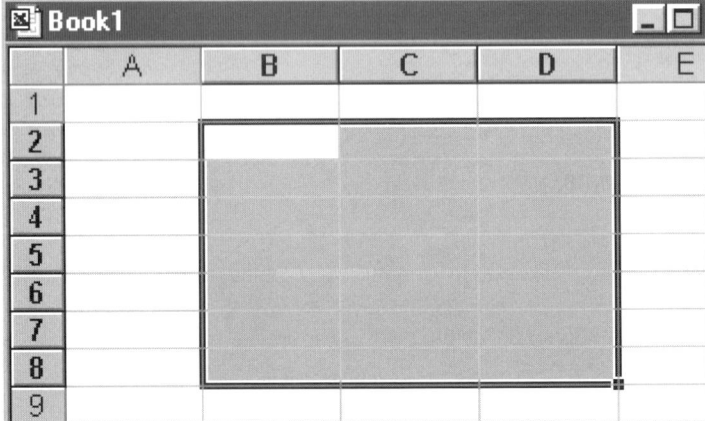

FIGURE 1.11

b. B2 is the active cell and remains white while the others go dark. The cell and column labels of the cell range selected (B – D and 2 – 8) appear in bold.

c. *De-select* the cell range – click anywhere on the worksheet.

(16) **Selecting Columns and Rows.** The letters and numbers identifying column and rows are called *designators*. Clicking or dragging on them can select a single column/row or a range respectively. Try this:

   a. Click the column designator for column B – all the cells in the column are selected.

   De-select by clicking anywhere on the worksheet.

   b. Use the mouse pointer to drag down on row designators 4 and 5 – all the cells in these rows are selected.

   c. Try selecting a few more individual columns/rows and ranges.

(17) **Moving Between Worksheets.** Often a workbook will contain a number of related worksheets. At the bottom of the workbook windows are a number of tabs labelling the different worksheets in the workbook – Sheet1, Sheet2 etc – you may need to enlarge the Excel window if these tabs are not displayed. Click on each tab in turn and the different worksheets are selected; at the moment all the sheets look identical as they contain no data. You can always tell which sheet is currently selected as its name tab appears in bold – see Figure 1.12.

Arrow buttons are placed to the left of the sheet tabs to allow you to move quickly between the different sheets. Experiment with these buttons, returning to Sheet1.

FIGURE 1.12

(18) **Using Excel Menus.** The pull-down menus at the top of the window are common to all Windows-based applications and offer a simple way to select options and issue commands, ie the two steps of 'opening' a menu and selecting an option.

   a. The main options, File, Edit etc, are placed on the *Menu Bar* at the top of the window. Use the mouse and screen pointer to click the word **EDIT**.

   The **EDIT** menu opens displaying a *pull-down* menu – see Figure 1.13. Edit is a typical menu – it offers a set of *options*, each of which executes a command.

   b. To close the **EDIT** menu simply click anwhere on the worksheet.

   c. Open the **EDIT** menu again; this time move the screen pointer onto the **GOTO** option – see Figure 1.13 – and click. A *dialog box* will appear – see Figure 1.14.

   The title of the dialog box should be 'Go To', if not then click the **CLOSE** button or the **CANCEL** button on the dialog box and try again.

(19) **DIALOG BOXES** are another standard Windows feature; they are used when you need to enter some further information before the command that

FIGURE 1.13

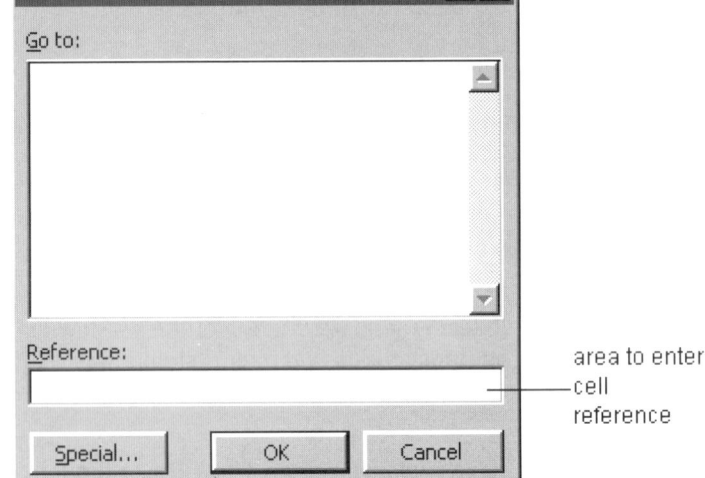

FIGURE 1.14

you have chosen can be executed. Sometimes this information is simply clicking further buttons, eg Yes, No, OK or Cancel, sometimes, as in the case of the Go To option, you will need to enter information from the keyboard.

a. Enter the cell reference **B6** in the Reference box – see Figure 1.14 above. If necessary click the reference section of the dialog box first to place the cursor there.

b. Click the **OK** button on the dialog box and the Go To option goes to cell B6.

 Using Keyboard Shortcut Keys. We saw above in section 13 that you can use combinations of keyboard characters to issue commands. This also applies to menu options. Look at the Menu Bar and you will see that each menu has a letter underlined – File, Edit, View etc. Holding down the **ALT**

Topic I • Finding your way around Excel

key (bottom left of the keyboard) and then typing the underlined letter will open the menu. All the menu options also have an underlined letter and can be executed in a similar way.

Try the following:

a. Hold down the **ALT** key and press the **E** key – the Edit menu opens.

b. Keeping the **ALT** key pressed down press the **G** key – the Go To dialog box opens.

c. Click the **CANCEL** button on the dialog box.

As this is an introductory book we will be using the mouse to make menu selections rather than keyboard shortcuts, which tend to take longer unless you are a competent typist.

21 **Opening Excel Help.** Microsoft no longer provides a full printed guide to Excel, so it is very important that you can use the comprehensive online help and tutorial facilities, provided as part of the Excel application.

a. Click the **HELP** menu on the Menu Bar – see Figure 1.15.

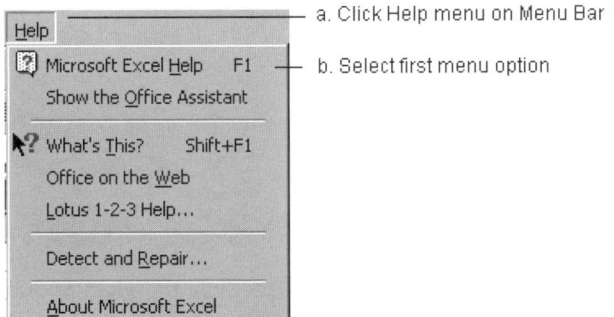

FIGURE 1.15

Click the first option **MICROSOFT EXCEL HELP** and a Help dialog box opens in its own window. You may need to maximise it.

b. At the top left hand corner of the dialog box are three tabs, **CONTENTS**, **ANSWER WIZARD** and **INDEX** – see Figure 1.16. Click each tab in turn and a new frame appears at the left hand side of the window.

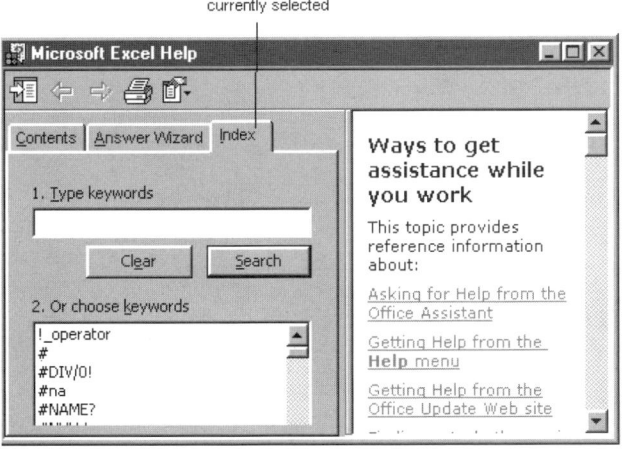

FIGURE 1.16

Topic I · Finding your way around Excel

 Help Contents. When you click the **CONTENTS** tab a number of Help topics are displayed. They are shown as chapters of a book, each of which can be opened by clicking – see Figure 1.17. You may need to use the scroll bars on the contents frame if the book icons are not visible.

    a.   To read one of these topics you need to click the '+' symbol next to the relevant book icon.

           Do this for the topic **GETTING HELP** and the '+' symbol changes to '-' and a number of subtopics are displayed, marked with '?' icons

FIGURE 1.17

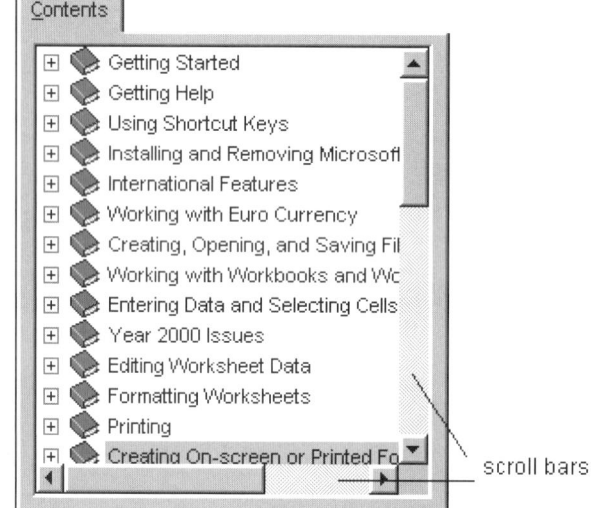

    b.   Click the '?' icons to read one or two of these subtopics; the Help text is displayed in the right hand frame. Finally click on the '-' symbol next to the **GETTING HELP** topic and the topic is closed.

 The Help Index. Click the **INDEX** tab at the top of the Help dialog box – see Figure 1.16 above if necessary.

You will see that the left hand frame is divided into three sections – let's experiment with them for a few minutes.

First let's use the second section, labelled 'Or choose keywords'. This allows us to scroll through an alphabetic list of help topics – see Figure 1.18. We will also use it to try out different ways of scrolling through a list.

FIGURE 1.18

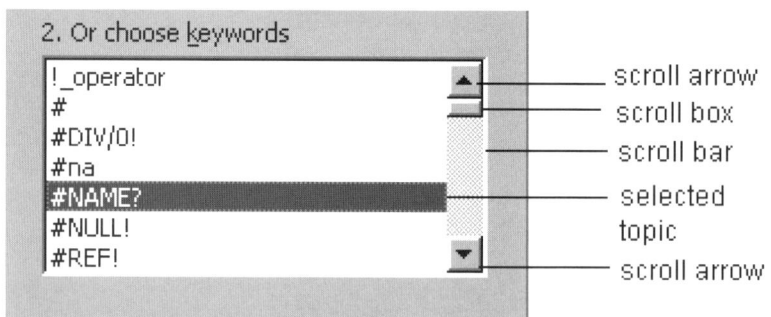

a. Place the screen pointer on the downwards pointing scroll arrow and hold it down – the list of Help topics scrolls continuously. Notice that the scroll box eventually moves too, keeping track of your position in the list.

b. Now try clicking on one of the scroll arrows, rather than holding the button down. The list will scroll more slowly, one line at a time.

c. The scroll box allows more rapid scrolling; first use the mouse to click on the scroll *bar* – either above or below the scroll *box*. The topics scroll in blocks.

d. Finally move the mouse pointer onto the scroll box and drag – you can rapidly scroll from top to bottom of the list.

24 Now scroll down to the topic **MENU** and double click it. Compare your help window with Figure 1.19 and try the following:

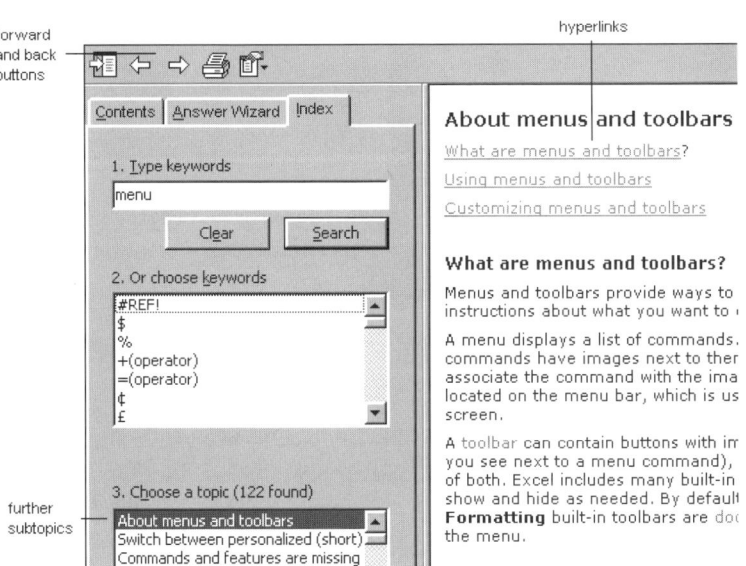

FIGURE 1.19

a. The right hand frame displays help text on the topic that you selected – Menus. Scroll through this text. When you are doing this you will notice various hyperlinks in blue (a common feature of Windows and the World Wide Web). Click on one of them and either a pop-up box or a complete window opens, providing further information or a definition. To close a pop-up box simply click on it; to close a complete window and return to the main help text click the **BACK** button – see Figure 1.19 above. You will find that once hyperlinks have been used their colour changes from blue to maroon.

b. *Note*: **FORWARD** and **BACK** buttons are used on Windows and the World Wide Web pages to re-visit previous pages – see Figure 1.19. If you find that you have gone forward or back too far simply click the appropriate button.

c. Read some of the further subtopics at the bottom left of the help window – see Figure 1.19 above. When you have done this use the **FORWARD** and **BACK** buttons to review the help topics that you have read.

d. Next we will try keying in a help topic rather than scrolling through a list – this is effective if you are fairly sure of your terminology.

Topic I · Finding your way around Excel

First click the **CLEAR** button at the top left of the Help window, then type in a help topic, eg Workbook, and click the **SEARCH** button. Experiment with the hyperlinks and the forward and back buttons.

 Answer Wizard. Excel offers a third Help feature – **ANSWER WIZARD** – which allows you to type the help topic in your own words, eg 'save a workbook'. This is offered as a tab at the left hand side of the Help dialog box. Click this tab.

Now using Figure 1.20 as a guide type the phrase save a workbook, click the **SEARCH** button and then select the topic that best fits your Help requirements.

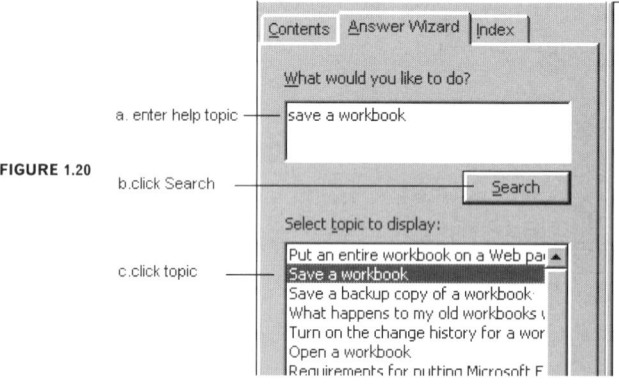

FIGURE 1.20

a. enter help topic
b. click Search
c. click topic

 Exiting Help. Click the **CLOSE** button on the Help window and you are returned to the workbook window.

 The Office Assistant. Open the **HELP** menu and select the menu option **SHOW THE OFFICE ASSISTANT**. The Office Assistant logo, an animated paper clip, is displayed; if necessary click it once to display a dialog box – see Figure 1.21.

a. The Search feature works in a similar way to the Answer Wizard. Simply type a search topic, eg 'tool bars' and then click the **SEARCH** button. The dialog box then shows a number of related topics. Clicking on one of these topics opens the relevant section of Excel Help. You may need to maximise it as before.

b. Close the Help dialog box; the Office Assistant Logo should still be displayed; click it and the **SEARCH** window is displayed again. To close the Office Assistant right click the paperclip logo and select the option **HIDE** from the pop up menu.

FIGURE 1.21

c. ***Note*: Closing Office Assistant**. Once you have used Office Assistant you may find it popping up every time you call up Help. If this gets irritating you can close it. Proceed as follows:

Right click the Office Assistant Logo and select **OPTIONS**. A dialog box appears.

You will see that that a number of options are selected or 'ticked', including 'Use the Office Assistant'.

Click the box next to this option and it is de-selected – the tick disappears.

Finally click the **OK** button and the Office Assistant logo will disappear. To use it again open the **HELP** menu and select the menu option **SHOW THE OFFICE ASSISTANT**.

(28) **Using 'What's This?'** If you forget what a particular Excel item does you can get a 'context sensitive' answer.

Open the **HELP** menu and select the menu option **WHAT'S THIS?**. The screen pointer is now question mark shaped. Click on any feature of the Excel window and a popup window opens, explaining what it does. Click it to hide it. To get help on another feature you must open the Help menu again and re-select What's This?.

(29) **Help on Buttons**. To find out what each button on the toolbar does simply rest the screen pointer on top of the button and a short description appears. **WHAT'S THIS?** will give you a fuller explanation

(30) **Exiting Excel – the Menu Method**. Open the **FILE** menu and select the option **EXIT**. If you have entered some data into the cells of the workbook you will be reminded to save it. If you need to do this then refer to Topic 2, page 27, otherwise click the **NO** button.

(31) **Exiting Excel Using the Close Button**. Open Excel again. This time exit Excel using the topmost **CLOSE** button. Refer to Figure 1.2 if necessary.

Summary of menu and keyboard commands

Notes:

Menu commands show the menu name first, followed by the command to choose from the menu, e.g. **EDIT-CLEAR** means open the Edit menu and select the Clear command.

Keyboard commands use the dash symbol to indicate keys that should be pressed down at the same time, e.g. `CTRL - HOME`

Keyboard commands

`ALT-TAB`	Display which tasks are running
`CTRL-HOME`	Go to cell A1
`CTRL-DOWN ARROW KEY`	Go to last row of the worksheet

Topic I · Finding your way around Excel

CTRL-RIGHT ARROW KEY   Go to last column of worksheet

Menu commands

EDIT-GOTO   Go to specified cell

FILE-EXIT   Exit Excel

HELP-MICROSOFT EXCEL HELP   Call up Help

HELP-SHOW THE OFFICE ASSISTANT   Call up Office Assistant

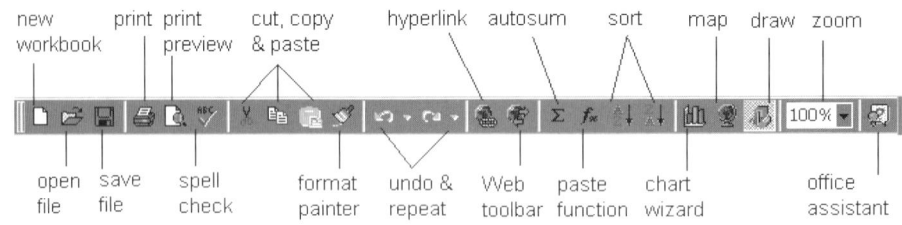

Formatting Toolbar

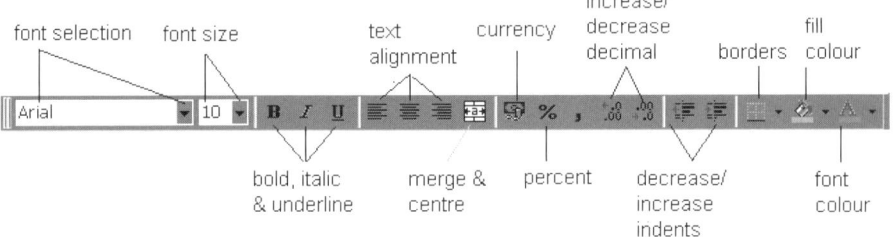

The Drawing Toolbar

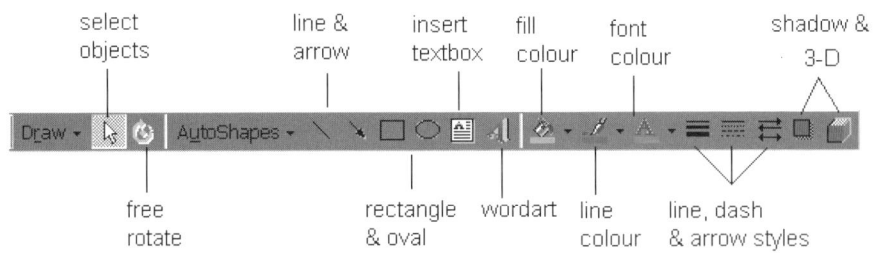

TOPIC 2

Creating your first worksheet

Introduction

This topic shows you how to enter some simple data into a worksheet and how to use formulae and functions to perform calculations. It also shows you how to delete, edit and copy data and how to save, close and open an existing workbook.

Topic objectives

- To enter and amend worksheet data.
- To use the spell checker.
- To adjust the dimensions of columns and rows.
- To make simple calculations using formulae.
- To save a workbook.
- To close and open a workbook.
- To delete worksheet data.
- To copy data using Paste, Fill and AutoFill commands.

Entering data into a worksheet

1 Our first worksheet will be based on the simple example of starting up a small business. The basic income from the business and the areas of expenditure are shown in Figure 2.1:

	A	B	C	D	E	F	G
1			Avon Garden Services - First 10 weeks				
2			Week 1				
3	INCOME						
4	Opening Balance						
5	Bank Loan						
6	Startup Grant						
7	Gardening						
8	Total Income						
9							
10	OUTGOINGS						
11	Food						
12	Accomodation						
13	Van Purchase						
14	Equipment						
15	Travel						
16	Total Outgoings						
17							
18	CLOSING BALANCE						

FIGURE 2.1

Topic 2 · Creating your first worksheet

We will gradually enter more detail for the first 10 weeks of business operation; for the moment enter the data exactly as shown here, it will help you check you have entered it correctly.

2 Use the **MAXIMISE** button to enlarge the workbook windows if necessary – see the previous topic page 6. Also if necessary make sure that **Sheet1** is the active sheet by clicking the sheet tab.

3 **Titles and Labels**.

a. Click cell **C1** so that it becomes the active cell – this is confirmed by the reference C1 displayed in the reference area; the cell will also have a heavy border.

b. Now simply start typing – enter the title shown in Figure 2.1 – **Avon Garden Services – First 10 weeks**. The text will display in the Formula Bar as you type – see Figure 2.2.

c. Next press the **ENTER** key – located on the right of the keyboard and marked with a curled arrow. The title is now displayed across several cells; this is normal.

d. We can now enter the cell labels in column A (a *label* is any text used to label cells). Click cell **A3** and enter the first label **INCOME**.

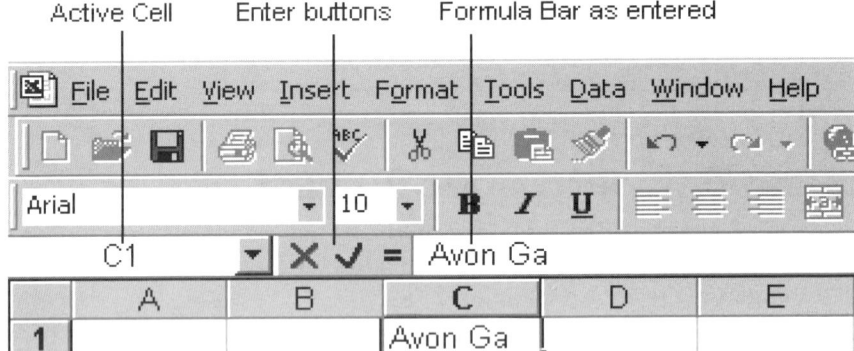

FIGURE 2.2

4 *Notes*: Whenever you enter data into a cell you have to complete the entry. You can do this in any of the following ways:

- press the **ENTER** key
- click another cell
- press an arrow key on the keyboard
- click the green 'tick' box that appears next to the Formula Bar (see Figure 2.2 above)

Text is automatically aligned to the left of the cell.

Forgetting to complete an entry will cause a number of problems, including menu options being dimmed and unavailable. Always check you have completed an entry if your next command fails to work properly.

5 Carry on entering all the cell labels in column A; include the wrong spelling of the word 'Accomodation'. Don't worry if some labels overlap into the next column.

Topic 2 • Creating your first worksheet

(6) **Correcting Errors**: Use the `BACKSPACE` key – this is the key at the top right of the keyboard, marked with a reverse arrow – to correct any errors that you notice whilst completing an entry. If you have just finished entering the data then use the **UNDO** button on the Standard Toolbar to remove it (see key at the end of previous topic).

Don't worry about errors that you notice at a later stage – we will correct them in later sections.

(7) **The Spell Checker**. First click on cell A1 then click the **SPELLING** button on the Standard toolbar; it is marked with a tick and 'ABC' – a small label appears to identify it – see Figure 2.3.

FIGURE 2.3

Excel checks all the text with its dictionary and a dialog box opens, telling you, eg, that 'Accomodation' is not in the dictionary as it has been misspelt with only one 'm'. Excel suggests the correct spelling. Click the **CHANGE** button.

A dialog box will inform you that all the text has been checked, click the **OK** button.

Note: Spell Checkers will also pick out most abbreviations and proper names for correction. You can click the **IGNORE** button or you can add frequently used words to the dictionary using the **ADD** button.

(8) **Using AutoCorrect**. Common errors such as misspelt words can be automatically corrected for you as you type. Click the menu **TOOLS** on the Menu Bar.

Select the option **AUTOCORRECT** and a dialog box appears – see Figure 2.4.

As you can see the dialog box offers to correct a number of common errors. If the various options are 'checked' or ticked then it is already turned on. An option can be turned off by clicking an option box to de-select it.

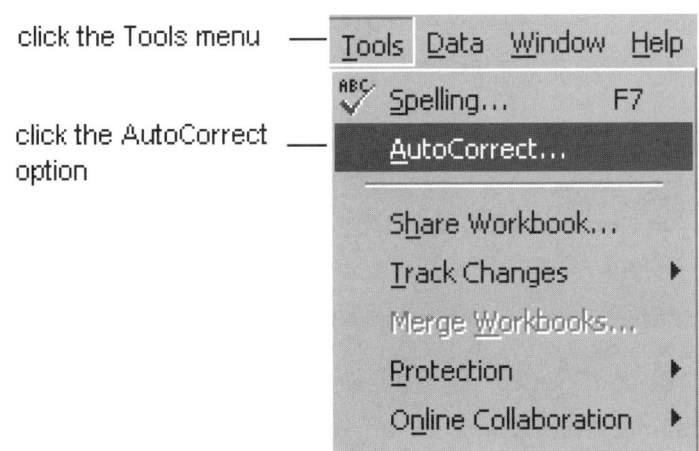

FIGURE 2.4

Topic 2 · Creating your first worksheet

(9) **Editing in the Formula Bar.** We will change the label in cell A7 from 'Gardening' to 'Gardening Work'.

    a. Click the cell and the Formula Bar displays whatever text is in the cell – see Figure 2.5.

    b. Place the screen pointer after the last letter of 'Gardening' in the Formula Bar as shown in Figure 2.5.

    c. Click *once* and a flashing cursor is placed there marking the *insertion point.*

       Type the word **Work**.

    d. Press the **ENTER** key on the keyboard and the cell label is amended.

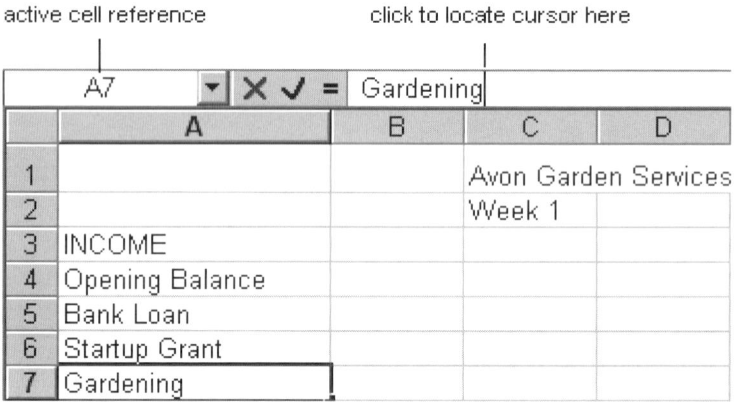

FIGURE 2.5

active cell reference   click to locate cursor here

	A	B	C	D
1			Avon Garden Services	
2			Week 1	
3	INCOME			
4	Opening Balance			
5	Bank Loan			
6	Startup Grant			
7	Gardening			

(A7 ▼ ✗ ✓ = Gardening)

(10) **Editing Directly in the Cell.** If you prefer you can amend cell contents directly in the cell rather than using the Formula Bar. We will practise this and alter the label 'Travel' in cell A15 to 'Fuel and Travel'.

This time move the mouse pointer over cell **A15**. *Double click* before the word 'Travel'.

The insertion point is marked by the flashing cursor – you may need to try more than once at first.

Now change the cell label to **Fuel and Travel** and press the **ENTER** key.

(11) **Notes on Deletion**: To delete text first click to place the insertion point as before, then:

    a. Use the **DELETE** key to delete to the *right* of the insertion point, or

    b. Use the **BACKSPACE** key (marked with a single reverse arrow) to delete to the *left* of the insertion point.

    c. Then simply use the mouse and click to select another cell.

    d. **Overtyping**: If you want to overtype the contents of a cell, ie type something new 'over' what is there, simply click the cell to select it and start typing. You don't need to delete the cell contents first.

(12) **Adjusting Column Width.** Some of the text labels in Column A are too wide to fit in single cells. We will find out how to widen columns using several methods:

Topic 2 · Creating your first worksheet

a. First use the mouse to place the screen pointer on the vertical line that separates column heading A from column heading B – see Figure 2.6.

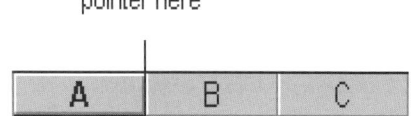

FIGURE 2.6

If correctly positioned the pointer will change to a double-headed arrow.

Now hold down the left mouse button and drag the column to the right until the width displayed is about 14.00.

b. Now use the mouse pointer to click the column designator; this is the 'A' labelling the column heading – the whole column will be selected (highlighted).

Now right click anywhere on column A and a popup menu appears – select the option **COLUMN WIDTH**. A special dialog box is displayed – see Figure 2.7.

Simply type the new column width, eg 13, then click the **OK** button and the width is re-adjusted.

c. Make sure that column A is still selected (highlighted). If not click the column designator A again.

This time click the **FORMAT** menu on the Menu bar and select the **COLUMN** option.

A further set of sub-options are offered – select **AUTOFIT SELECTION**. The width of the column is automatically adjusted to fit the longest label.

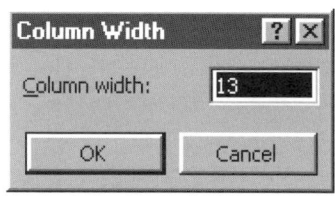

FIGURE 2.7

⑬ **Adjusting Row Height**. This uses the same principle as adjusting columns; we will try it for row 1 which holds the title.

Use the mouse to place the screen pointer on the horizontal line separating row designator 1 from row designator 2.

Now drag the mouse down until the row height is 18.00.

Now try this alternative method – click the **FORMAT** menu on the Menu bar and select the **ROW** option. Choose **HEIGHT** from the sub-options that are offered.

⑭ **Numeric Data**. Entering numbers is the same procedure as entering text:

a. Click cell **C4** and type *1250*.

b. When you press the ENTER key (or click the 'tick' box) the number is aligned to the right of the cell.

c. *Notes*: If the number is not aligned right make sure that you have entered the number 0 and not the letter O; this is a common mistake.

If a row of hash signs appears after you enter a number (######) this means that it is too wide for the cell and the column needs widening.

d. Carry on entering the rest of the income and expenditure items shown in

Topic 2 • Creating your first worksheet

Figure 2.8; remembering to complete each entry with the **ENTER** or **DOWN ARROW** key.

e. If you need to correct any of the entries refer to section 6 above. *Don't try to calculate the totals yet.*

15 **Optional**: If you wish to stop here and not proceed to the next task then save the workbook and exit Excel. This is is covered in detail in the task after next. Name the workbook **Business Startup**.

Formulae in Excel

At its simplest a formula is used for calculations such as addition and multiplication.

It is entered in a cell in the usual way and always starts with an equal (=) sign to indicate that a formula is about to follow.

Note: If you have exited Excel since the previous task then you will need to start Excel again and open the workbook **Business Startup** created in the previous task. If necessary refer to the next two tasks.

FIGURE 2.8

	A	B	C	D	E	F
1			Avon Garden Services - First 10 weeks			
2			Week 1			
3	INCOME					
4	Opening Balance		1250			
5	Bank Loan		1500			
6	Startup Grant		1000			
7	Gardening Work		180			
8	Total Income					
9						
10	OUTGOINGS					
11	Food		35			
12	Accommodation		80			
13	Van Purchase		60			
14	Equipment		20			
15	Fuel and Travel		25			
16	Total Outgoings					
17						

1 **An Addition Formula**. We have entered the first week's income and outgoings in the Business Startup workbook – refer to Figure 2.8 if necessary.

To add up the first week's income:

a. Click cell **C8** and enter an = sign. The = sign is displayed in the Formula Bar, next to four buttons, including a 'tick' and a 'cross' button.

b. Now type the formula **SUM(C4:C7)** next to the = sign – see Figure 2.9. The

Topic 2 · Creating your first worksheet

formula adds or sums the cell range C4 to C7.

c. Click the **TICK** button in the Formula bar (or press the **ENTER** key) and the result of the formula appears in cell C8 – the first week's income total is 3930.

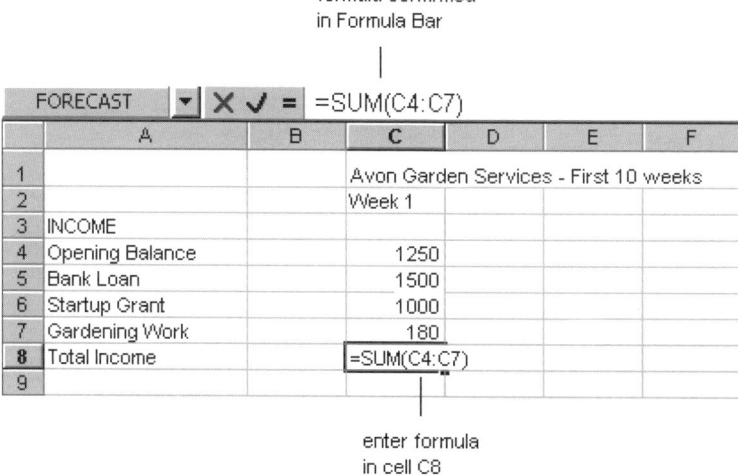

FIGURE 2.9

2. *Notes*:

a. SUM is an example of a function being used in a formulae. You can type functions and formulae in upper or lower case.

b. A formula can be corrected in the same way as any other cell entry. Make sure that the cell containing the formula (eg C8) is selected, then:

To delete the entire formula use the **DELETE** key or simply overtype.

To edit, move the screen pointer to the appropriate character in the cell and double click. Use the **BACKSPACE** or **DELETE** key to delete.

Remember to click the tick button again, or press the **ENTER** key.

c. SUM is much quicker than using the plus sign, eg =C4+C5+C6+C7. It is also expandable – if another income category were inserted into this range of 4 cells between rows 4 and 5, the new cell would automatically be included in the formula as part of the cell range. This would not happen if one used the + sign.

3. **Adding Up Columns Using Dragging**. We can use a second SUM formula to total up the first week's outgoings.

a. Click cell **C16** and enter the start of the formula *=SUM(*

b. Move the screen pointer onto cell **C11**.

c. Hold down the mouse button and drag down to cell **C15**.

The five cells holding the outgoings are enclosed by a dotted box – see Figure 2.10.

The formula should now read SUM(C11:C15 (if you have made a mistake then click the cross (X) box on the formula bar and start again).

Topic 2 · Creating your first worksheet

d. Click the tick box and the result of the formula – 220 – is displayed. Notice that there was no need to type the final bracket.

FIGURE 2.10

10	OUTGOINGS	
11	Food	35
12	Accommodation	80
13	Van Purchase	60
14	Equipment	20
15	Fuel and Travel	25
16	Total Outgoings	=SUM(C11:C15

4 **Error Messages**. If you enter an incorrect formula Excel provides a number of error messages. We will try out a couple.

a. Select cell **C8**; the Formula Bar reads SUM(C4:C7).

b. Amend the formula to SUM(C4:**C8**) and click the tick box to execute it.

An error dialog box appears. As C8 is the 'destination' cell – the cell containing the formula – it cannot also be one of the cells to be summed as this is 'circular'.

c. Click the **CANCEL** button on the dialog box and correct the formula to its original SUM(C4:C7) and execute it again.

d. *Note*: When you edit an existing formula you will notice that Excel's 'Range Finder' feature highlights the cell range in colour.

e. We'll try one more error message; select cell **C16** and amend SUM to SIM in the Formula Bar.

Execute this formula (use the **ENTER** key or tick box).

The error message #NAME? is displayed in place of the formulae. Leave it as it is for the moment.

5 **Deleting a Cell Entry**. Cell C16 should still be selected. Click the **EDIT** menu on the Menu bar.

When the Edit menu opens select the option **CLEAR** then the **ALL** option to delete the cell contents. You can use also the **DELETE** key to clear the contents of a selected cell.

6 **Adding Columns using AutoSum**. If you want to add a column or row of figures the **AUTOSUM** button can be quicker than entering a formula. It is on the Standard tool bar and is marked with the Greek letter Sigma (Σ – see key on page 18).

As we have just deleted the formula from cell C16 we can enter it again using AutoSum. Select the cell range C11 to C15 by dragging and click the **AUTOSUM** button once. The SUM formula is calculated and a total of 220 appears in cell C16.

7 **AutoCalculate**. Excel's AutoCalculate feature automatically records the total of any range of numeric cells selected. It appears in the Status Bar at the bottom right of the window. Whenever you select a range of cells

Topic 2 · Creating your first worksheet

holding numeric data Excel will automatically tell you the sum of their values. The total is for information only. Try this out by selecting a few cells in column C holding numeric data.

(8) Subtraction Using Formulae. We can now subtract total outgoings from total income to show the closing balance for the first week of trading. There is no need to use a function in the formula this time, merely a minus sign.

a. First enter a new cell label in cell A18 – see Figure 2.11. Widen column A if necessary.

b. Click cell C18 to select it and enter the formula *=C8-C16*

c. Execute the formula as usual – the closing balance for Week 1 should be 3710. Your worksheet should look like Figure 2.11.

	A	B	C	D	E	F
1			Avon Garden Services - First 10 weeks			
2			Week 1			
3	INCOME					
4	Opening Balance		1250			
5	Bank Loan		1500			
6	Startup Grant		1000			
7	Gardening Work		180			
8	Total Income		3930			
9						
10	OUTGOINGS					
11	Food		35			
12	Accommodation		80			
13	Van Purchase		60			
14	Equipment		20			
15	Fuel and Travel		25			
16	Total Outgoings		220			
17						
18	CLOSING BALANCE		3710			

FIGURE 2.11

Saving a workbook

If you have not saved the workbook yet then it is only saved in the computer's main memory. If the PC crashes or the power is turned off then all your work could be lost so it must be saved to disk permanently. I will assume in this book that you will be saving your work onto diskette or A drive rather than to hard disk. If you have saved it already then you should save the changes that you have made using the **Save** not the **Save as** command in the instructions that follow.

(1) Click the **FILE** menu on the Menu Bar – the File menu opens. Select the **SAVE AS** option. The **SAVE AS** dialog box opens – see Figure 2.12.

(2) Until it is saved the workbook is given a default name – Book1. We will give it the more descriptive name **Business Startup**.

(3) *A Note on Filenames*: A filename can be up to 218 characters long, and can contain combinations of letters, numbers and special characters such as spaces, dashes and underscores (_). They cannot contain the following characters: \ / < > * ? " ; or :

Topic 2 · Creating your first worksheet

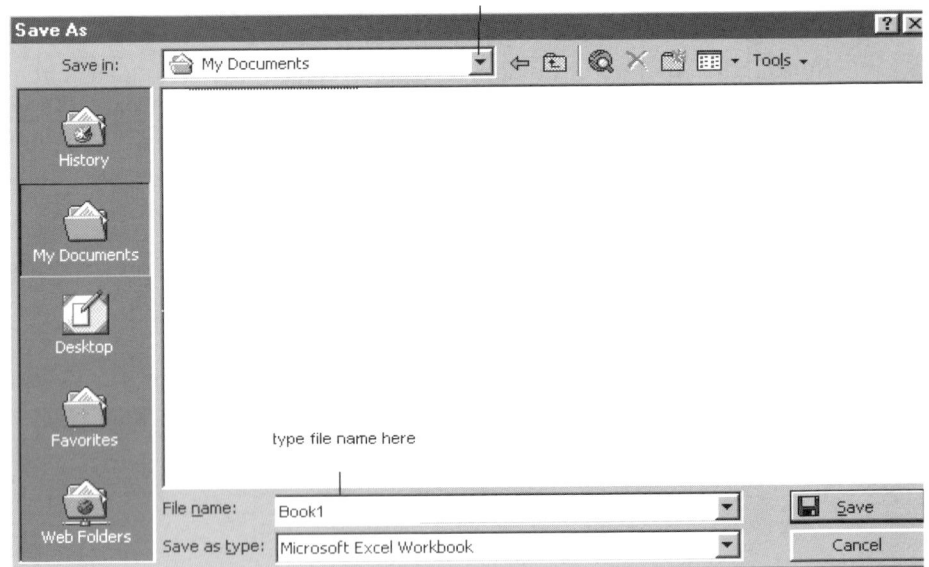

FIGURE 2.12

④ Place a formatted diskette in the drive then, using Figure 2.12 as a guide, do the following:

  a. Move the screen pointer onto the down arrow button on the **SAVE IN:** box and click; select 3½ **FLOPPY [A:]** from the drop-down list.

  b. Double click the existing file name – it should be highlighted. Amend the file name to **Business Startup** – simply overtype what is there.

  c. If you make a mistake click the **CANCEL** button on the dialog box and start again, otherwise click the **SAVE** button. The file takes a few seconds to save to diskette – the Status Bar at the bottom of the Excel window confirms that the workbook is being saved and the diskette drive light will also come on.

⑤ The name of the workbook – Business Startup – is now displayed in the Excel Title Bar.

⑥ **Hints on Saving**: Remember to save your workbook regularly as you work, eg every 5 or 10 minutes; don't leave it until you exit Excel. Any new work that you have done will be lost if the PC crashes or the power is turned off. Once the workbook has been saved under a filename you use the **Save** not the **Save as** command.

⑦ **Closing a Workbook**. Open the **FILE** menu and select the **CLOSE** option to close the workbook. The inner window goes blank. You will be reminded to save it if you have not already done so.

⑧ **Exiting from Excel**. Open the **FILE** menu and select the **EXIT** option to exit from Excel.

  Note: It is not necessary to close the workbook before exiting Excel as we did in step 6 above. Exiting from Excel will automatically close all open workbooks.

Topic 2 · Creating your first worksheet

Loading an existing workbook

In the previous task the workbook **Business Startup** was saved to diskette as a file on A drive. To use the workbook again it must be opened – retrieved from disk into main memory.

1 Start up Excel again. The new blank workbook **Book1** that appears when Excel is first opened can be ignored as we will be working with our existing workbook.

2 If you saved your **Business Startup** workbook to diskette then make sure that this disk is in the diskette drive.

Move the screen pointer onto the **FILE** menu then select **OPEN**. The **OPEN** dialog box appears – see Figure 2.13. It is very similar to the Save as dialog box- see Figure 2.12 above.

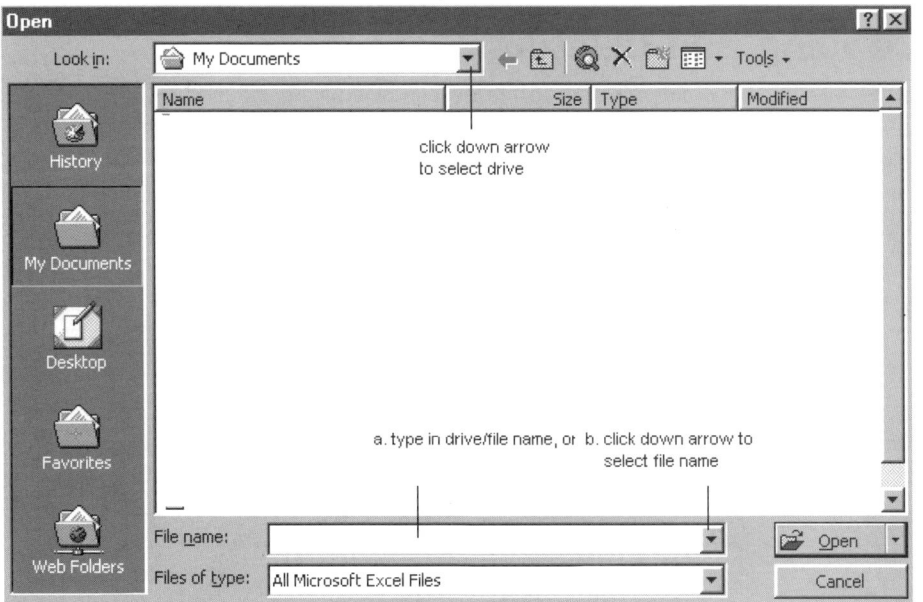

FIGURE 2.13

3 **Opening a Workbook by Entering the Name**. If you know the filename and the drive where it is stored as we do, then you can simply type this information in the File Name box. This box will already be selected.

So in this case type ***A:\Business Startup*** and then click the **OPEN** button.

The workbook will be retrieved from disk and be displayed. If not check the spelling of the filename, the colon and the back slash. Also check that you are using the correct diskette.

Open the **FILE** menu and select the **CLOSE** option again.

4 **Opening a Workbook from the File List**. If you don't want to type in the workbook name (if, for example, you are unsure of the spelling) you can open it by choosing it from a list:

a. Open the **FILE** menu and select **OPEN** – the dialog box opens again.

b. This time we will need to select the drive – see Figure 2.13 above.

Topic 2 · Creating your first worksheet

Move the screen pointer onto the down arrow button next to the **LOOK IN:** box and click. Click 3½ **FLOPPY [A:]** to select it.

c. The workbook **Business Startup** is now listed. Click to select it if necessary, then click the **OPEN** button again. The workbook will be retrieved from disk and be displayed.

5 **Independent Task**. Close the workbook as before. Open the **FILE** menu again and look at the bottom of the list of menu options. Excel displays a list of the last few workbooks that you (or another user of the application) have used.

You should see the workbook listed – you may need to scroll down the list to see it. If so click it to load the workbook again.

Copying and deleting

In this task we will create data for further weeks by copying the income and outgoings for Week 1. In doing so we will learn how to copy cells and columns and move and delete data. These are essential skills so make sure that you try them all out.

1 **Copying Cells**. To copy cells to another part of the worksheet you must first select them. To select all the cells containing the data for Week 1 move the screen pointer onto cell **C2**, and drag down to cell **C18** – see Figure 2.14. If you select the wrong range of cells then simply click anywhere on the worksheet to remove the selection and start again.

Open the **EDIT** menu and select **COPY** (not Cut). The copy command is confirmed by a flowing dotted line called the 'Marquee' that surrounds the cells.

FIGURE 2.14

	A	B	C	D	E	F
1			Avon Garden Services - First 10 weeks			
2			Week 1			
3	INCOME					
4	Opening Balance		1250			
5	Bank Loan		1500			
6	Startup Grant		1000			
7	Gardening Work		180			
8	Total Income		3930			
9						
10	OUTGOINGS					
11	Food		35			
12	Accommodation		80			
13	Van Purchase		60			
14	Equipment		20			
15	Fuel and Travel		25			
16	Total Outgoings		220			
17						
18	CLOSING BALANCE		3710			

Topic 2 · Creating your first worksheet

(2) **Pasting Cells.** Before we can paste the cells we must indicate where the cells are to be copied to.

a. Click cell **D2** – this is the cell where we want the copying to start.

b. Open the **EDIT** menu and select the **PASTE** option – the cells are copied to a new location. The Marquee remains around the original cells that have been copied; if you wanted you could paste them again.

c. If you have made a mistake then open the **EDIT** menu and select the **UNDO PASTE** command (or click the Undo button). If you keep using Undo you can reverse up to your last 16 actions – commands, key strokes etc.

d. Remove the Marquee by pressing the **ENTER** key on the keyboard.

(3) *Note*: When cells are copied or cut they are stored in a temporary memory area called the Clipboard until they are replaced by some other Copy or Cut command.

(4) **Copying Formulae.** When we copied the range of cells we copied not only the values but also the formulae. Click the cells **D8**, **D16** and **D18**. As you do so so their formulae are displayed in the Formula Bar. The cell references in the formulae are automatically adjusted to reflect their new location in Column D. These type of formulae contain *relative references*.

(5) **Cutting and Pasting Cells.** We have seen that *copying* cells leaves the original cells unchanged; *cutting* on the other hand physically removes the cell contents from their original location. They can be pasted to a new place in the worksheet. This apart, it is an identical operation to copying.

Select the cells that you have just pasted into column D, ie cell range **D2** to **D18**.

Open the **EDIT** menu and select **CUT**; the selected cells are enclosed by the marquee as before.

Select cell **E2**, then open the **EDIT** menu and select the **PASTE** option. This time the selected cells are moved into the adjacent column and column D is left blank.

(6) *Note – Toolbars*: Instead of the menu commands you may use the **CUT**, **COPY** and **PASTE** buttons on the Toolbar – there is a Toolbar key at the end of the first topic.

(7) **Clearing Cell Contents.** For practice we will clear the cells that we have just copied. If necessary select the cells range E2 to E18 again. Open the **EDIT** menu and select the **CLEAR** then the **ALL** options.

If you make a mistake remember that you can use the Edit – Undo command to reverse an unwanted action.

(8) **Filling Right.** An easier way of copying cell data into an adjacent column is to use the **FILL RIGHT** command.

Click cell **C2** to select it then hold down the mouse button and drag down the column to cell **C18**.

Keep the mouse button pressed down and drag the screen pointer across to select the same range of cells in the adjacent column. Now let go.

Topic 2 · Creating your first worksheet

You should now have selected 2 columns of cells - see Figure 2.15. You may need to try more than once to select the right cells.

FIGURE 2.15

	A	B	C	D
1			Avon Garden Services	
2			Week 1	
3	INCOME			
4	Opening Balance		1250	
5	Bank Loan		1500	
6	Startup Grant		1000	
7	Gardening Work		180	
8	Total Income		3930	
9				
10	OUTGOINGS			
11	Food		35	
12	Accommodation		80	
13	Van Purchase		60	
14	Equipment		20	
15	Fuel and Travel		25	
16	Total Outgoings		220	
17				
18	CLOSING BALANCE		3710	

9 Now open the **EDIT** menu and select the **FILL** then the **RIGHT** options.

The selected cells in column C – data and formulae – are copied across into column D.

If the Fill Right operation is incorrect then open the **EDIT** menu and select the **UNDO FILL RIGHT** option.

Amend the column label in cell D2 to **Week 2**.

10 The income items in cells **D4** to **D6** for Opening Balance, Bank Loan and Start-up Grant only apply to the first week of trading so they will need to be deleted.

Select cells D4 down to D6 by dragging, then press the **DELETE** key.

The totals in column D are automatically re-calculated, but the closing balance for Week 2 is now a negative amount of -40. However, we need to bring forward the closing balance of 3710 from Week 1 to become the opening balance for Week 2. We can do this with a formula.

11 We need to make the value held in cell D4 equal to the value held in cell C18 (the closing balance for Week 1).

Click cell **D4** and enter the formula **=C18**

Execute the formula in the usual way and all the totals for Week 2 are re-calculated, so that the closing balance for Week 2 is now 3670.

12 Now make the following changes to the outgoings for Week **2**:

Equipment   100
Fuel and Travel   60

The closing balance for Week 2 is now 3555.

13 We will now create the figures for Weeks 3 to 5, using Week 2 as a model.

Topic 2 · Creating your first worksheet

Use the mouse dragging technique again, this time selecting the data in Week 2.

Drag across to select the *3 adjacent* columns – 4 columns altogether.

Cells **D2** to **G18** should now be selected – see Figure 2.16.

```
Week 2
3710

180
3890


35
80
60
100
60
335

3555
```

FIGURE 2.16

(14) Now take the menu options **EDIT-FILL-RIGHT** as before. The values in column D are copied across into the 3 adjacent columns – E, F and G.

The closing balance for the fifth week should be 3090 – see Figure 2.17. Use the **UNDO** command to reverse a mistake.

At this point save the changed workbook – use the **FILE – SAVE** (not Save as) command.

	A	B	C	D	E	F	G
2			Week 1	Week 2	Week 2	Week 2	Week 2
3	INCOME						
4	Opening Balance		1250	3710	3555	3400	3245
5	Bank Loan		1500				
6	Startup Grant		1000				
7	Gardening Work		180	180	180	180	180
8	Total Income		3930	3890	3735	3580	3425
9							
10	OUTGOINGS						
11	Food		35	35	35	35	35
12	Accommodation		80	80	80	80	80
13	Van Purchase		60	60	60	60	60
14	Equipment		20	100	100	100	100
15	Fuel and Travel		25	60	60	60	60
16	Total Outgoings		220	335	335	335	335
17							
18	CLOSING BALANCE		3710	3555	3400	3245	3090

FIGURE 2.17

Topic 2 · Creating your first worksheet

(15) **Completing a Series Using AutoFill.** We need to amend the week numbers in row 2 for Weeks 3 to 5. As this is a series we can use AutoFill instead of typing them manually.

a. Select cell **D2** – at the bottom right hand corner of a cell there is a small square or 'handle'.

FIGURE 2.18

b. Move the screen pointer onto this handle and the shape changes to a cross – see Figure 2.18.

c. Now drag the cursor to select cells **E2** to **G2**. Release the mouse button and the cells are correctly labelled Week 3 to Week 5.

(16) Remember to save and close the workbook if you are not continuing with the next topic.

Summary of commands

Note:
Menu commands show the menu name first, followed by the command to choose from the menu, e.g. **EDIT-CLEAR** means open the Edit menu and select the Clear command.

Menu commands

EDIT-CLEAR	Clear cell contents
EDIT-COPY	Copy selected cells
EDIT-CUT	Remove selected cells
EDIT-DELETE	Delete selected rows or columns
EDIT-FILL-RIGHT	Copy selected cells into selected right hand columns
EDIT-PASTE	Insert cut or copied cells at a specified location
EDIT-UNDO	Undo previous operation(s)
FILE-CLOSE	Close current workbook
FILE-EXIT	Exit Excel
FILE-NEW	Open new, blank workbook
FILE-OPEN	Retrieve an existing workbook
FILE-SAVE AS	Save and name a new workbook
FILE-SAVE	Save an existing workbook
FORMAT	Format column, rows etc
TOOLS-AUTOCORRECT	Correct misspelled words automatically

Functions

=SUM()	Add a range of cells

TOPIC 3

Printing, formatting and copying your worksheet

Introduction

In this topic you will learn the basics of worksheet formatting, eg aligning text, adding borders and emboldening. You will also learn how to add drawing shapes to the worksheet and how to use printer and page settings. Finally we will create a copy of the worksheet.

Topic objectives

- To change fonts and character size.
- To embolden text.
- To format numbers.
- To delete and insert columns and rows.
- To add borders to cells.
- To hide gridlines.
- To freeze headings.
- To create text boxes and arrows.
- To set a print area.
- To change page settings.
- To insert headers and footers.
- To preview and print a worksheet.
- To copy a worksheet.

Worksheet formatting

1   **Text Emboldening.** If necessary open the workbook **Business Startup** – see previous topic. First we will put parts of the worksheet in bold.

     a. First select the column headings and the title – cells **A1** to **G2** (see Figure 3.1).

	A	B	C	D	E	F	G	H
1			Avon Garden Services - First 10 weeks					
2			Week 1	Week 2	Week 3	Week 4	Week 5	
3	INCOME							
4	Opening Balance		1250	3710	3555	3400	3245	
5	Bank Loan		1500					
6	Startup Grant		1000					
7	Gardening Work		180	180	180	180	180	
8	Total Income		3930	3890	3735	3580	3425	
9								
10	OUTGOINGS							

FIGURE 3.1

Topic 3 · Printing, formatting and copying your worksheet

  b. Now click the **BOLD** button – it is located on the Formatting Tool Bar, marked with a capital B (see Figure 3.2). The cells are now in bold – if you wish you can try the **ITALIC** or **UNDERLINE** buttons too.

  c. Embolden the row labels in cells A3 to A18 in the same way. If you need to widen column A see Topic 2 for guidance.

  d. Embolden the closing balances in cells C18 to G18.

② **Changing Fonts and Character Size**. Drag to select the row labels in column A again. Click the down arrow next to the **FONT SIZE** button on the Formatting Toolbar – see Figure 3.2. Change the default size from **10** to **8**.

Click the down arrow on the font button next and change the default Arial font to another one. Reverse the font changes using the **EDIT – UNDO** command.

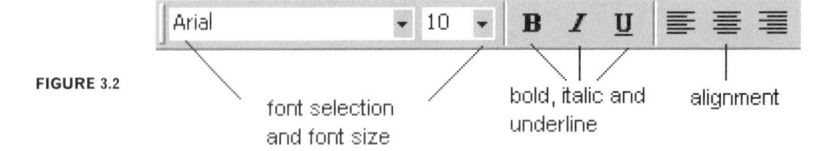

FIGURE 3.2

       Arial   10   **B** *I* U
    font selection   bold, italic and   alignment
    and font size   underline

③ **Aligning Cell Entries.** Excel places numeric values to the right of the cells and alphabetic characters to the left. A neater alternative can be to centre them under column headings.

First drag to select all the cells containing numeric values, ie cells **C4** to **G18**.

Click the **CENTRE** button on the Formatting Tool Bar – see Figure 3.2 above – and the values are centred.

④ **Formatting Numbers**. Re-select all the numeric cells again if necessary (C4 to G18).

Open the **FORMAT** menu and then select the option **CELLS**.

When the Format Cells dialog box is displayed make sure that the **NUMBER** tab is selected – see Figure 3.3.

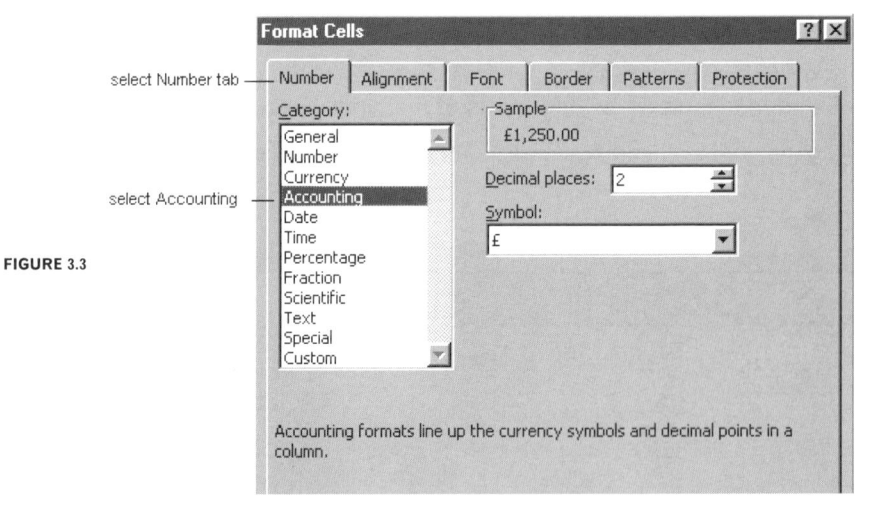

FIGURE 3.3

  select Number tab — Number | Alignment | Font | Border | Patterns | Protection

  Category: General, Number, Currency, **Accounting**, Date, Time, Percentage, Fraction, Scientific, Text, Special, Custom

  select Accounting

  Sample: £1,250.00
  Decimal places: 2
  Symbol: £

  Accounting formats line up the currency symbols and decimal points in a column.

36

Next select **ACCOUNTING** from the **CATEGORY** list. The format selected will display numbers to 2 decimal places.

Next select the **£** currency symbol and click the **OK** button.

Check that the formatting is correct. If a row of hash (#) symbols are shown you will need to widen the columns to show the whole entry.

(5) *Note*: To use a currency symbol in Excel (eg pound, dollar or Euro sign) you must use formatting; never type the symbol yourself or Excel will not treat the figures as numbers but as text, causing errors in calculations.

(6) **Columns and Rows – Deleting and Inserting**. As column B is blank at the moment it can be removed without affecting any data and formulae. Delete it by first clicking the column designator (the 'B') then using the **EDIT – DELETE** menu command. The remaining columns automatically shift to the left and any formulae are automatically amended to take account of their new position.

(7) We will now insert an extra row above row 2; click the row designator for Row 2 (the '2') and the whole row is selected.

Open the **INSERT** menu and select the **ROWS** option. A blank row is inserted, giving the worksheet an improved layout. Compare it with Figure 3.4.

	A	B	C	D	E	F
1		Avon Garden Services - First 10 weeks				
2						
3		Week 1	Week 2	Week 3	Week 4	Week 5
4	INCOME					
5	Opening Balance	£ 1,250.00	£ 3,710.00	£3,555.00	£ 3,400.00	£ 3,245.00
6	Bank Loan	£ 1,500.00				
7	Startup Grant	£ 1,000.00				
8	Gardening Work	£ 180.00	£ 180.00	£ 180.00	£ 180.00	£ 180.00
9	Total Income	£ 3,930.00	£ 3,890.00	£3,735.00	£ 3,580.00	£ 3,425.00
10						
11	OUTGOINGS					
12	Food	£ 35.00	£ 35.00	£ 35.00	£ 35.00	£ 35.00
13	Accommodation	£ 80.00	£ 80.00	£ 80.00	£ 80.00	£ 80.00
14	Van Purchase	£ 60.00	£ 60.00	£ 60.00	£ 60.00	£ 60.00
15	Equipment	£ 20.00	£ 100.00	£ 100.00	£ 100.00	£ 100.00
16	Fuel and Travel	£ 25.00	£ 60.00	£ 60.00	£ 60.00	£ 60.00
17	Total Outgoings	£ 220.00	£ 335.00	£ 335.00	£ 335.00	£ 335.00
18						
19	CLOSING BALANCE	£ 3,710.00	£ 3,555.00	£3,400.00	£ 3,245.00	£ 3,090.00
20						

FIGURE 3.4

(8) **Centring the Title**. The title would look better centred across columns A to F as these form the part of the worksheet that will eventually be printed.

Select cell range **1A** to **1F** and click the **MERGE AND CENTRE** button – it is on the Formatting Toolbar and marked with a small 'a' between two arrows – see key at the end of Topic 1.

The merge and centre feature in effect merges the 5 cells into one so they can no longer be individually selected. If you add more columns to the worksheet later then right click the merged cells and take the options **FORMAT-CELLS-ALIGNMENT**. You can then de-select the merged cells box.

Topic 3 · Printing, formatting and copying your worksheet

(9) **Cell Borders.** You can use borders to divide the worksheet into sections and make it more readable – see Figure 3.5 below.

   a. Select cells **A9** to **F9**. Open the **FORMAT** menu and select **CELLS**.

   b. Use Figure 3.5 as a guide when the Format Cells dialog box opens; click the **BORDER** tab first.

   c. Click the box in the Border section of the dialog box that shows a line along the bottom of the cell.

   d. Select a **THIN LINE** option from the **STYLE** box.

   e. Click the **OK** button – remove the highlighting from the cells and you will see a thin line along the bottom of cells A9 to F9.

(10) We will now put a thick border around all the cells in the worksheet.

   a. Click cell **A1** and drag down and across to cell **F19**.

   b. Open the **FORMAT** menu and select **CELLS**. When the Format Cells dialog box appears, click the **BORDER** tab if necessary.

   c. Select the **OUTLINE** option from the **PRESETS** section – see Figure 3.5.

   d. Select the **THICK LINE** in the **STYLE** box – see Figure 3.5.

   e. Finally click the **OK** button.

   f. Click to remove the highlight from the cells – the worksheet is enclosed in a thick line.

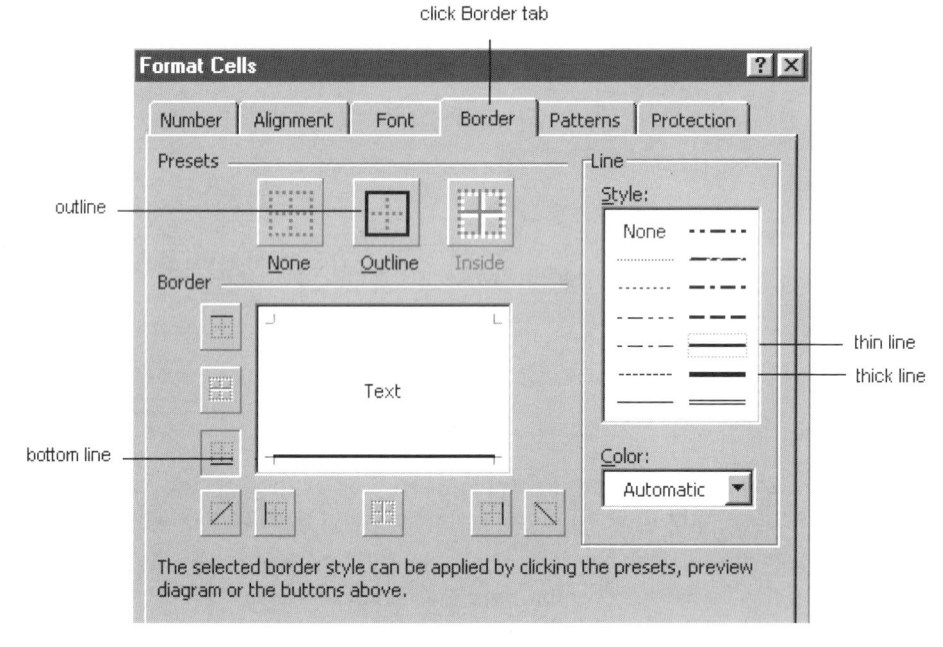

FIGURE 3.5

(11) ***Note***: To remove an unwanted border use the **EDIT – UNDO** command. Alternatively you can use the **FORMAT BORDER** dialog box to de-select the relevant border.

⑫ **Independent Task**. Find the **BORDERS** button on the Formatting Toolbar and click the down arrow next to it; use it to:

a. Draw a single thick line border under cells **A18** to **F18**.

b. Give the cell labels in cells **A2** to **A19** a right hand thick line border.

⑬ **Hiding the Gridline Display**. The gridlines are the horizontal and vertical lines that mark off each cell; now that the worksheet has borders they can be hidden.

a. Click on the **TOOLS** menu and select **OPTIONS**.

b. A dialog box appears, select the **VIEW** tab if necessary.

Find the **WINDOWS OPTIONS** section of the dialog box and click the box next to the **GRIDLINES** option to de-select the tick.

c. Now click the **OK** button on the dialog box; the gridlines on the worksheet are now hidden and our worksheet should now look like Figure 3.6. We can still show the gridlines when we print the worksheet if we wish.

	A	B	C	D	E	F
1		Avon Garden Services - First 10 weeks				
2						
3		Week 1	Week 2	Week 3	Week 4	Week 5
4	INCOME					
5	Opening Balance	£ 1,250.00	£ 3,710.00	£3,555.00	£ 3,400.00	£ 3,245.00
6	Bank Loan	£ 1,500.00				
7	Startup Grant	£ 1,000.00				
8	Gardening Work	£ 180.00	£ 180.00	£ 180.00	£ 180.00	£ 180.00
9	Total Income	£ 3,930.00	£ 3,890.00	£3,735.00	£ 3,580.00	£ 3,425.00
10						
11	OUTGOINGS					
12	Food	£ 35.00	£ 35.00	£ 35.00	£ 35.00	£ 35.00
13	Accommodation	£ 80.00	£ 80.00	£ 80.00	£ 80.00	£ 80.00
14	Van Purchase	£ 60.00	£ 60.00	£ 60.00	£ 60.00	£ 60.00
15	Equipment	£ 20.00	£ 100.00	£ 100.00	£ 100.00	£ 100.00
16	Fuel and Travel	£ 25.00	£ 60.00	£ 60.00	£ 60.00	£ 60.00
17	Total Outgoings	£ 220.00	£ 335.00	£ 335.00	£ 335.00	£ 335.00
18						
19	CLOSING BALANCE	£ 3,710.00	£ 3,555.00	£3,400.00	£ 3,245.00	£ 3,090.00

FIGURE 3.6

⑭ **Freezing Headings**. Once the worksheet gets over a certain size you can no longer see all the cells at once. In this situation you can freeze the row and column labels so that they are always in view when you scroll around the worksheet.

a. Click cell **B4** where the row and column labels intersect.

b. Open the **WINDOW** menu and select the option **FREEZE PANES**.

c. Now scroll across and down the worksheet; the column and row labels are frozen and remain as a reference.

d. *Note – Unfreezing Panes*: Open the **WINDOW** menu and select the **UNFREEZE PANES** option.

⑮ **Using Text Boxes**. A text box is used to hold blocks of text, such as brief notes, and can be used to explain a worksheet entry.

Topic 3 · Printing, formatting and copying your worksheet

    a. The Drawing Toolbar should be displayed at the bottom of the Excel Window – see key at the end of Topic 1. If it is not displayed then open the **VIEW** menu and select the **TOOLBARS** option. A list of toolbars is displayed, select **DRAWING**.

    b. Identify the **TEXT BOX** button by moving the screen pointer over each toolbar button in turn – a popup label identifies each button.

    c. Click the **TEXT BOX** button – the screen pointer changes to a cross shape.

    d. Move the screen pointer over cell **C21** and drag to draw a text box large enough to hold the text shown in Figure 3.7. The exact position of the box is not crucial.

    e. Type in the text – it is automatically aligned in the text box.

    f. When you have finished de-select the text box by clicking elsewhere on the worksheet.

    g. ***Notes on Text Boxes***: To alter a text box first select it by clicking it, you can then:

Move it by dragging the border of the box.

Re-size it by dragging one of the small square selection handles.

Delete the box providing that the selection border is dotted, rather than a diagonal line pattern – see Figure 3.7. Simply press the **DELETE** key.

The text within the box can be selected then edited, emboldened etc.

FIGURE 3.7

B	C	D	E
Avon Garden Services - First 10 weeks			
Week 1	Week 2	Week 3	Week 4
£ 60.00	£ 60.00	£ 60.00	£ 60.00
£ 20.00	£ 100.00	£ 100.00	£ 100.00
£ 25.00	£ 60.00	£ 60.00	£ 60.00
£ 220.00	£ 335.00	£ 335.00	£ 335.00
£ 3,710.00	£ 3,555.00	£ 3,400.00	£ 3,245.00

This workbook shows the income and outgoings for the first 5 weeks of trading.

16   **Using Shapes and Arrows**. We will experiment with adding arrows and encircling cells to draw attention to them. Use Figure 3.8 as your guide.

    a. Click the **OVAL** button on the Drawing Toolbar – if it is not displayed then open the **VIEW** menu and select the **TOOLBARS** option. A list of toolbars is displayed, select **DRAWING**.

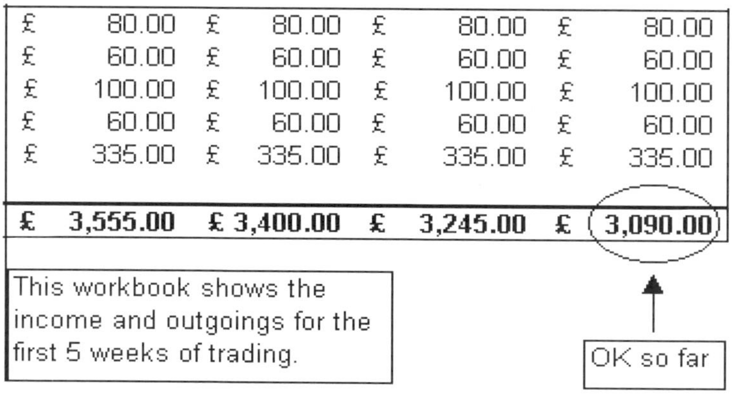

£	80.00	£	80.00	£	80.00	£	80.00
£	60.00	£	60.00	£	60.00	£	60.00
£	100.00	£	100.00	£	100.00	£	100.00
£	60.00	£	60.00	£	60.00	£	60.00
£	335.00	£	335.00	£	335.00	£	335.00
£	3,555.00	£	3,400.00	£	3,245.00	£	(3,090.00)

This workbook shows the income and outgoings for the first 5 weeks of trading.

OK so far

FIGURE 3.8

b. Drag the mouse pointer so as to encircle cell **F19**. If the cell contents within the shape become invisible see section f below. You can press the **DELETE** key to remove a wrongly drawn object.

c. Next click the **ARROW** button and drag to draw the arrow – arrows are drawn from tail to head.

d. Using the **TEXT BOX** button, draw a text box as shown in Figure 3.8. Enter the text.

e. Now try scrolling across and down. The arrow, oval and text box objects remain in their original positions relative to their underlying cells.

f. *Note*: If the contents of cell F19 are invisible then *right* click the oval object and select the option **FORMAT AUTOSHAPE** from the popup menu. Click the **COLORS AND LINES** tab if necessary. In the Fill section of the dialog box click the down arrow on the **COLOR:** box and select the option **NO FILL** then **OK**.

17 **Seeing More of the Worksheet**. To see the maximum number of worksheet cells:

a. Open the **VIEW** menu and select the option **FULL SCREEN**. However, this means that major components of Excel and Windows are hidden and unavailable, eg toolbars and the Taskbar. Repeat the **VIEW – FULL SCREEN** command to return to the normal view.

b. Use the **ZOOM** button on the Standard Toolbar to reduce the scale of the workbook. The default displayed is probably 100%; try changing it to 80 – 90%.

Worksheet printing

Printing a worksheet is similar to other Windows applications; you need to specify what and how to print – which cells, number of copies etc.

1 **Print Area Selection**. The first step is to select the worksheet cells that you want to print – in this case we will print all cells containing data – **A1** to **F24**.

Here is a simpler alternative to dragging if you want to select a large range of cells:

a. First click cell **A1** – the top left cell of the range that you want to print.

b. Scroll down until you can see cell **F24** (or whichever cell is the bottom right cell).

c. Hold down the **SHIFT** key (marked with an upwards arrow).

d. Select cell **F24** – the bottom right of the range that you want to select – and the complete cell range is selected.

2 **Print Area – Setting**. Open the **FILE** menu and select the option **PRINT AREA** then the option **SET PRINT AREA**. The print area is selected – surrounded with a dotted line. If you print without first setting the print area then the default area is the printed page, eg A4.

3 **Printing**.

a. Open the **FILE** menu and select the **PRINT** option – the Print dialog box appears.

b. Identify the **PRINT WHAT** section of the Print dialog box and click the **ACTIVE SHEETS** button. This ensures that the print area of the selected worksheet will be printed, not any blank cells outside it.

c. Now click the **PREVIEW** button so that you can see how the worksheet will look when printed on an A4 page. Check whether all 5 weeks can be printed on the page; if not see section 5 below.

4 **Page Setup**. At the top of the Preview window is the **SETUP** button. Click it and the Page Setup dialog box appears – select the **SHEET** tab if necessary – see Figure 3.9.

First check in the Print section that two option boxes **ROW AND COLUMN HEADINGS** and **GRIDLINES** are both de-selected, ie not ticked; as the worksheet is fairly small and simple we should be able to read it easily enough without them.

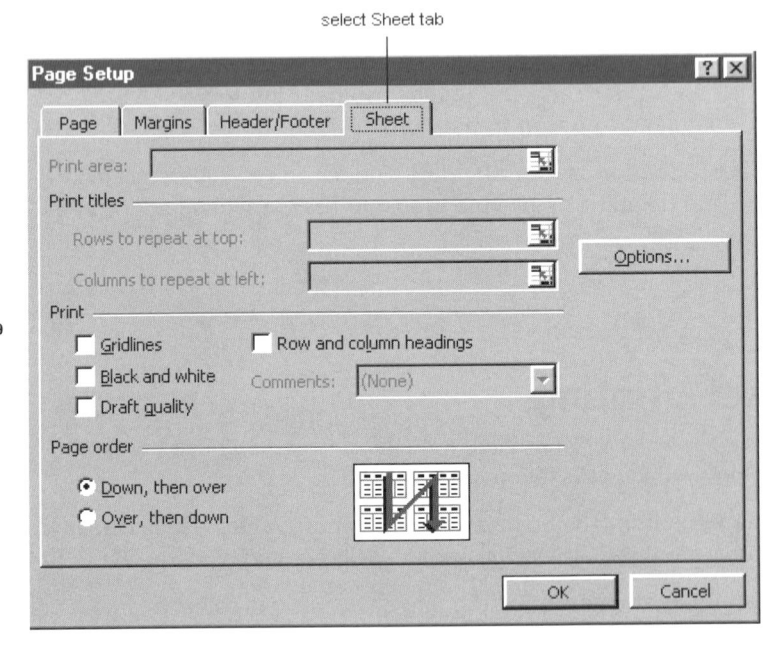

FIGURE 3.9

Topic 3 · Printing, formatting and copying your worksheet

5. **Further Page Settings**. Next click the **PAGE** tab and a new set of options are displayed. If your printer offers the following page settings they will be displayed in black; otherwise they will be dimmed or 'greyed out' to show that they are unavailable. Examine the following options:

   a. **Orientation**. The usual one is *portrait* – vertically down the page. If a worksheet is wider than it is long then you will fit more cells on the printed page in *landscape* – horizontally across the page. Change the orientation to landscape now if the worksheet will not fit onto the printed page – see section 3c above.

   b. **Paper size**. The current paper size in your printer is displayed, usually A4.

   c. **Scaling**. If the worksheet is too large to fit the printed page then you can reduce the scale to fit.

   d. **Fit to** is similar to the Scaling option; it will adjust the size of the printed area to fit on one or more pages.

6. **Margins and Alignment**. Next click the **MARGINS** tab on the **PAGE SETUP** dialog box. Click the **HORIZONTALLY** and **VERTICALLY** boxes in the 'Center on Page' section; this will centre the printout on the page.

7. **Headers and Footers**. Click the **HEADER/FOOTER** tab. Excel always allows blank space at the top and bottom of every printed page for headers and footers. We will add some extra information – eg page number, title, date and the name of the creator of the sheet.

   a. Click the **CUSTOM HEADER** button and a smaller dialog box is displayed – see Figure 3.10. It is divided into three sections.

   b. Select the centre section and type in a title – see Figure 3.10. Click the **OK**

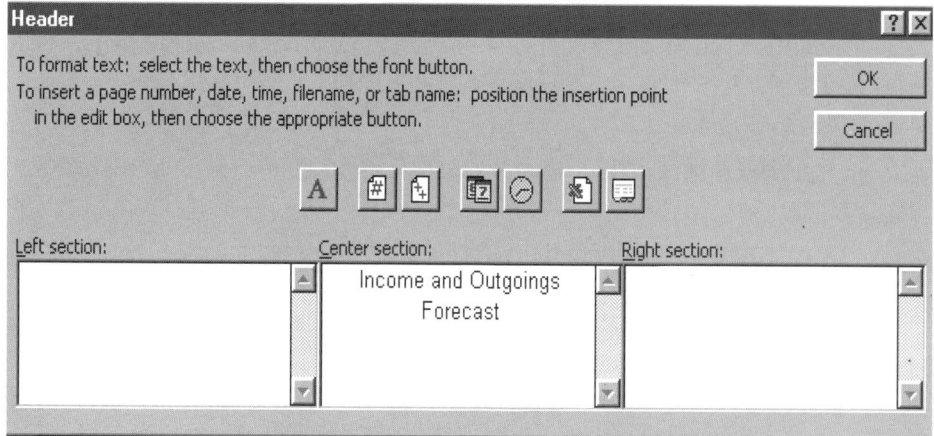

FIGURE 3.10

button and you are returned to the Page Setup dialog box.

   c. Now click the **CUSTOM FOOTER** button and insert the following, using Figure 3.11 as a guide.

   d. Click the left hand section and type your name.

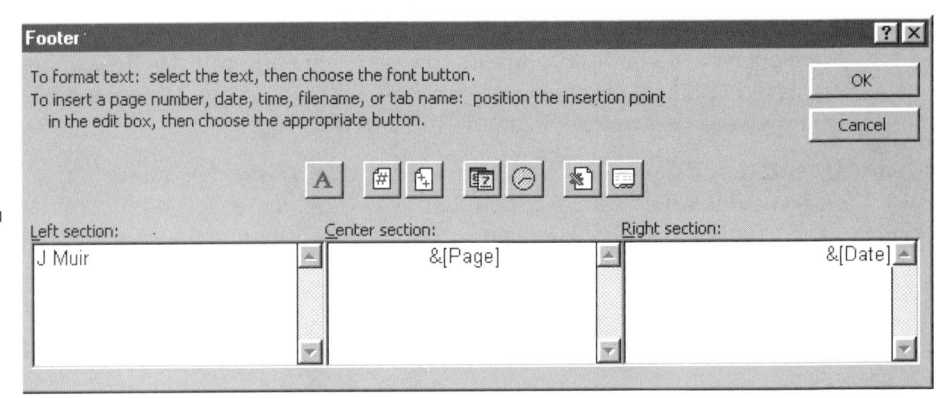

FIGURE 3.11

[Footer dialog box showing Left section: "J Muir", Center section: "&[Page]", Right section: "&[Date]"]

    e. Click the centre section and click the **PAGE NUMBER** button, marked with the '#' symbol.

    f. Click the right hand section and click the **DATE** button, marked with the number 7.

    g. When you have inserted these 3 items click the **OK** button. You will see that your custom header and footer are shown in the Page Setup dialog box. Click **OK** again.

    h. *Note*: If you are unsure of the function of any of the buttons used in the Custom Header or Footer dialog boxes click the **HELP** button (marked with a question mark) then click the button and its purpose will be explained.

8   **The Printer**. Make sure that your printer is turned on, connected via cable to your computer and has paper in it. Check each of these in turn if the next section does not produce a printout.

9   **Print Preview**. Open **PRINT PREVIEW** again – if you scroll you can now see the headers and footers as they will appear on the printed page. There are various option buttons at the top of the dialog box:

For information only:

NEXT and **PREVIOUS** are for worksheets that take up more than one page.

MARGINS displays margin settings for the printed sheet.

PAGE BREAK PREVIEW is also for multi-page worksheets; you can reset both the print area and the page breaks simply by dragging them. You can also cut and paste cells between different printed pages and Excel will automatically re-scale the cells to fit.

PRINT and **SETUP** take you to either the Print or the Page Setup dialog boxes.

10   **Zoom**. Click the **ZOOM** button once or twice – you can switch between a full-size and a reduced view of the worksheet. Select the reduced view and move the screen pointer over the worksheet – it becomes magnifying glass shaped. Click and the area under the pointer is enlarged. You can scroll around to look at other parts of the worksheet.

11   When you are happy with the print preview, click the **PRINT** button at the top of the dialog box. If you are not happy then click the **CLOSE** to return to the worksheet.

The print dialog box appears; select **ALL** from the **PRINT RANGE** section and **ACTIVE SHEETS** in the **PRINT WHAT** section.

Click **OK** and the worksheet should start printing now.

12 *Note – If your worksheet won't print*: Check the previous stages again.

If you still have no success check that the correct printer is selected as follows:

a. Open the **FILE** menu and select **PRINT** as before. Check in the **PRINTER NAME**: section that the correct printer is selected.

b. If the print area is incorrect and not all the worksheet has been printed then you will need to reset it. Select the menu options **FILE – PRINT AREA – CLEAR PRINT AREA**. The dotted print area line is removed; see section 1 above to re-set it.

Independent task – Check your progress

For further practice we will extend the worksheet to cover a 10 week trading period. In this task I shall keep the instructions to a minimum. Make sure that the **Business Startup** workbook is opened and that **Sheet1** is selected.

1 First select the column for Week 5 – cells **F3** to **F19**. Drag across the worksheet to select the next 5 columns G to K.

2 Now use the **EDIT-FILL-RIGHT** command to copy the columns into the selected columns.

If the totals are displayed as a row of hash symbols – ##### – then widen the selected columns using the command **FORMAT-COLUMNS-AUTOFIT SELECTION**.

Remember to use the **UNDO** command if you make a mistake.

3 Make the following amendments now:

a. Change the week numbers for Weeks 6-10.

b. Remove the oval shape surrounding the Weeks 6-10 totals in row 19 – click each shape in turn so that the oval is selected and then use the **DELETE** key.

c. Amend the note in the rectangular text box to reflect 10 weeks of trading.

d. Use the **FORMAT-CELLS** menu or the **BORDERS** button to extend the cell borders.

4 The worksheet for Weeks 6-10 is reproduced in Appendix 1 – check it with your version.

Copying a worksheet

1. At the moment the **Sheet1** tab should be selected. Hold down the **CTRL** key on the keyboard, locate the screen pointer on the **Sheet1** tab and drag with the mouse.

The cursor changes to show a tiny copy of the worksheet, marked with a '+' sign.

2. Drag the cursor onto the **Sheet2** tab.

Release the mouse button then the **CTRL** key. Sheet1 is copied, renamed **Sheet1 (2)**.

3. Click the tab for **Sheet1 (2)** – it is now the active worksheet, a replica of Sheet1.

4. *Note*: If you didn't hold down the **CTRL** key, or released it too soon, then Sheet1 may have been moved to a new position instead of being copied. In this case drag it back to its original position, using only the mouse, and try again.

Testing out assumptions

Using an Excel worksheet you can test out various assumptions simply by altering cell values and noting the results. We will experiment with the income and outgoings for the first 10 weeks of trading, using the copied worksheet **Sheet1 (2)**.

1. Make the following changes to **Sheet1 (2)**:

   a. Delete the bank loan of £1500 from cell B6.

   b. Increase the cost of van purchase to £90 from Week 4 onwards.

   You will now end the trading period with a balance of £605.

2. Let's assume that you employ a part-time worker from Week 6 onwards and that their wages cost you £80 per week.

   a. Use the **INSERT-ROWS** command to insert a new row above the row that holds total outgoings (row 17 if your worksheet is the same as Appendix 1).

   b. Label the row **Part-time wages** and insert the £80 for Weeks 6 to 10. If you have used the **FILL-RIGHT** command check that the formulae for the closing balance have been adjusted so that total outgoings are still subtracted from total income.

   c. Obviously the part-time worker will increase your income from gardening work, so increase this from £180 per week to £300 per week for Weeks 6 to 10.

3. Compare your worksheet with Appendix 2; we have now created two alternative models, based on different sets of assumptions. In later topics we will use more sophisticated methods.

Summary of commands

Note:
Menu commands show the menu name first, followed by the command to choose from the menu, e.g. **EDIT-CLEAR** means open the Edit menu and select the Clear command.

Menu commands

EDIT-CLEAR-ALL	Delete cell contents
EDIT-DELETE	Delete selected rows or columns
EDIT-FILL-RIGHT	Copy column into adjacent columns
EDIT-UNDO	Undo previous operation
FILE-NEW	Open new, blank workbook
FILE-OPEN	Retrieve an existing workbook
FILE-PAGE SETUP	Amend page settings for printing
FILE-PRINT	Print worksheet
FILE-PRINT PREVIEW	Preview worksheet before printing
FILE-SAVE	Save current workbook
FORMAT-CELLS-BORDER	Add cell borders
FORMAT-COLUMN-WIDTH	Adjust column width
FORMAT-CELLS-FONT	Embolden, italics, character size and style
FORMAT-CELLS-ALIGNMENT	Align text blocks
FORMAT-CELLS-NUMBER	Format numbers, percentages etc
FORMAT-ROW-HEIGHT	Adjust row height
INSERT-ROWS	Insert a blank row
TOOLS-OPTIONS	Do/do not display gridlines etc
VIEW-FULL SCREEN	Turn on/off full screen mode
VIEW-TOOLBARS	View a toolbar
WINDOW-FREEZE PANES	Freeze row and column headings
WINDOW-UNFREEZE PANES	Unfreeze row and column headings

TOPIC 4

Further worksheet activities

Introduction

This topic completes the topics on basic worksheet skills; you will learn how to name and delete worksheets and how to calculate averages and percentages. We will also look at absolute references and some further Excel formatting features, including automatic and conditional formatting.

Topic objectives

- To practise naming and deleting worksheets.
- To calculate averages and percentages.
- To use an absolute refererence in a formula.
- To use automatic and conditional formatting.
- To copy formats.
- To indent and rotate cell data.

Naming worksheets

The workbook **Business Startup** consists of two worksheets named **Sheet1** and **Sheet1 (2)**. We will change these default names for the more descriptive ones 'first model' and 'second model'.

A sheet name can have up to 31 characters. It can contain spaces, but not the following characters: [ ], /, \, ? and *

❶ Open the workbook **Business Startup** and make sure that **Sheet1** is selected.

Open the **FORMAT** menu and select the options **SHEET** then **RENAME**.

The sheet tab is highlighted. Simply type the new name ***first model***.

Press **ENTER** and the sheet name appears on the sheet tab.

❷ Name **Sheet1 (2)** 'second model'. This time use the alternative method – double click the sheet tab and then type the name.

❸ *Note*: The longer the name, the longer the sheet tab becomes, meaning that fewer tabs can be seen at a time. If this happens you should use the arrow buttons to the left of the sheet tabs to select the correct sheet.

Deleting a worksheet

As well as our two renamed worksheets your workbook will contain other blank, unused worksheets that we can delete:

1 Click the sheet tab of one of the unused worksheets – it is now the active sheet.

2 Open the **EDIT** menu and select the option **DELETE SHEET**.

3 A dialog box is displayed, warning you that the deletion will be permanent. Check again that that you have selected the correct sheet, then click **OK**.

Calculating percentages and averages

1 Open a new blank workbook and create the worksheet shown in Figure 4.1.

Close any other open workbook. To open a new workbook use the **FILE – NEW** command. When the **NEW** dialog box opens click the **WORKBOOK** icon then **OK**.

2 Format the worksheet as follows, using the skills learned in Topic 3:

a. Put the cell labels and title in bold.

b. Centre the cell labels and monthly values as shown.

c. Put a border around the cells shown and add the text box.

d. Widen column A.

e. Centre the title across columns A to E.

3 We will now calculate the totals, using skills learned in Topics 2 and 3:

a. Use the SUM function to calculate the April sales total in cell **E4**.

b. Use the command **EDIT-FILL-DOWN** to copy the formula to cells **E5** and **E6**.

c. Similarly calculate the totals in row 9 next using SUM and **EDIT-FILL-RIGHT**.

	A	B	C	D	E
1	Insurance Sales - Second Quarter			
2					
3		Home	Business	Holiday	Total Sales
4	April	587	148	89	
5	May	695	241	168	
6	June	734	198	207	
7					
8	Average Sales per Quarter				
9	Total Sales per Quarter				
10	% of Total				
11					
12		This worksheet shows a sales analysis of the three major insurance categories.		
13					
14					

FIGURE 4.1

Topic 4 · Further worksheet activities

(4) Save the workbook as **Insurance Sales** (save it in the same folder/drive as our first workbook Business Startup).

(5) Averages. Row 8 will hold the average sales for each type of insurance; select cell **B8** and enter the formula *=AVERAGE(B4:B6)*.

Remember to click the tick box or press `ENTER`.

Use **EDIT-FILL-RIGHT** to copy the formula to cells C8 to E8.

(6) Use the **FORMAT-CELLS** command to remove the decimal places from cells B8 to E9: Select the **NUMBER** tab then **NUMBER** from the **CATEGORY** list.

Set **DECIMAL PLACES** to 0 then click **OK** – see Figure 4.2.

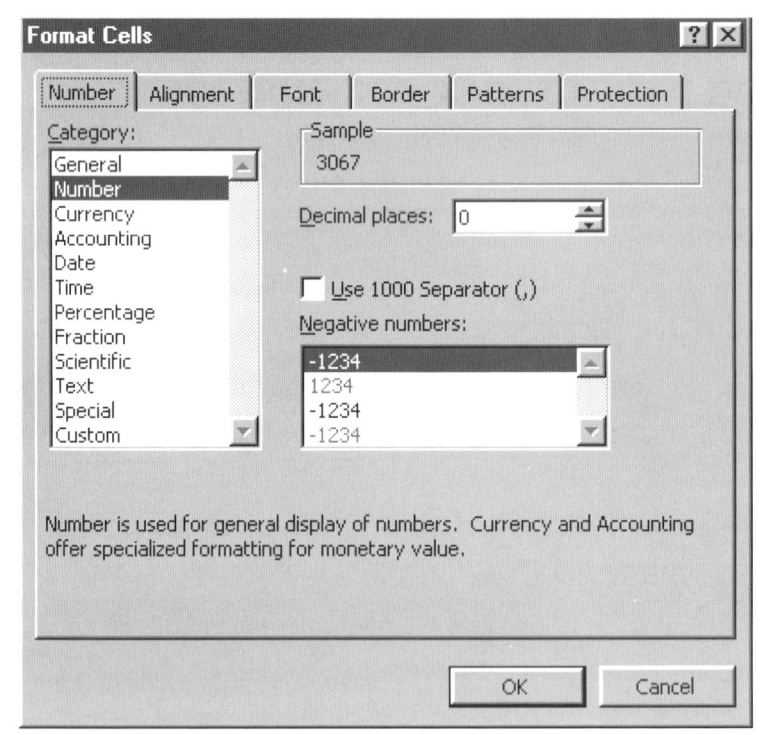

FIGURE 4.2

(7) First we will calculate the quarterly totals – cells **B9** to **D9** – as fractions of the total sales – cell E9.

Enter the formula *=B9/$E$9* in cell B10 (the '/' sign represents division, the dollar sign an absolute reference – see below).

The value 0.65732 is shown in cell B10 – this is the quarterly total for home insurance as a decimal fraction of the overall quarterly total.

(8) *Note: Absolute and Relative References.* We have been using *relative* references in formulae so far; this is very useful as it means that whenever a cell containing a formula is copied or moved the cell references in the formula are automatically adjusted. However, there are situations where we would not want this to happen; the percentages we are calculating are a case in point as they must all be based on one cell – E9. So we must have a way of making this clear, otherwise the formula would be adjusted when we used the Fill right command. This is the reason for the dollar sign in the formula =**B9/$E$9** – E9 becomes an *absolute* reference while B9 remains a relative reference as we want it to change when it is copied to another cell. A quick way to convert a cell reference to an absolute one is to select the cell reference in the Formula Bar and press the F4 function key. Pressing it more than once gives a combination of relative and absolute references, called a *mixed* reference.

(9) Percentages. Now to turn the B10 total into a percentage; open the **FORMAT** menu and select **CELLS** then **NUMBER**.

Select the **PERCENTAGE** option and make sure that **DECIMAL PLACES** are set to 2.

Home insurance is now shown as 65.73% of total sales.

(10) Use **EDIT-FILL-RIGHT** to express Business and Holiday in cells **C10** and **D10** as percentages too.

Centre the values in rows 8 to 10.

Compare your worksheet with Figure 4.3.

	A	B	C	D	E
1		Insurance Sales - Second Quarter			
2					
3		Home	Business	Holiday	Total Sales
4	April	587	148	89	824
5	May	695	241	168	1104
6	June	734	198	207	1139
7					
8	Average Sales per Quarter	672	196	155	1022
9	Total Sales per Quarter	2016	587	464	3067
10	% of Total	65.73%	19.14%	15.13%	
11					
12		This worksheet shows a sales analysis of the			
13		three major insurance categories.			
14					
15					

FIGURE 4.3

Automatic worksheet formatting

AutoFormat offers a range of pre-set formats which save you the time and effort of designing your own. You can choose a complete worksheet or a range of cells and the various sections – headings, data, totals – will be correctly identified and formatted.

(1) Select all the cells in the **Insurance Sales** worksheet, ie cell range **A1** to **E10**. Open the **FORMAT** menu and select **AUTOFORMAT**.

A dialog box appears showing a range of sample formats.

(2) Selecting a Format. Use the scroll bar to review the formats, then select the **CLASSIC 3** format and click **OK**.

Click the worksheet to remove the cell selection – the worksheet is automatically converted to the chosen format.

Topic 4 · Further worksheet activities

③ **Undoing AutoFormat**. Open the **EDIT** menu and select **UNDO AUTOFORMAT** – your worksheet is restored to its previous format.

④ *Notes*: If the **UNDO** command does not work then select **FORMAT-AUTOFORMAT** again and scroll down the Formats list and select the **'NONE'** option. You may find, however, that you have lost such original formatting as bold and centring.

A last resort is to close the worksheet without saving it – but you will also lose any other changes made since the worksheet was last saved.

⑤ **Sub-Formats**. Select all the worksheet cells again and open the **AUTOFORMAT** menu.

Select another format then click the **OPTIONS** button on the dialog box.

In the **FORMATS TO APPLY** section there are 6 options offered; experiment with de-selecting and re-selecting each option. You will see that the format selected changes to reflect this.

⑥ Click the **OK** button on the dialog box when you have chosen your options.

The worksheet is reformatted minus the options that have been deselected. Click the worksheet to remove the cell selection. Use the **EDIT – UNDO** command again to restore the worksheet to its original format.

Save the workbook at this point before proceeding with the next task.

Indenting, rotating and aligning cell data

① **Indenting**. Select cells **A4** to **A10** in the **Insurance Sales** worksheet.

Open the **FORMAT** menu and select **CELLS**. The Format Cells dialog box is displayed. Select the **ALIGNMENT** tab – see Figure 4.4.

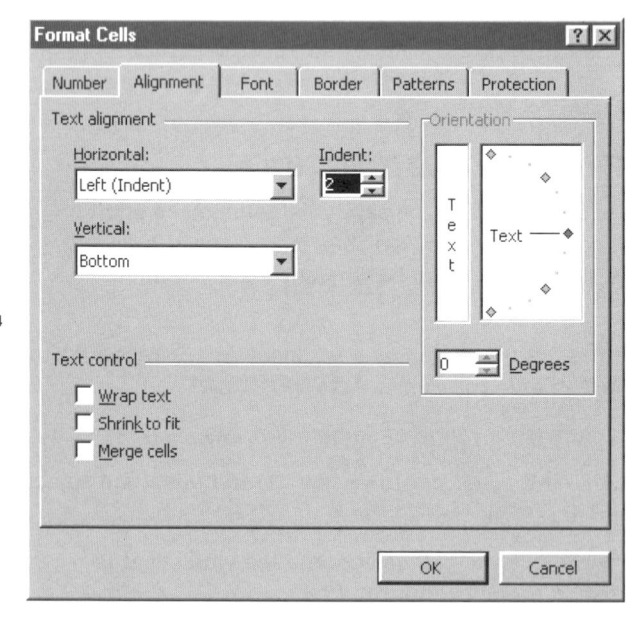

FIGURE 4.4

You can indent text by up to 15 steps. Use the arrows on the **INDENT** box to increase the indent steps to 2.

Click **OK** and the text is indented in the cells.

② Text Rotating. Use the **EDIT-UNDO** command to remove the indent.

a. Select cells **B3** to **D3**.

b. Open the **FORMAT** menu and select **CELLS**. The Alignment tab should still be selected.

c. This time use the arrows on the **DEGREES** box to set it to -1.

d. Click **OK** and the column headings are rotated.

③ Text Aligning. Undo the rotation using the **EDIT** menu. Select cells **B3** to **E3**.

Use the **ALIGNMENT** dialog box to centre the text horizontally and vertically. If the vertical centring is not apparent you could experiment with a smaller font size.

Conditional formatting and copying formats

① The conditional formatting feature lets you format only those cells whose values conform to certain limits.

Select cell range **B4** to **D6** in the **Insurance Sales** workbook.

② Open the **FORMAT** menu and select **CONDITIONAL FORMATTING** – a dialog box appears – see Figure 4.5. Let's say that we wish to pick out which of the values in the selected cells fall between 100 and 300.

③ Using Figure 4.5 as a guide enter these values into the dialog box.

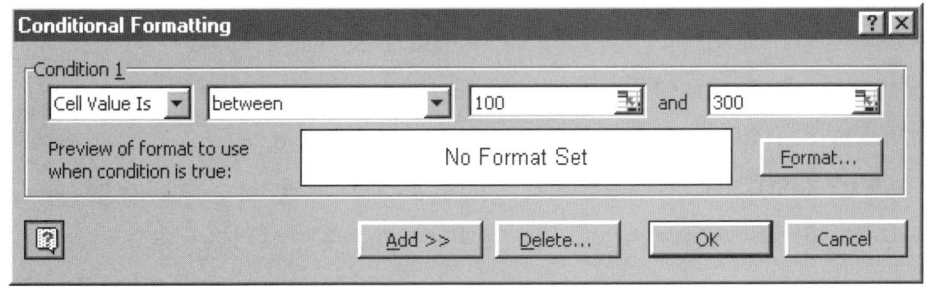

FIGURE 4.5

④ Click the **FORMAT** button on the dialog box and the Format Cells dialog box is displayed.

a. Select the **BORDER** tab on this dialog box.

b. Click the **OUTLINE** button then the **OK** button – you are returned to the Conditional Formatting dialog box. Click the **OK** button on this dialog box.

c. You are returned to the worksheet; de-select the cells – you will see that the cells whose values fall between 100 and 300 have a border.

(5) Copying Formats. Using Format Painter you can copy complex formats quickly.

   a. First apply the following formats to cell **A4**: Text font size 12, italic and cell coloured red.

   b. Make sure that this cell is still selected. Now identify the **FORMAT PAINTER** button, marked with a paintbrush on the Standard Toolbar. Click this button.

   c. Select a cell or cell range to copy this format to, eg cells **A5** and **A6**.

   The format is copied – use **EDIT-UNDO** if it doesn't work correctly.

Summary of commands and functions

Note:
Menu commands show the menu name first, followed by the command to choose from the menu, e.g. **EDIT-CLEAR** means open the Edit menu and select the Clear command.

Menu commands

EDIT-CLEAR-ALL	Delete cell contents
EDIT-DELETE SHEET	Delete selected worksheet
EDIT-FILL-DOWN	Copy selected cells into selected lower cells
EDIT-FILL-RIGHT	Copy selected cells into selected right hand columns
EDIT-UNDO	Undo previous operation
FILE-NEW-WORKBOOK	Open new, blank workbook
FORMAT-AUTOFORMAT	Apply Excel built-in format
FORMAT-CELLS-ALIGNMENT	Indent and rotate cell data
FORMAT-CELLS-NUMBER	Format numeric data
FORMAT-CONDITIONAL FORMAT	Format cells meeting certain conditions
FORMAT-SHEET-RENAME	Rename Selected Sheet

Functions

=AVERAGE()	Average range of cells

TOPIC 5

Excel charts

Introduction

In the next few topics we will use charts to present worksheet data in a more visual way (chart is Excel's preferred word for graph). Excel uses its special ChartWizard feature which lets you create a wide variety of different chart types in a few simple steps – line graphs, pie charts, bar charts etc, as well as many sub-types. You can either embed a chart in your worksheet or create it as a separate chart sheet. We will be looking at both approaches and also learning how to format charts for the best results.

Topic objectives

- To create a column chart using ChartWizard.
- To create a pie chart.
- To change the size of a chart.
- To format chart text.
- To understand fundamental chart concepts.
- To change one chart type into another.
- To display multiple worksheet windows.
- To demontrate the dynamic relationships between chart and worksheet data.
- To re-position chart elements.
- To display values on a chart.

Some initial worksheet data

1. We will create the worksheet shown in Figure 5.1 as the basis for our first charts. It shows the number of companies who have responded to a national marketing campaign. Start with a new blank workbook.

	A	B	C	D	E	F
1		Number of Responses to Marketing Campaign					
2						
3		Week 1	Week 2	Week 3	Week 4	Total
4						
5	TV Campaign	876	1056	1348	985	4265
6	Web Site	325	278	167	339	1109
7	Telephone	416	178	529	472	1595
8	Newspapers	276	238	318	287	1119
9	Trade Press	43	52	38	34	167
10						
11	Total	1936	1802	2400	2117	8255
12						

FIGURE 5.1

Topic 5 · Excel charts

(2) Format it as shown, ie adjust the column widths and put the cell labels and headings in bold.

(3) Total up the first column using a formula or the **AUTOSUM** button, placing the result in cell **B11**.

(4) Use **FILL RIGHT** or **AUTOFILL** to copy this formula to the 3 adjacent cells (C11 to E11).

(5) Similarly total cells **F5** to **F9**; as a check calculate the overall total for all responses in cell **F11**. It should be 8255, as shown in Figure 5.1.

(6) Save the workbook as **Marketing Campaign**. We will use the worksheet to create a number of different chart types.

Using ChartWizard to create a chart

Excel's ChartWizard feature offers a host of options and features to create the chart of your choice; however, they all use 4 basic steps: first you select the worksheet cells you want to base your chart around, then:

(1) Choose the chart type you prefer – column chart, line chart etc.

(2) Confirm the cells that you wish to use in your chart.

(3) Choose the chart's horizontal and vertical axis, title, etc.

(4) Select either an 'embedded' chart forming part of the worksheet or a chart as a separate sheet.

These steps may sound complicated but Excel dialog boxes help you along. If you make a mistake at any stage you can cancel the step, get help or return to a previous step.

(1) Our first chart will be a column chart of the first week's responses:

Select the cell range **A3** to **B9**.

To start ChartWizard issue the menu command **INSERT – CHART** (or use the **CHARTWIZARD** button – see key at the end of Topic 1).

(2) *Note: The Office Assistant*: The **OFFICE ASSISTANT** dialog box may appear too at this stage; you may find it a useful addition to the ChartWizard instructions. If it is not displayed it can be called up by clicking the Office Assistant button (marked with a '?') at the bottom left of the ChartWizard dialog box. If you want to hide it right click the Office Assistant paperclip logo and select **HIDE**.

(3) **ChartWizard – Step 1 of 4 – Chart Type** is displayed now.

a. First select the **STANDARD TYPES** tab if necessary.

This is the stage where you select the Chart type. Make sure that **COLUMN** is selected – see Figure 5.2.

b. 7 sub-types of the column chart are shown on the right of the dialog box. Click to select each sub-type in turn and Excel explains its purpose underneath.

Topic 5 • Excel charts

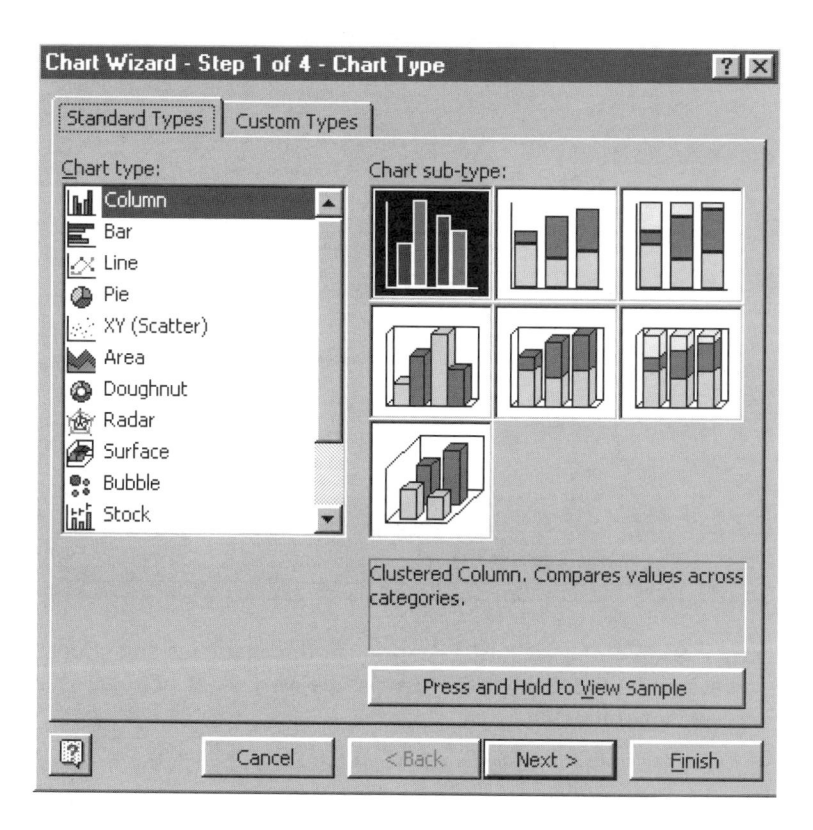

FIGURE 5.2

    c.   Click the **PRESS AND HOLD TO VIEW SAMPLE** button – your chart is previewed.

    d.   Finally re-select sub-type 1, the standard clustered column chart, and click the **NEXT** button.

4   **ChartWizard – Step 2 of 4 – Chart Source**.

First select the **DATA RANGE** tab if necessary; you will see that the range of worksheet cells that you selected is confirmed – A3 to B9. Excel shows them as a formula and includes absolute references and the sheet number, ie =Sheet1!$A$3:$B$9. If the cells in the worksheet are hidden by the dialog box then place the screen pointer on the title bar and drag it to one side.

At this stage we could amend the range of cells we wanted to chart if they were incorrect, or simply press the **CANCEL** button and start again. Assuming that the cell range is correct click the **NEXT** button.

5   **ChartWizard – Step 3 of 4 – Chart Options.**

    a.   Make sure that the **TITLES** tab is selected first.

    b.   Using Figure 5.3 as a guide, add titles and axis labels to the chart, eg start with the Chart title box and enter ***Week 1 Responses***.

    c.   As this chart will not need a legend, click the **LEGEND** tab on the dialog box and de-select the option **SHOW LEGEND**.

Click the **NEXT** button.

Topic 5 · Excel charts

FIGURE 5.3

⑥ **ChartWizard – Step 4 of 4 – Chart Location**. At this stage we can choose whether to have an 'embedded' chart – part of the worksheet – or place the chart in its own separate sheet.

Select the **AS NEW SHEET** option – see Figure 5.4 – and click the **FINISH** button. The chart appears in its own sheet, with the default name **Chart1** shown on the sheet tab.

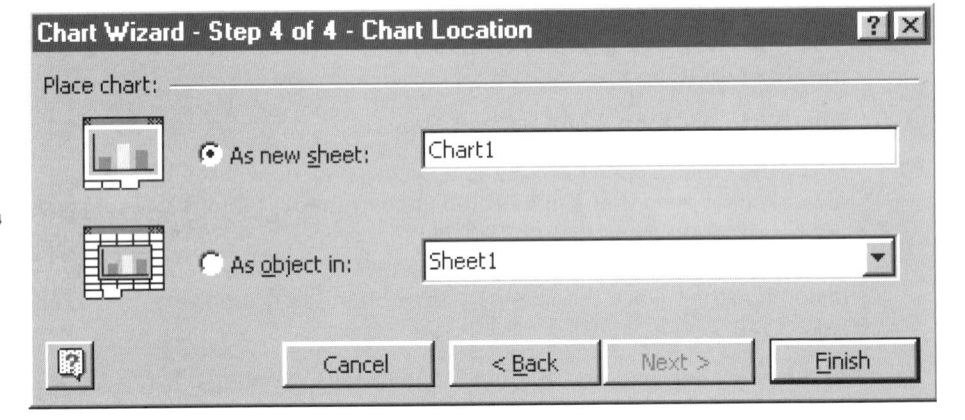

FIGURE 5.4

Altering the chart size

You may find that when you first create a chart it is too small, and some of its elements are unreadable. You can alter its overall size with the View menu.

① Make sure that the chart window is maximised then issue the menu command **VIEW – SIZED WITH WINDOW**. This command enlarges the chart to fill the window.

Next issue the menu command **VIEW – FULL SCREEN**; the chart is larger but you lose Excel menus and other features. Re-select the **VIEW – FULL SCREEN** option to de-select it.

Topic 5 · Excel charts

2 Click the window **RESTORE** button; as we have selected the **SIZED WITH WINDOW** command the complete chart is still displayed but some of the text may be too small to read.

3 Issue the menu command **VIEW – SIZED WITH WINDOW** command again; this has the effect of de-selecting it.

Now try the **VIEW – ZOOM** command which allows you to choose your own chart size.

Try out the **FIT SELECTION** option on the Zoom dialogue box – the chart fits to the current window size.

Note: The View – Zoom command is not available if Sized with Window is selected.

4 Finally open the **VIEW** menu and select the **SIZED WITH WINDOW** option.

5 *Note: The Chart Toolbar*. If the Chart Toolbar appears close it for these activities as we will be using ChartWizard.

6 **Enlarging the Font Size**.

  a. To make the chart labels more readable *right* click the white space around the chart (not the chart or the axes).

  b. Select the option **FORMAT CHART AREA** – a dialog box appears.

  c. Select the **FONT** tab.

  d. Change the font, eg to 8 point bold – see Figure 5.5. You can also change the font and the colour if you wish. Click **OK**.

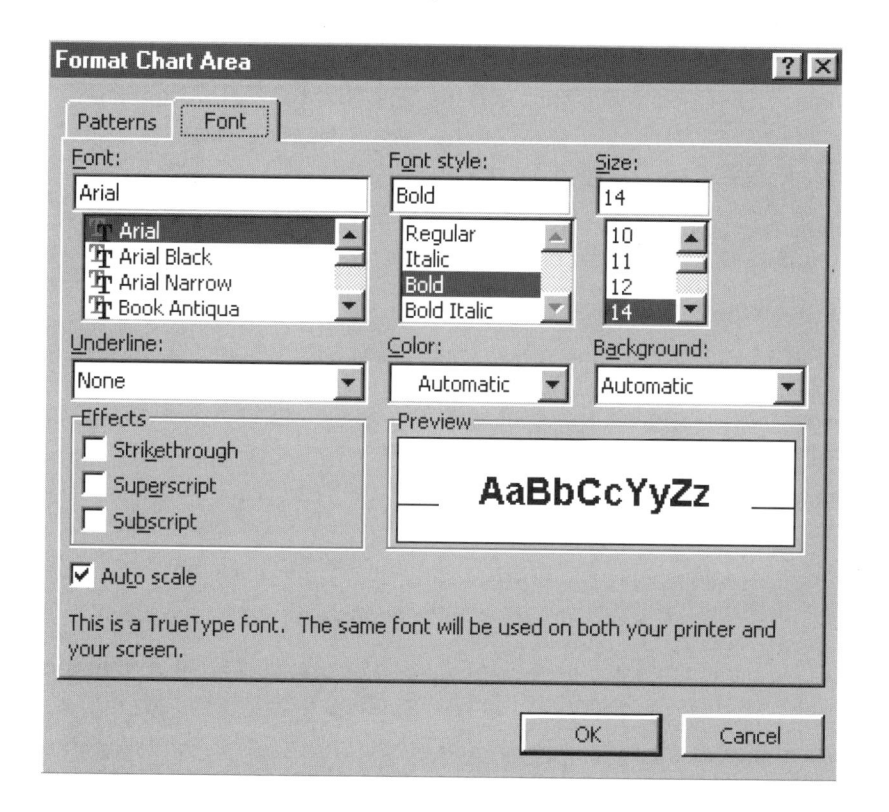

FIGURE 5.5

Chart concepts

We have created a column chart, based on the data in cells A3 to B9 of Sheet1 of the Marketing Campaign workbook. We will briefly review some key chart concepts.

a. The 5 columns represent the values of the 5 worksheet cells plotted – cells B3 to B9. Place the mouse pointer on a column and a text box identifies it.

   Each value is represented by a **data point**, collectively they form **a data series**.

   This is a very simple column chart consisting of only one data series – the number of responses to each type of marketing for one week.

b. It is usual to show the values on the **Y** or **vertical axis**, as in this chart; for this reason it is also called the **value** axis.

c. The categories are placed on **X** or **horizontal axis**; in this chart we have 5 categories – TV Campaign, Web Site etc. Notice that Excel automatically takes the labels from column A of the worksheet. The X axis is also called the **category** axis.

d. As we will see later some other chart types do not use any axes, eg pie charts.

Changing the chart type

1. We can convert the column chart to any other type of type of chart.

   a. With **Chart1** as the active sheet in the workbook, open the **CHART** menu and select the **CHART TYPE** option.

   b. A dialog box opens, make sure that the **STANDARD TYPES** tab is selected.

   c. Select **PIE** from the list of Chart Type options.

   d. A choice of pie chart sub-options are now displayed on the right of the dialog box. Make sure that option 1 is selected (in black).

   e. Click **OK** and the column chart changes to a pie chart.

2. **Adding a Legend.** Pie charts show clearly the contribution of each value to the total, in this case the proportion of each response to the total 'pie'. However, as a pie chart has no X or Y axis a legend or key is essential to explain the meaning of the various pie sections.

   a. Select the menu options **CHART – CHART OPTIONS** and then select the **LEGEND** tab.

   b. Select the options **SHOW LEGEND** and **RIGHT** and click **OK**.

3. Notes:

   a. If the legend is too small it can be enlarged by first clicking it so that it is surrounded by a selection box then by dragging a selection 'handle'.

   b. The font size can be enlarged by right clicking the legend and taking the option **FORMAT LEGEND**. Make sure that the **FONT** tab is selected, then use the **SIZE** box to change the font size.

c. Open the **VIEW** menu and check that the **SIZED WITH WINDOW** option is still selected.

Displaying multiple windows

1. The Marketing Campaign workbook contains two separate documents, the pie chart **Chart1** and the worksheet **Sheet1**. At the moment the chart is the 'active' sheet.

   It is often useful to see worksheet and related chart side by side in two separate windows – see Figure 5.6.

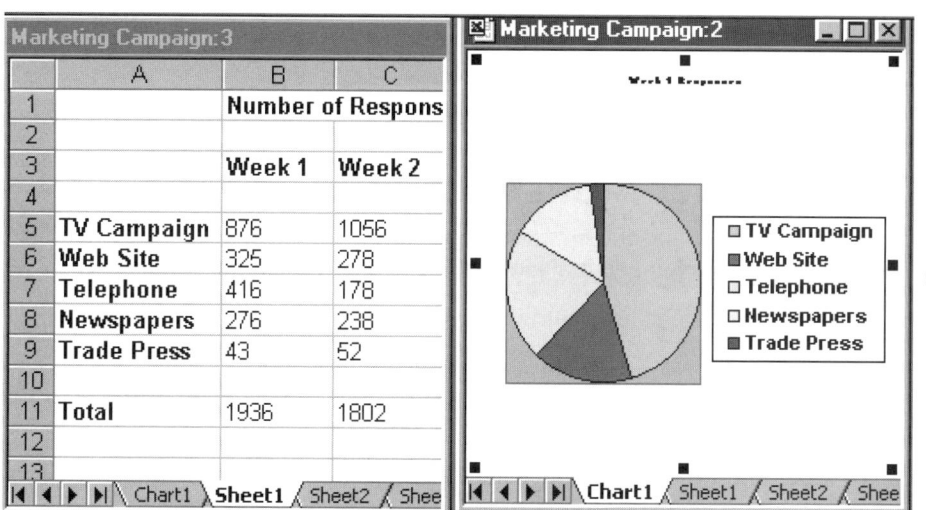

   FIGURE 5.6

2. Open the **WINDOW** menu and select the option **NEW WINDOW** – nothing appears to happen.

   However, open the **WINDOW** menu again and two sheets are listed at the bottom of the menu – **Marketing Campaign:1** and **Marketing Campaign:2**. A second window has been opened. If both windows are the same then simply use the sheet tab to select the other document, ie Sheet1 or Chart1.

3. **Re-arranging Windows**. We will now try out different ways of displaying the two windows.

   a. Open the **WINDOW** menu and select the **ARRANGE** option. The Arrange Windows dialog box is displayed. Select the **CASCADE** option.

   b. The two windows are arranged in an overlapping pattern – see Figure 5.7. Try clicking on the border of each window – it will select each window and bring it to the top.

FIGURE 5.7 click on overlapping corners

Marketing Campaign:2
Marketing Campaign:3

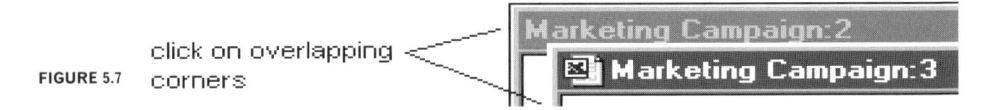

4 Open the **WINDOW** menu and select the **ARRANGE** option again.

Select the **VERTICAL** option this time and click **OK**. The two windows are now displayed side by side – see Figure 5.6 above. If the correct windows are not displayed then simply select them using the sheet tabs.

5 **Changing the Window Size**. We now have two windows side by side. Only one window can be active at a time. Click a window and it becomes active – its title bar is blue. To move or re-size a window use the normal procedure – drag the title bar to move it and drag the sides to change the size. You will find that the chart may become 'squashed' if you make it too small.

6 **Enlarging Chart Text**. To increase the size of any chart text right click on it and select the **FORMAT** option. When the dialog box is displayed, click the **FONT** tab and select a different font size.

Chart and worksheet links

1 A worksheet and the chart based on it are dynamically linked; when the data in one changes it also does in the other. Click the worksheet to activate it.

2 Select cell **B5** and amend the responses for the TV Campaign to **600**.

Press the **ENTER** key on the keyboard. When the change is executed the related section of the pie chart changes too.

3 Open the **EDIT** menu and select the option **UNDO TYPING**.

The pie chart returns to its original form.

4 We will now the close the extra window; simply click the **CLOSE** button on one of the windows. Maximise the remaining window if necessary.

Saving and opening a chart

1 The chart is part of the Marketing Campaign workbook and will be saved along with it as **Chart1**. Open the **FILE** menu and select **SAVE**. If you have had several attempts at creating the chart then the default name will be a higher number – Chart2, Chart3 etc.

2 Now open the **FILE** menu and select **CLOSE**. If you need to save the workbook a dialog box will prompt you. If so click the **YES** button.

3 Now open the workbook **Marketing Campaign** again using the File menu – the workbook is listed at the bottom of the menu. The last few workbooks that have been used will also be listed.

Topic 5 · Excel charts

Re-positioning pie chart segments

1 Check that the pie chart is the active sheet.

Click the pie chart once (not the space around it) – a dotted circle will enclose it.

2 Click the segment denoting Newspapers once – handles appear on the segment – see Figure 5.8. If you make a mistake press the `ESC` key on the keyboard and start again.

selection handles enclose the pie segment

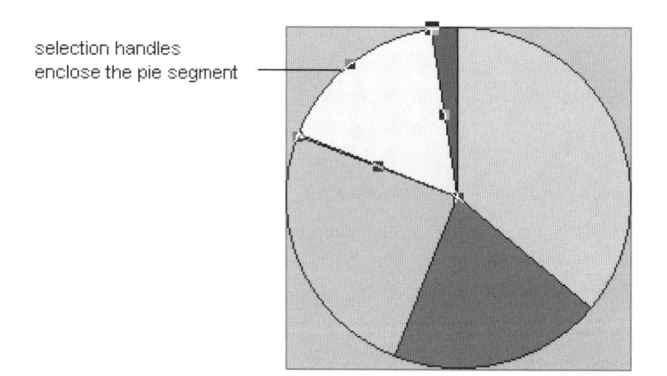

FIGURE 5.8

3 Use the left mouse button to drag the segment slightly away from the rest of the pie – this has the effect of emphasising this segment.

4 *Notes*: This sequence of selections can be fiddly at first; remember to use **EDIT-UNDO** if necessary. If you double click you will call up a dialog box which you can cancel.

Remember to check that the correct part of the chart is selected – enclosed in selection handles. Use the `ESC` key to remove the selection handles.

Displaying values on a chart

If pie chart segments are similar in size you can add values or percentages to the chart to make their relative proportions clearer.

1 Open the **CHART** menu and select **CHART OPTIONS**. Make sure that the **DATA LABELS** tab is selected.

2 Experiment with each of the options in the dialog box, finally selecting the **SHOW PERCENT** option. Click **OK** and the chart should now resemble Figure 5.9.

3 To enlarge the size of the font double click on one of the percentages. The **FORMAT DATA LABELS** dialog box is displayed.

Make sure that the **FONT** tab is selected then choose a different font size, eg 9 or 10.

Do the same for the legend and title if necessary.

4 Save the workbook at this point.

Week 1 Responses

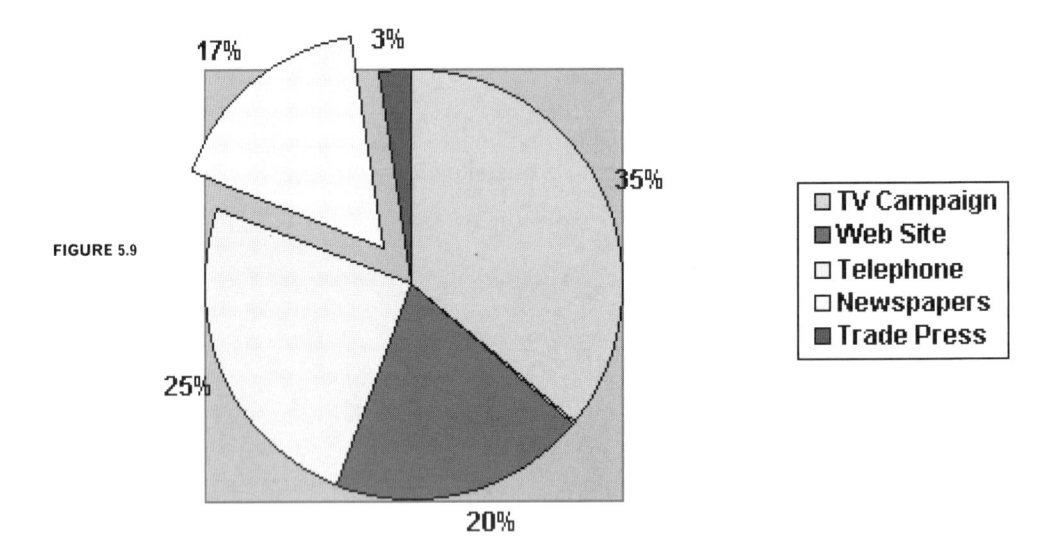

FIGURE 5.9

- 17%
- 3%
- 35%
- 20%
- 25%

☐ TV Campaign
■ Web Site
☐ Telephone
☐ Newspapers
■ Trade Press

Summary of commands

Note:
Menu commands show the menu name first, followed by the command to choose from the menu, e.g. **EDIT-CLEAR** means open the Edit menu and select the Clear command.

Menu commands

CHART-CHART OPTIONS	Change title, legend, data labels etc
CHART-CHART TYPE	Change the chart type
EDIT-UNDO	Reverse previous operation
INSERT-CHART	Create a new chart
VIEW-FIT SELECTION	Chart fits window size available
VIEW-FULL SCREEN	Sheet increases to full screen size
VIEW-ZOOM	Specify a particular chart size
VIEW-SIZED WITH WINDOW	Re-size chart to window size
WINDOW-ARRANGE	Arrange layout of windows
WINDOW-NEW WINDOW	Open extra window

TOPIC 6

Formatting, copying and naming charts

Introduction

In this topic we will be learning how to alter the size and position of chart components, how to add text boxes and how to print charts. We will learn how to change the colours and patterns of chart pie segments and columns and how to draw charts from non-adjacent cells. We will also be naming and copying charts.

Topic objectives

- To re-size and re-position chart components.
- To change the fonts and styles of chart text.
- To use text boxes and arrows in charts.
- To print charts.
- To vary chart colours and patterns.
- To draw a line chart.
- To add titles and legend to an existing chart.
- To re-name charts.
- To plot a chart from non-adjacent cells.
- To copy charts.

Re-sizing and re-positioning chart components

In the previous topic we learnt how to edit individual chart components, eg pie segments, title or legend. It is simply a matter of clicking the item to select it, then either dragging with the mouse or using a menu option. This topic extends these techniques further. Here are some simple guidelines before we start:

- It takes practice to select the right item – particularly when several items are close together.
- An item is only selected if it is enclosed in selection 'handles' – see previous topic.
- To remove selection handles simply click elsewhere on the chart or press the **ESC** key.
- If you make a mistake while making a change to the chart then use the **EDIT-UNDO** option.
- Single clicking selects a component, double clicking calls up a dialog box; cancel an unwanted dialog box using the **CANCEL** or the **CLOSE** button.

1 Open the Workbook **Marketing Campaign** created in the previous topic.

Make sure that **Chart1** is the active sheet.

First try clicking the various parts of the chart in turn to select them – pie segments, percentages, title and legend. Try deselecting them with the **ESC** key.

Now click the **LEGEND** box – the sides of the box display a number of square 'selection handles'.

2 Move the screen pointer onto the the top left handle; when correctly placed the pointer changes to a double-headed arrow and a tip box appears to identify it – see Figure 6.1.

Drag the selection handle up to the left to enlarge the legend.

FIGURE 6.1

3 Click the outside edge of the grey area that surrounds the pie chart; make sure that the whole pie area is selected rather than an individual segment or label – see Figure 6.2.

Drag the selection handle on the bottom right hand corner down to to the right to enlarge the chart. If you drag anywhere else on the chart you will move it rather than copy it; use the **EDIT-UNDO** command to reverse this.

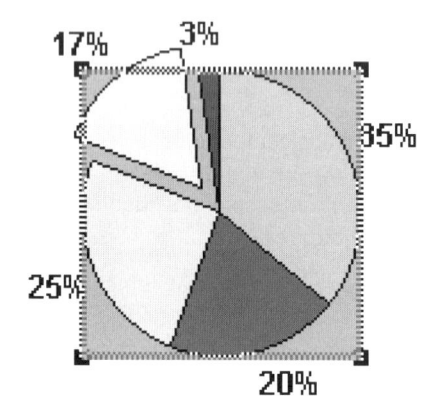

FIGURE 6.2

4 **Re-positioning the Title**. Use the same technique to move the title, ie:

a. Click the title to surround it with a selection rectangle.

b. Use the mouse on the edge of the rectangle and drag it to a new position; you cannot change the size of the title by dragging – this is dealt with in the next task.

Topic 6 • Formatting, copying and naming charts

    c.   Next click in front of the word 'Responses' in the title to place a flashing line there – the text insertion point.

    d.   Insert the word **Marketing** in the title.

More chart formatting

1   **Fonts and Styles**. First we will make the title more prominent.

    a.   Right click the title and select the option **FORMAT CHART TITLE**.

    b.   Make sure that the **FONT** tab in the dialog box is selected – you can select various fonts, sizes and styles.

    c.   Select a font size of **12** and another font type, select **BOLD**, then **OK**.

    d.   The title is reformatted – press the **ESC** key to deselect it.

2   **Using Text Boxes and Arrows**. In the pie chart the number of responses in the trade press is rather low; we can add a comment to emphasize this. If the Drawing Toolbar is already displayed at the bottom of the screen then skip section a.

    a.   Open the **VIEW** menu and select **TOOLBARS** – you are offered a selection of further toolbars to display. Select **DRAWING** and it is displayed at the bottom of the window.

    b.   Click the **ARROW** button on the Drawing Toolbar – marked with a downwards-pointing arrow.

    c.   The screen pointer changes to a cross; drag to draw the arrow as shown in Figure 6.4 on page 68. You draw the arrow from the base to the tip.

    Note: You can delete an arrow if it is still selected by pressing the **DELETE** key on the keyboard.

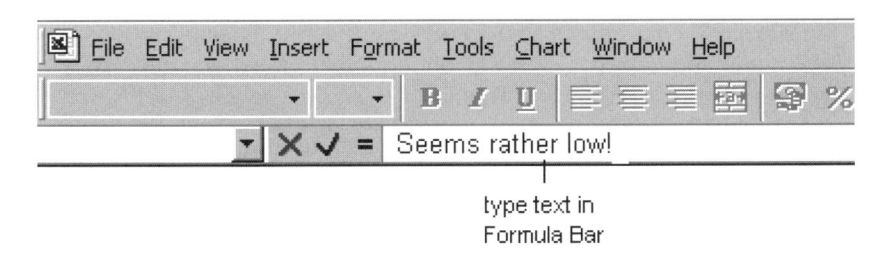

FIGURE 6.3

    d.   To add text to the arrow first press the **ESC** key first if necessary to de-select the arrow. Then select the Formula Bar at the top of the screen and type the comment ***Seems rather low!*** – see Figure 6.3 above.

    e.   Click the **TICK** box next to the Formula Bar to complete entering the text.

    The text now appears on the screen, enclosed by selection handles.

    f.   Now drag *the selection rectangle itself* but not one of the handles to move the text next to the arrow.

    g.   Enlarge the text if necessary; first select the text by dragging, then right

FIGURE 6.4

Week 1 Marketing Responses

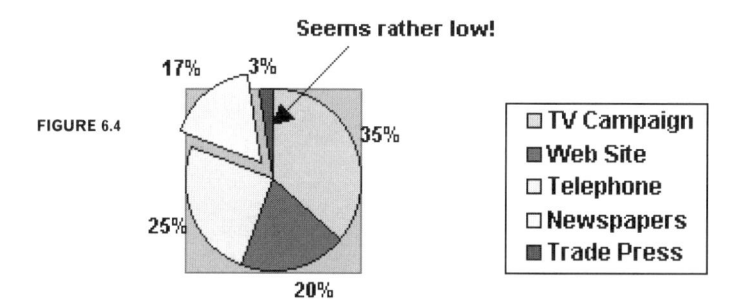

Seems rather low!

17% 3%
35%
25%
20%

☐ TV Campaign
■ Web Site
☐ Telephone
☐ Newspapers
■ Trade Press

click it and proceed as in section 1 above. You may need to re-position it once you have done this. To delete the text select it and press the **DELETE** key.

3 *Note – Formatting All Chart Text*. If you wish to apply a format change to all the chart text proceed as follows:

a. Click the outside edge of the chart window so that all the chart is selected – small square 'handles' appear around it.

b. Right click or open the **FORMAT** menu and select the option **SELECTED CHART AREA**. Any formatting options that you select will apply to all the chart elements

4 **Independent Task**. Format the percentage labels on the pie chart to make them more readable.

Printing charts

1 Printing charts involves the same basic operations as printing worksheets – see Topic 3. First ensure that **Chart1** is the active sheet, then open the **FILE** menu and select the **PRINT** option. If you prefer you can use the Print button on the Standard Toolbar instead.

2 *Note*: If you open the File menu and find that the Print option is 'dimmed', ie in pale grey rather than black, this means that it is unavailable. The usual reason for this is that you have not completed an operation. Check whether the tick box next to the Formula Bar, or some other part of the chart, is selected and complete the action.

3 The Print dialog box is displayed:

a. First select the number of copies if you wish to print more than one.

b. Click the **PREVIEW** button to see how the chart will appear when printed.

To enlarge or reduce the size of the image simply click it or use the **ZOOM** button at the top of the window.

c. To check the page setup click the **SETUP** button – this offers you the usual range of options using a number of tabs, eg margins, headers, footers, scaling, portrait and landscape – see Topic 3 for more information on this.

Topic 6 · Formatting, copying and naming charts

d. If you are satisfied click the **PRINT** button, otherwise close the dialog box.

If nothing happens then check that the printer is switched on, the cable from the computer to the back of the printer is connected and there is paper in the trays.

Chart colours and patterns

If you decide to print charts in black and white you can add contrast to the segments, columns etc by using suitable patterns.

1 Click on one segment of the pie chart so that it is enclosed in selection handles. Do not select the whole chart – see Figure 6.5.

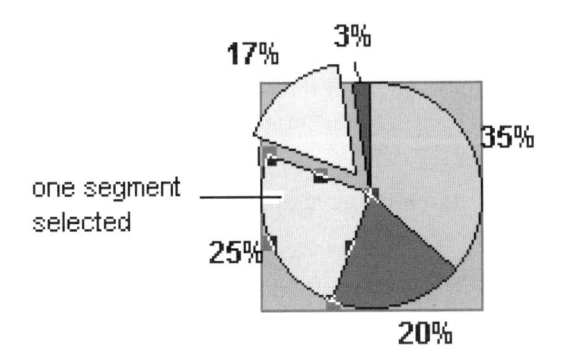

FIGURE 6.5

2 Right click the selected segment and take the option **FORMAT DATA POINT**.

   a. Select the **PATTERNS** tab from the dialog box that appears.

   b. In the **BORDER** section of the dialog box select a different edge for the segment.

   c. In the **AREA** section of the dialog box click the **FILL EFFECTS** button. A new dialog box is displayed.

   d. First click the **GRADIENT** tab and select the option **ONE COLOR** – see Figure 6.6.

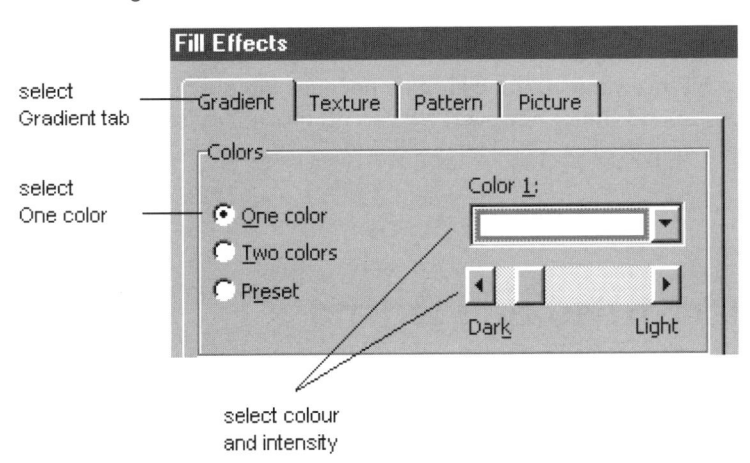

FIGURE 6.6

Click the down arrow on the **COLOR 1** box and select a colour. A slide bar under this box allows you to vary the intensity of the colour that you have chosen.

e. Click the **PATTERN** tab and choose a suitable pattern.

f. Click **OK** to return to the first dialog box, then click **OK** on this dialog box to return to the chart – the selected segment has changed its colour and pattern.

③ **Independent Task.** Re-format the rest of the pie chart segments with suitable patterns and save the changes.

Line charts

We will use the **Insurance Sales** worksheet, created in Topic 4, to create a line chart. Line charts are especially useful for displaying trends over time, eg comparing sales of different types of insurance over 3 months. The 3 values for each type of insurance are shown by points on a line.

① Make sure that the workbook **Insurance Sales** is open and that **Sheet1** is the active sheet.

② Let's compare the sales of all types of insurance for the 3 months. Select cell range **A3** to **D6**, ie 16 cells in all.

③ Open the **INSERT** menu and select the **CHART** option.

④ The first ChartWizard dialog box is displayed. Select **LINE** – sub-type 4 (the default); this should be already selected. Click the **NEXT** button.

⑤ In the second dialog box check that data range Sheet1!$A$3:$D$6 is displayed. The formula looks complex because it includes the sheet name and uses absolute references (the dollar signs). Click the **NEXT** button.

⑥ We will add titles etc later so click the **NEXT** button on the third dialog box.

⑦ On the fourth and final dialog box select the **AS NEW SHEET** option then click the **FINISH** button.

⑧ The line chart is displayed in its own window, named **Chart1**.

Open the **VIEW** menu and select **SIZED WITH WINDOW**. The line chart expands to fill the window. It lacks titles because we did not use ChartWizard to add them; however, we can do this at any stage, eg in our next task.

Adding chart titles and legend

① Make sure that the line chart created in the previous task is still the active document.

Open the **CHART** menu and select **CHART OPTIONS**.

Topic 6 · Formatting, copying and naming charts

② Click the **TITLES** tab on the Chart Options dialog box.

③ Enter *Sales of Insurance Policies* in the **CHART TITLE** box.

④ Add the title *Current Year* to the **CATEGORY (X) AXIS** box.

⑤ Similarly in the **VALUE (Y) AXIS** box type the title *Policies Sold*.

⑥ Now click the **LEGEND** tab to ensure that the **SHOW LEGEND** option is selected. Click **OK**.

Re-positioning titles and legend using the format menu

You can drag titles and legends to new positions with the mouse but the Format menu offers further options which we will try out now. Remember that you can call up the menu directly by right clicking the chart component, or double click it to call up the dialog box.

① Click the title for the Y axis, 'Policies Sold' to select it.

Open the **FORMAT** menu and select the option **SELECTED AXIS TITLE**.

② The **FORMAT** dialog box opens, click the **ALIGNMENT** tab. You are offered various options. Make sure that horizontal and vertical text alignment are both set to **CENTER** – see Figure 6.7.

Change the **TEXT ORIENTATION** TO 0 DEGREES IF NECESSARY.

Use the **FONT** tab to make the text larger then click **OK**.

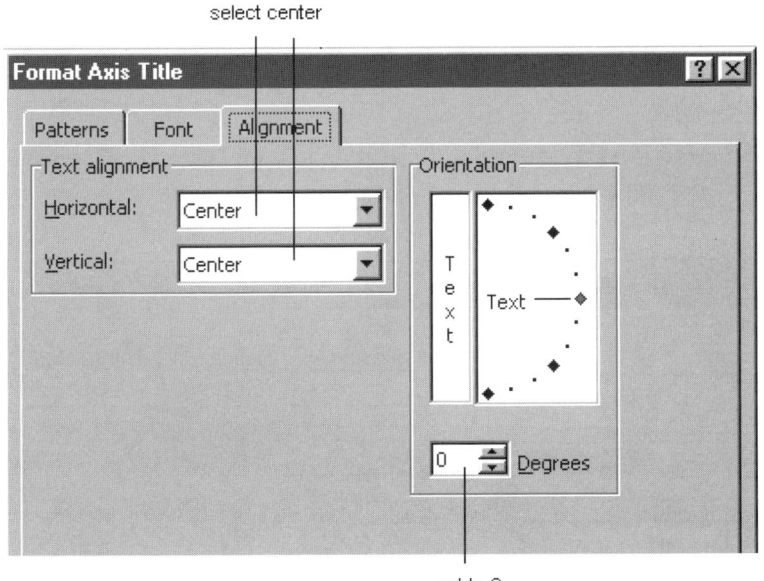

FIGURE 6.7

Topic 6 · Formatting, copying and naming charts

3 The title 'Policies Sold' is now displayed horizontally – more readably but it may overlap the chart itself. You can select the title then drag it and/or re-size it if this is a problem. You can see in Figure 6.8 that it is also possible to split the title over two lines using the **ENTER** key.

4 **Independent Tasks**.

a. Using the above operations adjust the font size, style or colour for:
the X axis title,
the X and Y axes themselves,
the legend.

b. Use the **CHART TYPE** option on the **CHART** menu to try out other line chart types – return to sub-type 4 when you have finished.

c. Finally print the line chart and compare it with Figure 6.8.

FIGURE 6.8 Policies Sold

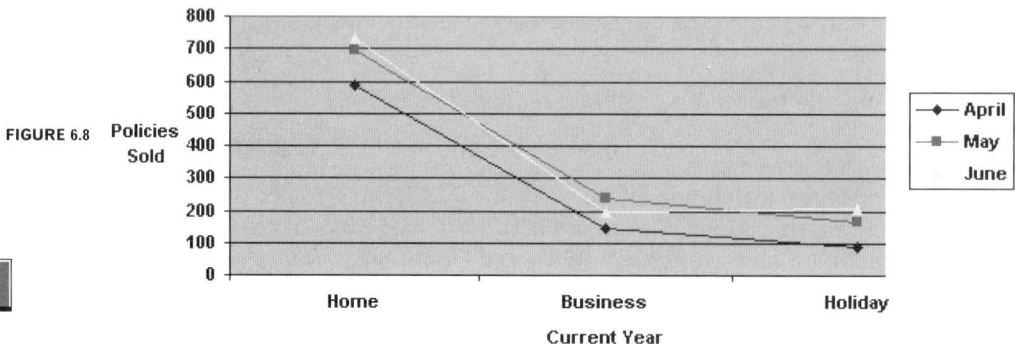

Drawing a chart from non-adjacent cells

If we wanted to create a new chart from the **Insurance Sales** worksheet comparing the sales of home and holiday insurance we would need to select non-adjacent cell ranges from the worksheet, using the **CTRL** key.

1 First select the cell range **A3** to **B6**, holding the row labels and the data for Home Insurance.

2 Next hold down the **CTRL** key and select cell range **D3** to **D6**. Compare your selections with Figure 6.9.

FIGURE 6.9

	A	B	C	D	E
1		Insurance Sales - Second Quarter			
2					
3		Home	Business	Holiday	Total Sales
4	April	587	148	89	824
5	May	695	241	168	1104
6	June	734	198	207	1139
7					
8	Average Sales per Quarte	672	196	155	1022
9	Total Sales per Quarter	2016	587	464	3067
10	% of Total	65.73%	19.14%	15.13%	

Topic 6 · Formatting, copying and naming charts

③ You can now use ChartWizard, as before, to create another line chart on a separate sheet. It should have the default name **Chart2**. Add a suitable title and format the text to enlarge it – see previous tasks and Figure 6.10 as a guide.

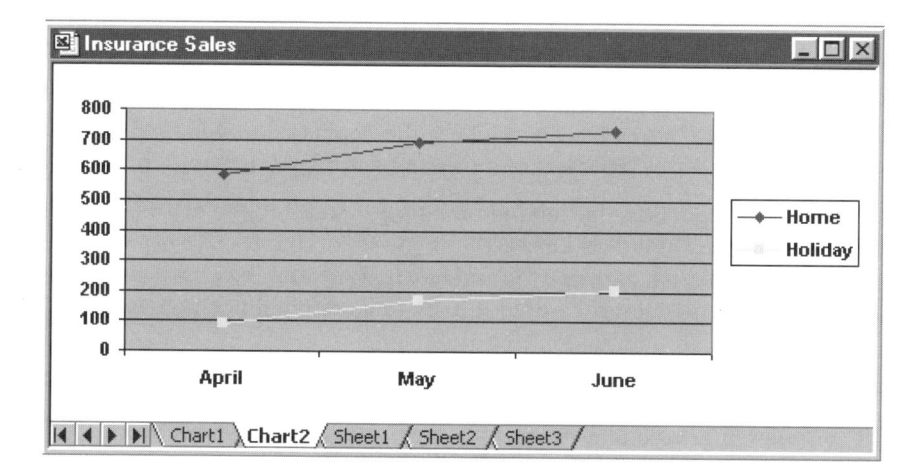

FIGURE 6.10

Naming charts

At the moment the workbook **Insurance Sales** consists of one worksheet and two line charts. We will give them more descriptive names than the default ones Sheet1, Chart2 etc. The rules for naming charts are the same as for worksheets, ie a chart name can be up to 31 characters long, can contain spaces, but not the following special characters: [ ], /, \, ? and *

① First select the sheet tab for **Sheet1**, if it not visible then you may need to maximise the window.

② Open the **FORMAT** menu and select the options **SHEET** then **RENAME** (a quicker alternative is to right click the sheet tab). The name on the tab is now selected.

③ Type the new name **Sales Data**.

④ Repeat these operations for the two charts, renaming them **Line 1** and **Line 2** respectively. The sheet tabs at the bottom of the window should now look like Figure 6.11.

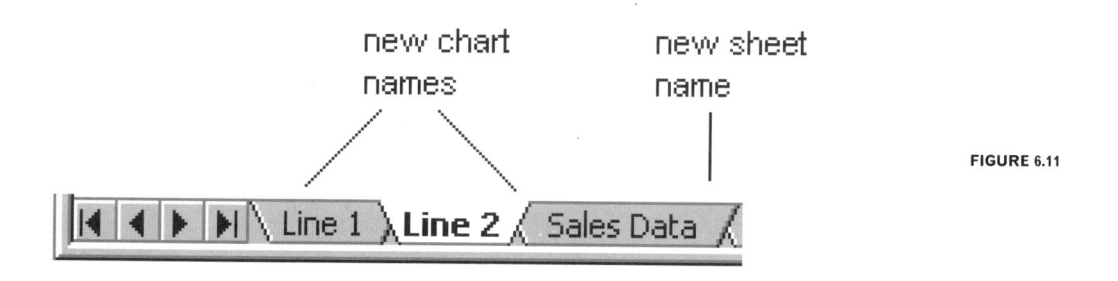

FIGURE 6.11

Copying charts

① We will use the same drag and drop technique to copy a chart as we used in Topic 3 to copy a worksheet – see page 46. We can then modify the copy.

  a. Select the name tab for Line 2 – it is now the active window.

  b. Hold down the **CTRL** key – the cursor changes to an icon marked with a + sign.

  c. A small triangle marks the place where the copied chart will be placed; drag the mouse so that the cursor moves past the next sheet tab.

  d. First release the mouse button *then* the **CTRL** key and the chart is copied – the name tab is marked Line 2 (2). If you let go the **CTRL** *before* releasing the mouse then you may merely have moved the Line 2 sheet to a new position, in which case drag it back to its original position and try again.

② Now rename the copied chart Line 3.

③ If you are not proceeding to the next topic then save and close your workbook.

Summary of commands

Note:
Menu commands show the menu name first, followed by the command to choose from the menu, e.g. **EDIT-CLEAR** means open the Edit menu and select the Clear command.

Menu commands

CHART-CHART OPTIONS	Change title, legend, data labels etc
FILE-PRINT	Print chart
FORMAT-SELECTED.....	Format selected chart element
FORMAT-SHEET-RENAME	Name a chart sheet
INSERT-CHART	Create a new chart
VIEW-SIZED WITH WINDOW	Re-size chart to size of window
VIEW-TOOLBARS	Show or hide a toolbar

TOPIC 7

Further chart skills

Introduction

In this topic we learn to create some other types of chart, to add and remove chart values and reverse and re-scale the axis of a chart. We will also deal with chart gridlines and trendlines and use goal seeking in a chart.

Topic objectives

- To change the scale of a chart axis.
- To delete chart sheets.
- To create area, bar, 3-D and doughnut charts.
- To add and remove chart values.
- To reverse the axes of a chart.
- To add gridlines and trendlines to a chart.
- To use goal seeking in a chart.
- To add arrows and text boxes to charts.
- To create an embedded chart.

Changing the scale of a chart

1 Select the worksheet **Sales Data** in the workbook **Insurance Sales**. We will create a new line chart for Business and Holiday insurance.

2 First select cell range **A3** to **A6**, holding the row labels.

3 Next hold down the **CTRL** key and select cell range **C3** to **D6**. Compare your selections with Figure 7.1.

	A	B	C	D	E
1		Insurance Sales - Second Quarter			
2					
3		Home	Business	Holiday	Total Sales
4	April	587	148	89	824
5	May	695	241	168	1104
6	June	734	198	207	1139
7					
8	Average Sales per Quarter	672	196	155	1022
9	Total Sales per Quarter	2016	587	464	3067
10	% of Total	65.73%	19.14%	15.13%	

FIGURE 7.1

4 You can now use ChartWizard, as before, to create another line chart on a separate sheet. Add a suitable title and format the text to enlarge it – see the previous topic as a guide if necessary.

(5) Rename the new chart **Line 4**. You will see that the two lines are quite close together at points, but we can improve the chart's readability by changing the default scale for the vertical axis. At the moment the minimum and maximum values for the vertical axis are 0 and 300.

(6) Right click the vertical 'Y' axis and select the option **FORMAT AXIS**; select the **SCALE** tab.

Change the maximum and minimum values to 75 and 250.

Click the **OK** button and the chart axis is re-scaled, making the two lines easier to compare.

Open the **EDIT** menu and choose the **UNDO** and **RE-DO** commands to review the difference.

(7) Open the **FILE** menu and select **SAVE** to save the changes.

Deleting charts

(1) The workbook Insurance Sales contains two identical charts – **Line 2** and **Line 3**. We will delete **Line 3**.

(2) Right click the sheet tab for **Line 3** and select the **DELETE** option from the popup menu.

(3) A dialog box warns you that the sheet will be permanently deleted.

Check that the correct sheet is selected then click **OK**. The sheet is now deleted – check that the name tab has disappeared.

(4) *Note*: If you find that you have deleted a sheet containing vital data then the last resort is to exit Excel without saving your work. If you have saved your work recently then not too much work will be lost.

Creating area charts

Our next chart type is the area chart as shown in Figure 7.2. An area chart can be regarded as a number of line charts stacked on top of each other to form separate areas. It shows not just the trend in sales for each policy type but the contribution of each policy type to overall sales.

(1) Open the workbook **Insurance Sales** if necessary. Make sure that the worksheet **Sales Data** is the active sheet.

Select cells **A3** to **D6**, ie all insurance types, all months.

(2) Use ChartWizard to create a standard area chart, ie select **AREA** as the chart type.

Try out all the types of area chart by using the **SAMPLE** button on Step1 of ChartWizard. Finally select area chart sub-type 2.

(3) *Note: The Office Assistant*: The **OFFICE ASSISTANT** dialog box may

appear too at this stage; you may find it a useful addition to the ChartWizard instructions. If it is not displayed it can be called up by clicking the Office Assistant button (marked with a '?') bottom left of the ChartWizard dialog box. If you want to hide it right click the Office Assistant paperclip logo and select **HIDE**.

4 At Step 2 of ChartWizard check that the correct cell range is chosen.

5 At Step 3 of ChartWizard select the **DATA LABELS** tab and then select the **SHOW LABEL** option.

6 At Step 4 of ChartWizard select the **AS NEW SHEET** option.

7 When you finish ChartWizard use the **VIEW – SIZED WITH WINDOW** command to fit the chart to the the window size.

8 Select the **CHART-CHART OPTIONS** command and add a title to the chart – see Figure 7.2.

9 **Formatting All Chart Text**. Click the white space at the edge of the chart window so that all the chart is selected, ie small selection 'handles' enclose it.

Right click the chart and select **FORMAT CHART AREA**.

Select the **FONT** tab from the dialog box that appears and change the fonts to 9 point bold.

10 Name the chart **Area 1** (see previous topic if necessary).

11 Finally delete the legend.

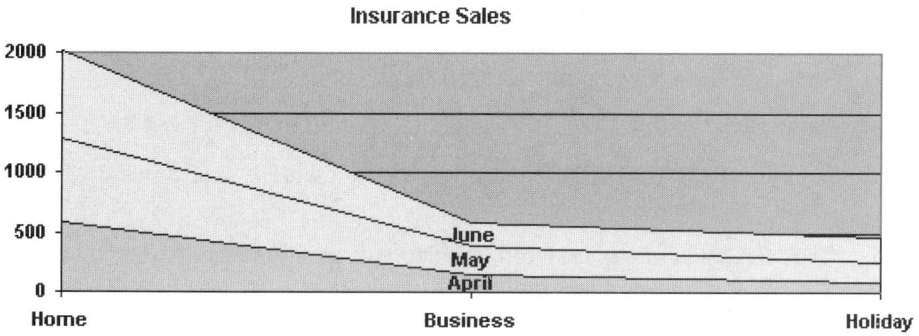

FIGURE 7.2

Removing and adding chart values

In Excel it is easy to remove a range of chart values, eg a segment from a pie chart or an area from a pie chart; it is equally easy to add new data range to a chart.

1 **Removing Values from a Chart**. Click once on the area for June on the **Insurance Sales** area chart, (not on the label). Selection handles appear on the area and the formula for the corresponding cell range is shown in the Formula Box at the top of the chart window, with the sheet names and absolute reference symbols ($) added – see Figure 7.3.

Topic 7 · Further chart skills

Formula Bar shows the cell references for selected month

=SERIES('Sales Data'!$A$6,'Sales Data'!$B$3:$D$3,'Sales Data'!$B$6:$D$6,3)

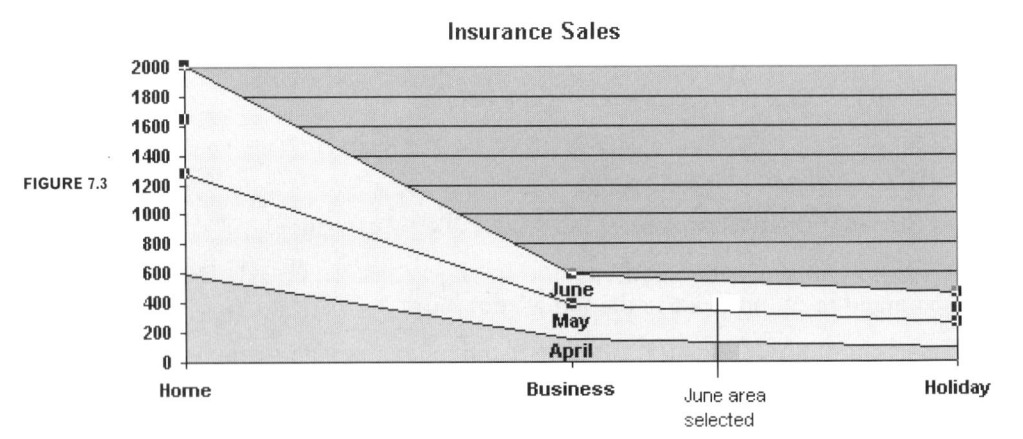

FIGURE 7.3

Insurance Sales

[Chart showing area chart with values 0-2000 on Y-axis; categories Home, Business, Holiday on X-axis; series June, May, April labeled; "June area selected" annotation]

② Press the **DELETE** key on the keyboard and the June values are removed (use the **EDIT – UNDO CLEAR** command to reverse any mistake).

③ **Adding Values to a Chart.** Select the worksheet **Sales Data** and select the cell range **A6 – D6**, ie for the month that we have just deleted.

Right click the selected cells and select the **COPY** option.

④ Now make the **Area 1** chart the active window again.

Open the **EDIT** window and select the **PASTE** option. If the the values are pasted back in an incorrect position, then follow section 6 below.

⑤ **Changing the Positions of Chart Values.**

a. Click the June area again so that it is selected.

b. Right click the June area and select the option **FORMAT DATA SERIES**.

c. Click the **SERIES ORDER** tab and use the dialog box to move it to its correct position.

d. Click **OK** and June is restored to its correct position as in Figure 7.3 above. If necessary re-size the window.

Reversing the axes on a chart

The **Area 1** chart plots the insurance types along the **X** or horizontal axis – these are our 3 categories. The number of each insurance type sold per month is plotted on the **Y** or vertical axis. However we could find it useful to reverse the axes, ie to have the months along the X axis and the number of different types of insurance sold shown on the Y axis. Comparing Figures 7.3 and 7.4 will make this distinction clear. It is easy to reverse the axes either in a new chart or for an existing one.

① With **Area 1** the active sheet click the **CHARTWIZARD** button on the Standard Toolbar.

Topic 7 · Further chart skills

(2) Check that Area Chart sub-type 2 is still selected in the dialog box, then click the **NEXT** button.

(2) ChartWizard – Step 2 is displayed next; make sure that the **DATA RANGE** tab is selected.

(3) Click the **COLUMNS** button and the chart axes are reversed – this is previewed for you.

Click the **FINISH** button.

(4) We now have 2 views of the same data:

Data Series in Rows – insurance types are categories, the months are plotted on the value axis – see Figure 7.3 above.

Data Series in Columns – the months are categories, the insurance types are plotted on the value axis – see Figure 7.4 below.

Note: You can reverse the axes for other chart types too.

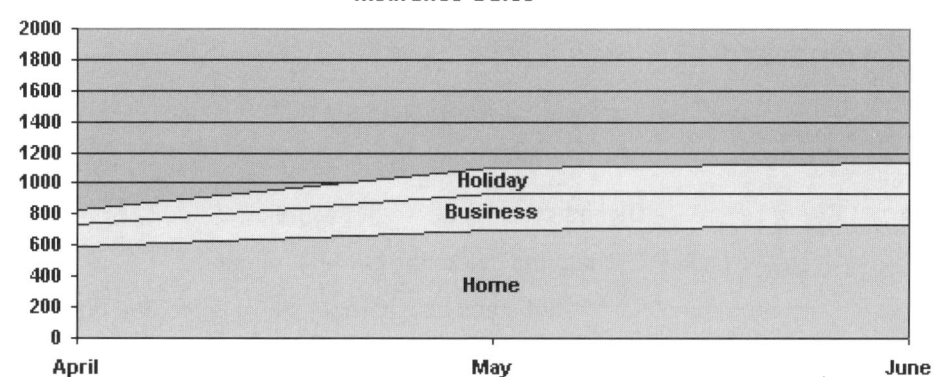

FIGURE 7.4

(5) **Independent Task**. Reverse the changes to the chart axes, showing the data in rows again – see Figure 7.3 above.

Using gridlines

(1) Gridlines can help you to read the values from a chart more easily – sometimes they are added to a chart by default, as in the case of area charts.

Make sure that the chart **Area 1** is selected.

Open the **CHART** menu and select **CHART OPTIONS**. Select the **GRIDLINES** tab.

(2) Experiment with selecting and deselecting the various gridlines options for both the Category Axis and the Value Axis, noting the effects. Cancel the dialog box when you have finished.

(3) Save and close the **Insurance Sales** workbook.

Topic 7 · Further chart skills

Creating bar and column charts

We have already created a column chart in Topic 5; at its simplest it shows the worksheet values as vertical columns and is especially useful for showing change over time. Bar charts are similar, showing worksheet values as a series of horizontal bars and are useful in comparing the sizes of items at a single point in time.

1 We will use another worksheet as the basis for these charts – see Figure 7.5. Create it in a new workbook – if Excel is open already simply open the **FILE** menu and select **NEW**. A dialog box appears, double click on the **WORKBOOK** icon.

When you have entered the data save the workbook as **Video Sales** and the worksheet as **Sales Data**.

FIGURE 7.5

	A	B	C	D	E
1		Video Sales - Current Year			
2					
3	Month	No. Sold	Revenue	Advertising	
4	June	750	1915	280	
5	July	910	3054	401	
6	August	1075	3447	498	
7	September	1330	4450	733	
8	October	1618	5009	801	
9					

2 Select cells **A3** – **D8** and create a new chart as follows:

a. Open the **INSERT** menu and select the **CHART** option.

b. Follow the four ChartWizard steps as before; at step 1 select the options **BAR CHART, SUB-TYPE 1**.

At step 2 select the **ROWS** option.

At step 4 select the **AS A NEW SHEET** option.

c. Open the **VIEW** menu and select the **SIZED WITH WINDOW** option.

d. If the text labels are too small then click the whole chart area to select it.

Right click the chart and select the option **FORMAT CHART AREA**.

Click the **FONT** tab and select the options **BOLD, SIZE 9**.

3 The chart produced is the standard clustered bar chart – see Figure 7.6.

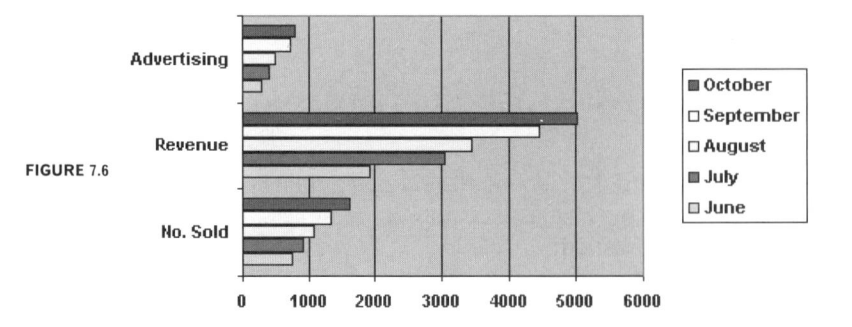

FIGURE 7.6

④ Name the bar chart **Bar 1**.

⑤ Return to the worksheet **Sales Data** and, making sure that the same set of cells are still selected, create a second type of bar chart. Proceed exactly as before but this time select the 2nd sub-type of bar chart – stacked bars.

⑥ The 3rd sub-type, the 100% stacked bar, can also be useful in showing the chart values as percentages. Preview this option and re-select the 2nd sub-type.

Format and re-size the chart as before.

Name it **Bar 2** – see Figure 7.7.

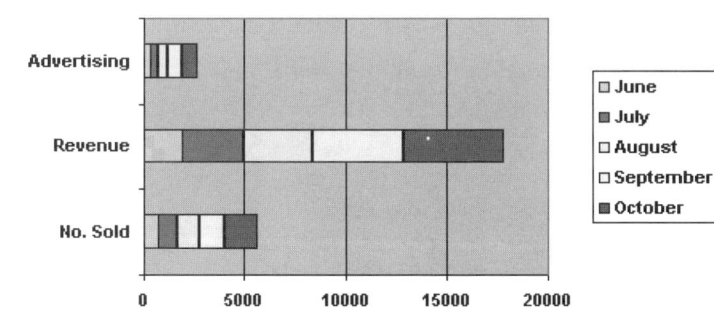

FIGURE 7.7

⑦ Each bar shows the sum of the smaller bars so that you can judge the contribution of each month to the overall category.

Independent task – column charts

① Make sure that cells **A3** to **D8** in the worksheet are still selected. Use this data to try out different types of column chart.

② Create the column chart shown in Figure 7.8.

Open the **VIEW** menu and select **SIZED WITH WINDOW**. Format and re-size the chart as before.

Save the sheet as **Column 1**.

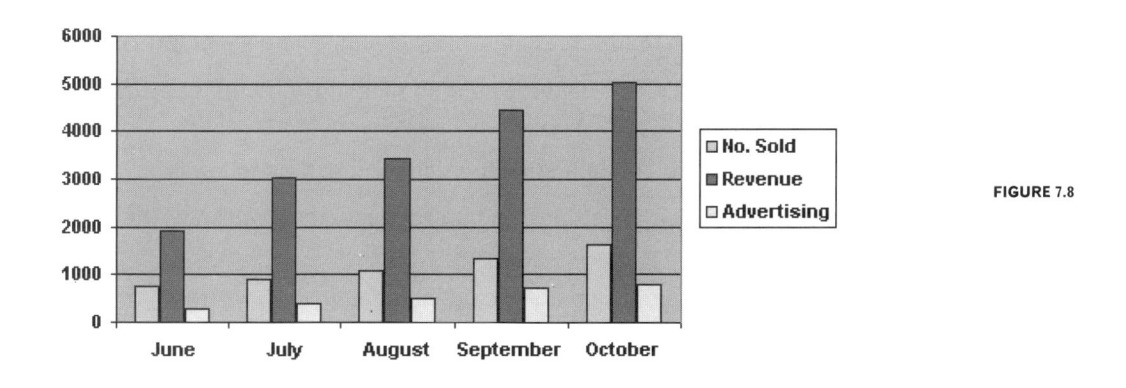

FIGURE 7.8

Topic 7 · Further chart skills

Adding trendlines to a chart

1 We can add trendlines to emphasise trends or relationships between different sets of chart values.

    a. Make sure that the chart **Column 1** is still selected and click one of the columns representing advertising – all 5 advertising columns should now be selected.

    b. Right click one of the columns and select the option **ADD TRENDLINE**.

    c. The **ADD TRENDLINE** dialog box appears – make sure that the **TYPE** tab is selected.

    d. Select **LINEAR** and then select the **ADVERTISING** series if necessary.

    e. Click **OK** – a trendline is added to the chart – see Figure 7.9.

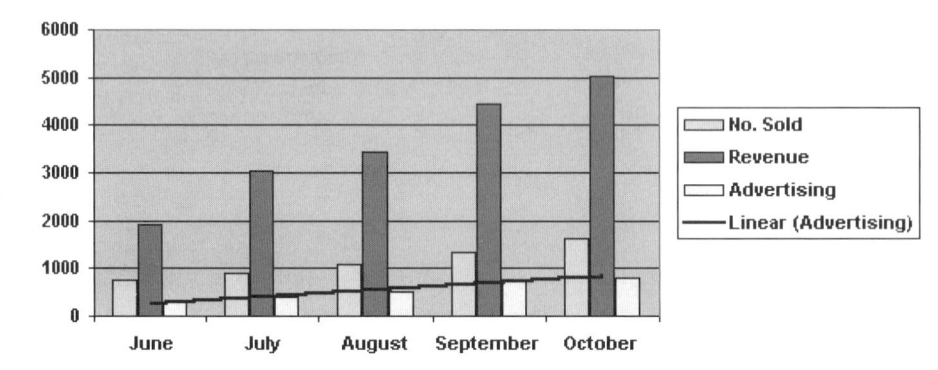

FIGURE 7.9

2 The trendline shows the relationship between advertising, sales and revenue. Sales and revenue continue to rise whilst the money spent on advertising has started to level off.

Goal seeking

1 We have seen that a chart and the worksheet on which it is based are linked, ie any changes in the worksheet are automatically reflected in the chart. The reverse is equally true – amending chart values will change the worksheet.

2 Open the workbook **Insurance Sales** and select the worksheet **Sales Data**.

3 Select cells **A3** to **E4** that hold the column headings and the sales data for April.

Use ChartWizard to create a standard column chart as follows:

    a. Accept the default axis settings so that the insurance types are the categories on the X axis.

    b. Give the chart a title but do not include a legend.

    c. Create it as a new sheet.

Topic 7 · Further chart skills

d. Open the **VIEW** menu and select **SIZED WITH WINDOW**. Format the text labels as before.

e. Name the chart **Goal Seek 1**. It should resemble Figure 7.10.

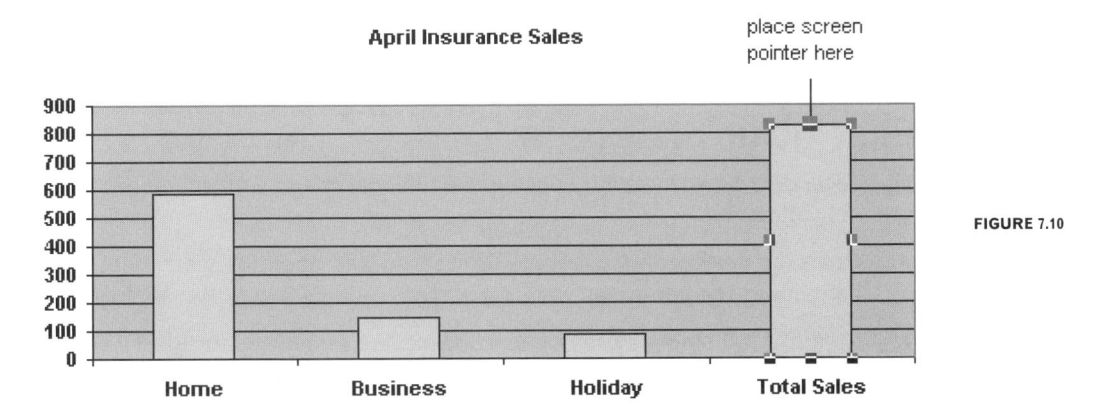

FIGURE 7.10

④ Move the screen pointer onto the 4th (total sales) column and click it once - a single selection handle appears.

Click again and the column is now enclosed in selection handles – see Figure 7.10.

Now move the pointer onto the top of the column and the screen pointer changes to a double-headed arrow. An information box should also open.

⑤ Use the mouse to drag the column upwards until its value equals 900. A goal seek dialog box opens – see Figure 7.11 – and the worksheet is displayed.

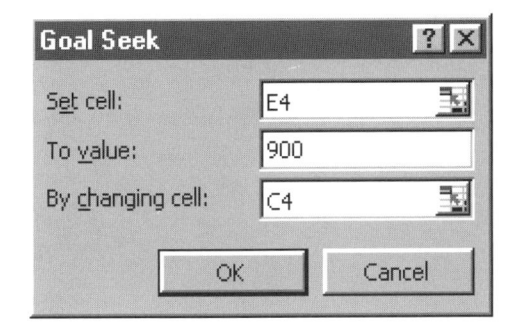

FIGURE 7.11

⑥ Using the **GOAL SEEK** dialog box we can change any cell in the range **B4** to **D4** to achieve the sales goal of 900 insurance policies sold. Complete the dialog box as shown above and click **OK**.

The value of cell **C4** is changed to 224 – the number of business insurance policies sold to achieve the goal of 900 in cell E4.

⑦ Click the **CANCEL** button on the new dialog box that is displayed to restore the cells to their original values. Save and close the workbook.

⑧ *Notes on using Goal Seek*: In the example of goal seeking that we have just tried the cell whose value we set (C4) contained a value, not a formula.

The cell was related by a formula to the cell whose target value we changed – E4. These two conditions are essential for Goal Seek to work successfully.

You can also goal seeking in worksheets as well as charts – see Topic 11.

Check your progress

In this independent task you will try out some additional charts and techniques that we have not yet covered.

1 Open the workbook **Marketing Campaign** and open the worksheet containing the campaign data.

   a. Create a 3-D stacked area chart showing the responses for the TV Campaign, Web Site and Telephone for all 4 weeks. Do not include the **Totals** column in the chart.

   Compare your chart with Appendix 3.

   b. Name the chart **3-D Area**.

   c. Add titles, embolden the chart text and change the order of the 3 areas so that they are all visible – see previous task 'Removing and Adding Chart Values' on page 77.

2 Open the workbook **Video Sales**. Add a further column to the worksheet, using formulae to calculate advertising as a percentage of the revenue – see Figure 7.12

FIGURE 7.12

	A	B	C	D	E
1		Video Sales - Current Year			
2					
3	Month	No. Sold	Revenue	Advertising	Adv as % of Revenue
4	June	750	1915	280	15%
5	July	910	3054	401	13%
6	August	1075	3447	498	14%
7	September	1330	4450	733	16%
8	October	1618	5009	801	16%
9					

   a. Create a line chart based on the percentages; name it **Line 1**.

   b. Add titles and axis labels as shown. Embolden the text.

   Remove the gridlines (**CHART-CHART OPTIONS**).

   c. Compare your chart with Appendix 4.

   d. Open the **CHART** menu and select the **ADD TRENDLINE** option.

   Add a linear trendline that forecasts forward for a month.

   e. Use the **CHART-CHART OPTIONS** menu to show the data table on which the chart is based.

   f. Compare your chart with Appendix 5.

Topic 7 · Further chart skills

③ Creating Doughnut Charts. A doughnut chart is like an extended pie chart; it shows the contribution of a number of elements to an overall total, but, unlike a pie chart, it can show more than one data series.

a. Open the workbook **Video Sales** if necessary and highlight cells **A3** to **C6** in the worksheet – the columns showing revenue and numbers sold for June to August.

b. Use ChartWizard to create the doughnut chart shown in Figure 7.13. Note that the percentages are added at Step 3 of ChartWizard and the sections representing August have been given an alternative pattern to make the percentages more visible. We add the lines and arrows in the next section.

c. Name the chart **Doughnut 1**.

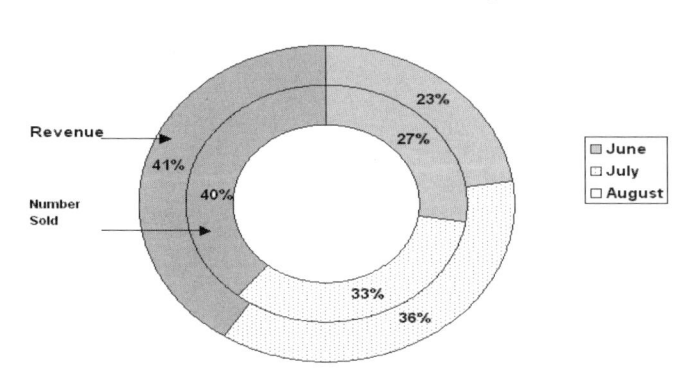

FIGURE 7.13

④ Adding Arrows. As it is not clear what the two doughnut rings represent we will add notes to them. If necessary display the Drawing toolbar using the **VIEW** menu and the **TOOLBARS** option.

Use the arrow and the text box tools to create the labels above – refer back to Topic 6, page 67 if necessary.

⑤ Custom Charts. Select a range of cells in the **Video Sales** worksheet to chart and call up ChartWizard. Step 1 of ChartWizard offers a second tab **CUSTOM TYPES**. Select it and review the charts offered:

a. Some are just more colourful versions of standard charts, eg 'Blue Pie' and 'Colored Lines'.

b. Others offer monochrome versions of standard charts, useful if you don't have a colour printer.

c. A few offer genuinely alternative ways of presenting data, eg 'Logarithmic' or 'Lines on 2 Axes'.

d. If you do not wish to create a custom chart then cancel the dialog box, otherwise the other 3 ChartWizard steps are similar to those for standard Charts.

⑥ Save and close the **Video Sales** workbook.

Topic 7 · Further chart skills

Creating an embedded chart

So far all the charts that we have created have been displayed as separate sheets in the workbook. You can also create create embedded charts, ie forming part of the worksheet upon which they are based. This is useful if you want to view or print a chart and worksheet on the same page. The ChartWizard steps remain the same until you reach Step 4 where you select the 'As option in' option.

1   Open the worksheet **Insurance Sales** and maximise the worksheet **Sales Data** if necessary.

Select cells **A4** to **D5**.

2   Use ChartWizard to create a standard bar chart. At Step 4 leave the option **AS OBJECT IN** selected and press **FINISH**.

3   The embedded chart is created as part of the worksheet – see Figure 7.14.

a. Chart and worksheet can be selected in turn by clicking. Try moving and re-sizing the chart by dragging border and the selection handles.

b. Select one of the bars on the chart and Excel's Range Finder outlines the corresponding worksheet elements.

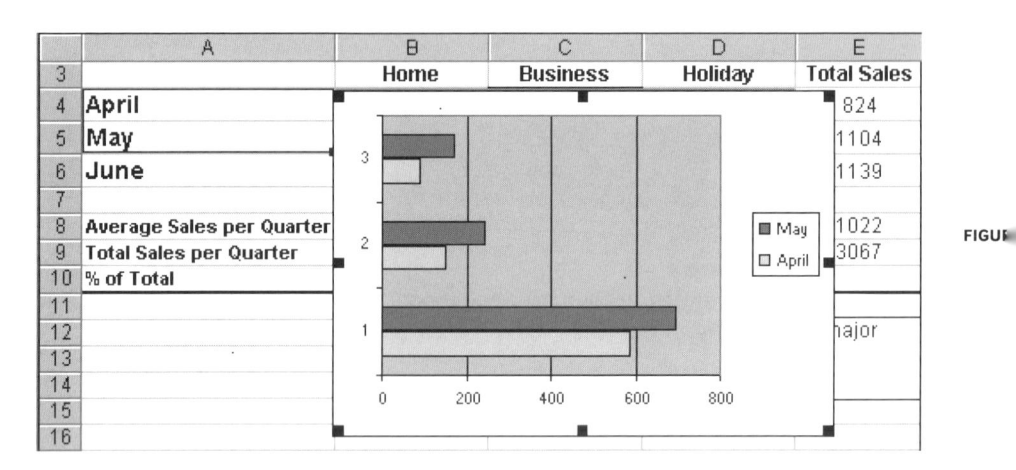

FIGURE

4   **Drag and Drop** as a technique is used extensively in Microsoft Office applications. In Excel you can drag a range of cells and 'drop' them onto a chart. We can add the figures for June to the chart in this way.

a. Select cells **A6** to **D6** on the worksheet.

b. Move the screen pointer onto the bottom edge of this cell range – see Figure 7.15.

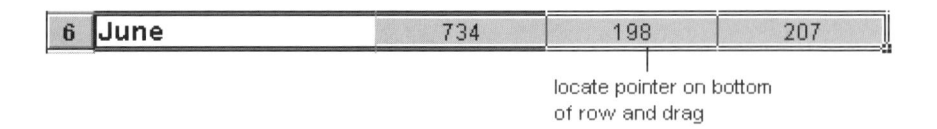

locate pointer on bottom of row and drag

FIGURE

c. Use the mouse to drag the cell range (represented by a dotted rectangle) onto the chart. The chart is re-plotted to include a third set of bars.

Use the **EDIT-UNDO** command if you have made a mistake.

5 Format the embedded chart now – double click the white space at the edge of the chart. A dialog box will then be displayed and the chart can be formatted in the usual way.

6 **Printing Embedded Charts**. Select the embedded chart and select **PRINT PREVIEW** from the **FILE** menu; if the chart is selected then the worksheet will not be printed.

Close Print Preview and return to the worksheet. Press the **ESC** key on the keyboard to remove the selection and select Print Preview again; you can now print chart and worksheet as one document.

7 *Notes*

a. To place an embedded chart in a separate window temporarily first select it then take the options **VIEW – CHART WINDOW**.

b. To transfer an embedded chart to its own separate sheet open ChartWizard and at Step 4 select the **AS NEW SHEET** option.

c. An embedded chart can be deleted using the **DELETE** key.

8 Exit from Excel, saving any changes.

Summary of commands

Note:
Menu commands show the menu name first, followed by the command to choose from the menu, e.g. **EDIT-CLEAR** means open the Edit menu and select the Clear command.

Menu commands

Command	Description
CHART-CHART OPTIONS	Change title, legend, data labels etc
CHART-ADD TRENDLINE	Add a trendline to selected chart data
EDIT-COPY...PASTE	Copy data from worksheet to chart
EDIT-DELETE SHEET	Delete a chart sheet
EDIT-UNDO/REDO	Undo/redo a change to a chart
FILE-NEW	Create new workbook
FILE-SAVE	Save workbook
FORMAT-SELECTED.....	Format selected chart element
INSERT-CHART	Create a new chart
INSERT-CHART-ON THIS SHEET	Create an embedded chart
INSERT-TITLES	Insert chart or axis title
VIEW-SIZED WITH WINDOW	Re-size chart to window size
VIEW-CHART WINDOW	View embedded chart in own window

TOPIC 8

Excel databases

Introduction

We have now covered worksheets and charts and are ready to deal with Excel's third main component, databases.

In Excel a database is really a special type of list, a list being defined as a set of related data stored in the rows of a worksheet, eg a list of invoices, details of club members or a file of employees. Once organised in this way the list can be sorted or searched in various ways, ie it becomes a simple database.

Figure 8.1 shows an example of a simple list or database holding details of customer invoices. We can use it to introduce certain key database terms.

FIGURE 8.1

	A	B	C	D	E
1	Invoice Ref	Invoice Date	Customer No.	Customer Name	Invoice Value
2	A5418	08-Jun-00	2134	Singh Developments	658.00
3	A5419	05-Mar-00	1579	Berger Products	1437.00
4	A5420	31-Jan-00	2111	Webb Joinery	654.87
5	A5421	31-Jan-00	1093	Singh Electrical	2349.00
6	A5422	12-Apr-00	2198	Wilson's Golf	138.65
7	A5423	13-Apr-00	1532	Harris Publishing	2568.12
8	A5424	09-May-00	1579	Berger Products	188.00
9	A5425	09-May-00	2134	Singh Developments	19.91
10	A5426	20-Feb-00	1579	Berger Products	789.00
11	A5427	08-Mar-00	1478	Hamilton Media	905.99

Record. Each invoice occupies a row in the worksheet and is called a record.

Field. Each record holds the same 5 fields or data items – Invoice Ref, Invoice Date, Customer No, Customer Name and Invoice Value. Each field takes up a single column. The first row holds the field names, the other rows contain the actual data – the field values.

Database. The database consists of a list or table of 10 records.

Excel is primarily a spreadsheet application, not a database, and does not offer the relational, multi-table features of a special-purpose database management system such as Access. However, you can perform simple database-related tasks such as searching for individual records, adding and deleting records, editing existing records and sorting records into different sequences.

Database rules in Excel

Database size. A database can occupy the entire worksheet, but cannot take up more than one worksheet. The same worksheet can hold several different databases.

Fields. Every record must have the same fields, but fields can be left blank. Do not enter extra blanks at the start of fields as this will affect searching and sorting.

Capitalization. Excel databases are not 'case sensitive', ie Excel ignores upper or lower case when searching or sorting, so entering, e.g. 'SMITH', 'smith' or 'Smith' will locate the same records.

Topic objectives

- To use Fill Series to comlete a data series.
- To enter and format dates.
- To sort database records using different fields.
- To create database calculated fields.
- To search using a data form.
- To search using AutoFilter.
- To subtotal a database.

Creating the database

Ideally you should plan the database structure before you start entering data, in particular plan which fields you intend to use. Figure 8.1 above shows a database set up to record customer invoices, so we need to know both the customer details – name and reference code – and the order details too – date, reference code and value. Each of these items of information represents one field.

1 **Entering Field Names.** Starting with a new workbook, enter the 5 field names shown shown in Figure 8.1 (cells **A1** to **E1**).

Widen the columns if necessary, and centre and embolden the field names.

2 **Using AutoComplete.** Complete columns C and D – the **Customer No.** and **Customer Name** fields – as shown in Figure 8.1 above. When you enter a customer name for the second time, eg Singh Developments, Excel completes the entry automatically. When this happens stop typing and continue with the next entry. If there there are two different companies starting with the same characters, eg 'Singh'; you would need to complete the rest of the company name.

Note: AutoComplete can be set on or off by opening the **TOOLS** menu and selecting **OPTIONS**. Select the **EDIT** tab and choose 'Enable AutoComplete for Cell Values'.

3 Now complete column E, the **Invoice Value** field. Don't enter .00 after a value – see Section 4 below.

4 **Formatting the Fields.** Now we will format the invoice values to 2 decimal places.

  a. Select the 10 value fields, ie cells **E2** to **E11**.

  b. Open the **FORMAT** menu and select the **CELLS** option, a dialog box appears.

c. Click the **NUMBER** tab and then the **NUMBER** category if necessary.

d. Select **2** from the **DECIMAL PLACES** list and click the **OK** button – see Figure 8.2.

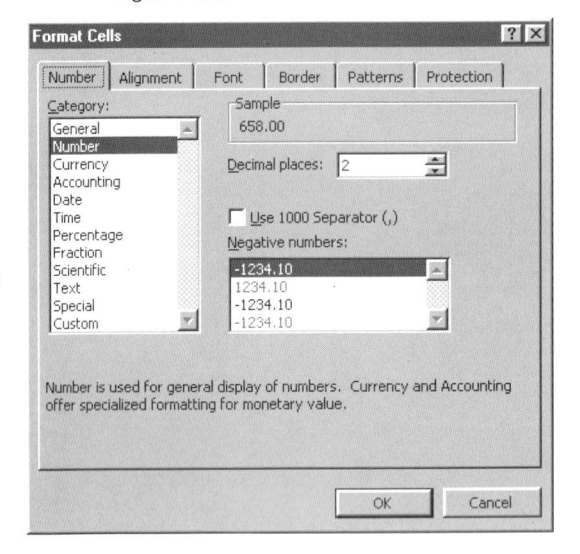

FIGURE 8.2

5. **Data Series**. The **Invoice Ref** field is an alphanumeric sequence – increasing by 1 for every new invoice record. The **FILL SERIES** command is quicker to use when numbers, dates etc increase or decrease by a constant factor. For the fill operation to work they must be in adjacent cells.

   a. Enter the start value *A5418* in cell **A2**, then select the whole range, **A2** to **A11**.

   b. Open the **EDIT** menu and select the options **FILL** – **SERIES**.

   c. A dialog box appears; make sure that the options are selected as in Figure 8.3; ie,

   SERIES IN: COLUMNS (the data series will occupy a column)
   TYPE: AUTOFILL
   STEP VALUE: 1 (the numbers will increase by 1 each time)

   d. Click the **OK** button and the column is filled with a data series for the invoice references.

   e. *Note*: A data series can also be based on weeks, dates and fractional numbers

6. **Entering Dates**. You will find that you can enter dates in a number of formats and Excel will automatically recognise and format them.

   Enter the first invoice date in cell **B2** as *08jun* – Excel automatically converts it to 08-Jun; if it doesn't then check what you have entered.

   Enter the remaining dates and check the status bar as you do so. Whatever the date format in the cells the status bar displays dates in a numeric format, eg 08/06/00.

7. Format all the dates to the one shown in Fig 8.1 using the **FORMAT** command and selecting the option **CELLS**. Click the **NUMBER** tab and

FIGURE 8.3

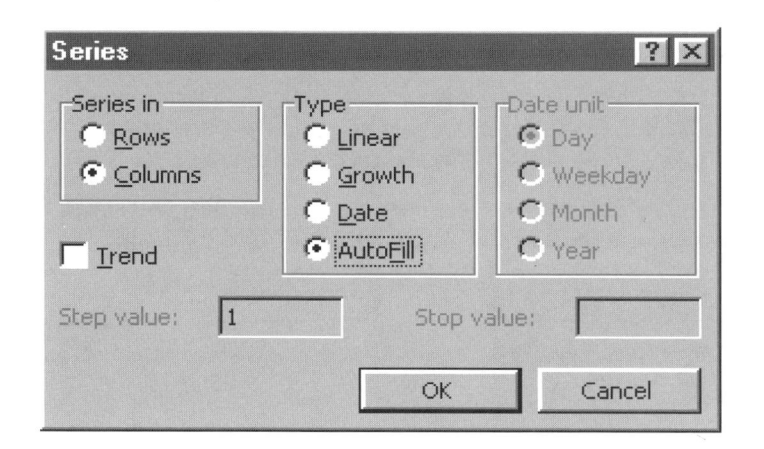

select the **DATE** category from the dialog box. Excel 2000 lets you use 4 digits for the year if you prefer.

8 Finally enter the rest of the data shown in Figure 8.1 above.

9 Name the worksheet **Customer Invoices** and save the workbook as **Databases**.

Sorting records

Often one needs to arrange the same list in different orders, eg in invoice number sequence (as at present) or in customer name sequence. Excel's Sort command can be used with any field or fields to place the records in a new sequence. This is useful in speeding up searching once the database gets larger.

Hints for sorting

If there are different types of data in the fields that you are sorting then the sort order is as follows: Numbers, text, logical values, error values, blanks. This will not be an issue in the database that we have created.

Use the **EDIT – UNDO SORT** command to reverse an incorrect sort.

Remember to include all the rows and columns in the sort, ie all fields, all records. If you leave any columns out they will become attached to the wrong record.

1 To sort the customer invoices into date sequence select the whole database, ie cells **A1** to **E11** including the field names in the header row.

Open the **DATA** menu and select **SORT** – the Sort dialog box appears.

If necessary, locate the mouse pointer on the title bar and drag the dialog box down so that the database is visible.

2 Complete the Sort dialog box as shown in Figure 8.4:

a. **Sort by**: We will sort by **Invoice Date**; select this field from the **SORT BY** box.

Leave **ASCENDING** selected (ie earliest dates first).

b. **Then by**: We are only sorting by one field so leave these 2 options unselected.

c. **My list has**: **HEADER ROW** should remain selected – we do not want the field names in row 1 to be sorted, only the records. Click **OK**.

d. The records in the database are sorted into date order, earliest dates first. If you have made a mistake use **EDIT – UNDO SORT** and try again.

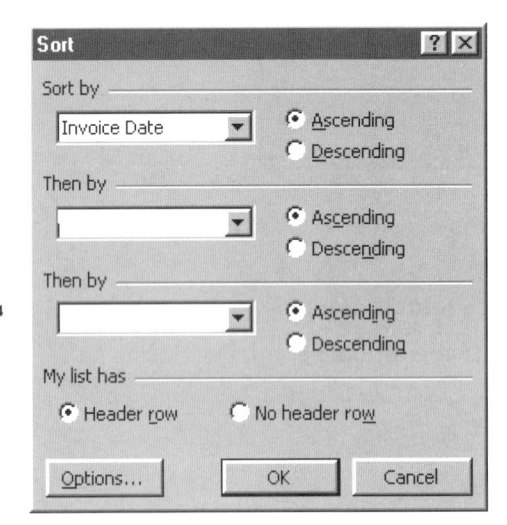

FIGURE 8.4

③ **Re-sorting**. Check that cells A1 to E11 are still selected and sort the records by **Customer Name**.

Notice that strict alphabetical sequence is followed, the record for Singh Developments is placed before Singh Electrical.

④ **Sorting by Multiple Fields**. If we sort the records in date order by customer we use two fields or 'keys' in database parlance. The primary key is the customer name and the invoice date the secondary key.

Select all the database cells as before and issue the **DATA-SORT** command again.

Make the following entries in the Sort dialog box using Figure 8.5 as a guide:

a. In the first **SORT BY:** box select **Customer Name**.

b. In the first **THEN BY:** dialog box select **Invoice Date**.

c. Select the **DESCENDING** button next to the first **THEN BY:** box; this will place them in reverse date order, ie latest invoices displayed first.

d. Click **OK** and check that the records are sorted into this new sequence.

e. Click on the worksheet to remove the selection highlighting from the database – it should resemble Figure 8.6.

⑤ **Consolidation**. Try the following sorts:

a. Invoices in descending order of value, ie largest value invoices first.

b. By **Customer No.** in ascending date order.

Topic 8 · Excel databases

FIGURE 8.5

	A	B	C	D	E
1	Invoice Ref	Invoice Date	Customer No.	Customer Name	Invoice Value
2	A5424	09-May-00	1579	Berger Products	188.00
3	A5419	05-Mar-00	1579	Berger Products	1437.00
4	A5426	20-Feb-00	1579	Berger Products	789.00
5	A5427	08-Mar-00	1478	Hamilton Media	905.99
6	A5423	13-Apr-00	1532	Harris Publishing	2568.12
7	A5418	08-Jun-00	2134	Singh Developments	658.00
8	A5425	09-May-00	2134	Singh Developments	19.91
9	A5421	31-Jan-00	1093	Singh Electrical	2349.00
10	A5420	31-Jan-00	2111	Webb Joinery	654.87
11	A5422	12-Apr-00	2199	Wilson's Golf	138.65
12					

FIGURE 8.6

Calculated fields

We will add two new database fields:

    a. A field calculating **VAT** at 17.5%.

    b. A **Total** field which adds the VAT field to the **Invoice value** field.

    Both fields are calculated fields, ie produced by formulae in the usual way.

1   Enter the field names **VAT** and **Total**, in cells **F1** and **G1** – see Figure 8.7.

2   In cell **F2** enter a formula that calculates VAT at 17.5%, ie =**E2*0.175**

    Note: The symbol * is used for multiplication.

    Copy the formula to the rest of the records in cells **F3** to **F11** now.

    Select cells **F2** to **F11** then open the **EDIT** menu and select the options **FILL** then **DOWN**.

3   Now enter a SUM formula in cell **G2** to add the **VAT** field in cell **E2** to the **Value** field in cell **F2**. Fill down as before.

4   Format the two new fields to 2 decimal places – see previous task.

93

Topic 8 · Excel databases

FIGURE 8.7

	B	C	D	E	F	G
1	Invoice Date	Customer No.	Customer Name	Invoice Value	VAT	Total
2	31-Jan-00	1093	Singh Electrical	2349.00	411.08	2760.08
3	08-Mar-00	1478	Hamilton Media	905.99	158.55	1064.54
4	13-Apr-00	1532	Harris Publishing	2568.12	449.42	3017.54
5	20-Feb-00	1579	Berger Products	789.00	138.08	927.08
6	05-Mar-00	1579	Berger Products	1437.00	251.48	1688.48
7	09-May-00	1579	Berger Products	188.00	32.90	220.90
8	31-Jan-00	2111	Webb Joinery	654.87	114.60	769.47
9	09-May-00	2134	Singh Developments	19.91	3.48	23.39
10	08-Jun-00	2134	Singh Developments	658.00	115.15	773.15
11	12-Apr-00	2199	Wilson's Golf	138.65	24.26	162.91
12						

5 Calculated fields can be searched and sorted in the same way as any other fields; to try this, sort the database by the **Total** field (ascending order).

Using a data form

As the information changes the database will need updating and records will need adding, deleting and amending. You can use a special data form to search and update the database.

1 Select one of the cells in the Customer Invoices database – there is no need to select the whole database.

2 Open the **DATA** menu and select the **FORM** option.

A data form is displayed. The field names and field values for the first record are displayed on the left of the form and the number of the current record is also displayed, at the moment Number 1 of 10 – see Figure 8.8.

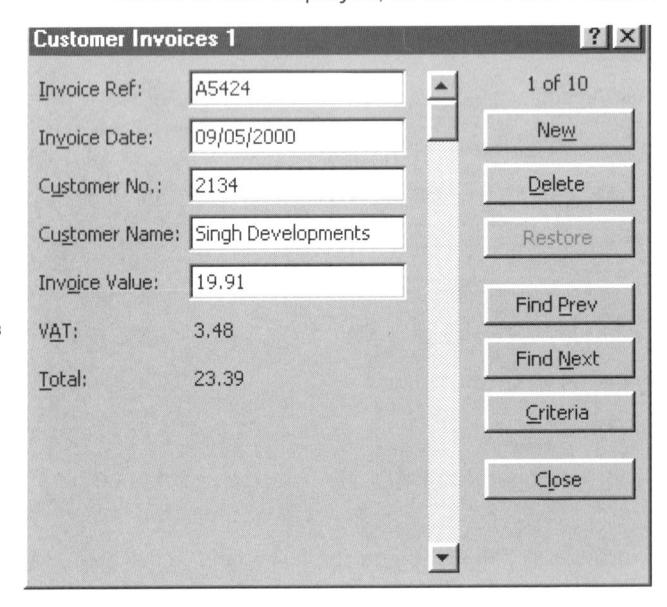

FIGURE 8.8

Customer Invoices 1

- Invoice Ref: A5424
- Invoice Date: 09/05/2000
- Customer No.: 2134
- Customer Name: Singh Developments
- Invoice Value: 19.91
- VAT: 3.48
- Total: 23.39

1 of 10

New | Delete | Restore | Find Prev | Find Next | Criteria | Close

3 We will now carry out some database maintenance tasks using the buttons on the right hand side of the form:

a. **FIND NEXT** button: Click this and you scroll forward a record at a time. When the record changes the Record Counter displays the current record number 2 of 10, 3 of 10 etc.

b. **FIND PREV.** button: Click this button to scroll backwards in the database.

c. The **SCROLL BAR**: scrolls through records more quickly. Move to the last record in the database – 10 of 10. After this record a new, blank record is provided.

d. **DELETE** button: Click it once and a message warns you that the selected record will be permanently deleted. We do not want to do this so click the **CANCEL** button. Records deleted using a data form cannot be restored, so you will need to be careful before going ahead.

e. **CRITERIA** button: Allows you to locate records using search criteria. Try this in the next section.

5 Try the following searches:

a. Click the **CRITERIA** button on the data form – the blank record allows you to enter search criteria.

Enter *Singh* in the **Customer Name** field in either upper or lower case.

b. Click the **FIND NEXT** button and the first record that meets this search criterion is displayed; click **FIND NEXT** again to find any further matching records. Click the **FIND PREV.** button to scroll back again. There are 3 records in all.

Note: Both company names beginning in 'Singh' are located – to narrow the search further we would have to enter the complete company name.

c. Click the **CRITERIA** button again. 'Singh' is still displayed in the **Customer Name** field.

Enter the second criterion *<1000* in the **Invoice Value** field.

We are now searching using 2 criteria, ie customer name = Singh *and* invoice value less than £1000.

Click the **FIND NEXT** and **FIND PREV.** buttons. Two records match these criteria.

d. Click the **CRITERIA** then the **CLEAR** button to delete the search criteria, then click the **FORM** button to display the data form.

Notes: The two calculated fields, **VAT** and **Total**, cannot be edited in the data form as they are based on formulae which should not be overwritten.

Care needs to be used when editing records in a data form as amendments are saved *permanently* as soon as you move to another record. Make sure that you use the **RESTORE** button *before* you move to another record if you do not want the changes to be permanent.

e. Press the **CLOSE** button to exit from the data form.

6 **Consolidation**. Using the operations you have just learned, open the data form again and use the **CRITERIA** button to locate records matching the following conditions:

a. Invoice Total greater than or equal to 2000 (>=)
b. Invoices placed before 10-April (enter the full date, eg 10/04/2000 and use the '<' sign)
c. Customer No = 1579 and Invoice Date = 9th May.
d. Remember to erase any previous search criteria before entering new ones.

Subtotalling a database

Excel has a special subtotal command for databases; this is not only quicker than using the SUM function but also lets us outline the database and just display the subtotals.

1 Select all the cells in the **Customer Invoices** database and sort it in **Customer Name** order – we will subtotal the invoices for each customer.

2 Open the **DATA** menu and select the **SUBTOTALS** option. Complete the dialog box as follows, using Figure 8.9 as a guide.

a. **AT EACH CHANGE IN**: Select **Customer Name**.
b. **USE FUNCTION**: Leave this as **SUM** as we are adding the value of invoice values.
c. **ADD SUBTOTAL TO**: Select **Total** – the the field values we are adding.
d. Click the **OK** button.

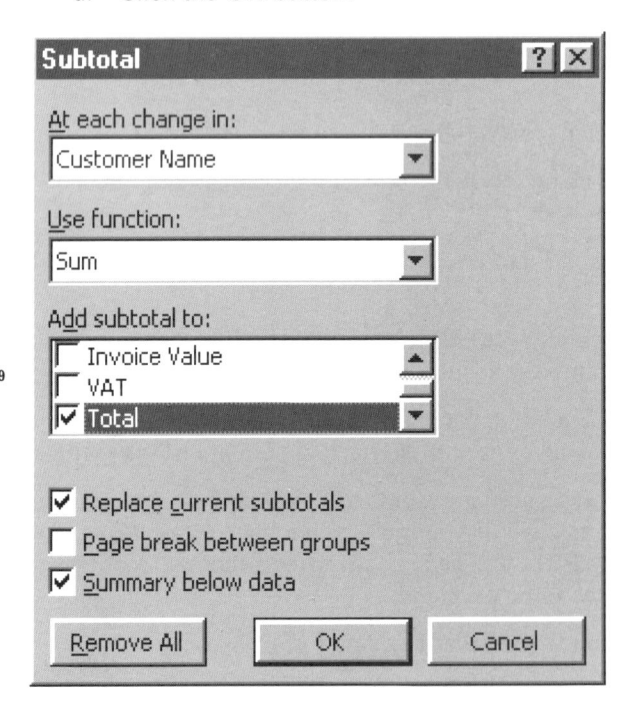

FIGURE 8.9

Topic 8 · Excel databases

(3) Click the mouse to remove the highlighting. Your database should resemble Figure 8.10 below. You will see that after each customer a new row holds the customer name and a subtotal for the value of their invoices. A grand total for all invoices is displayed at the end of the database – you may need to scroll down and widen the total column to see this.

subtotal and
outline buttons

1 2 3		C	D	E	F	G
	1	Customer No.	Customer Name	Invoice Value	VAT	Total
	2	1579	Berger Products	188.00	32.90	220.90
	3	1579	Berger Products	789.00	138.08	927.08
	4	1579	Berger Products	1437.00	251.48	1688.48
	5		Berger Products Total			2836.45
	6	1478	Hamilton Media	905.99	158.55	1064.54
	7		Hamilton Media Total			1064.54
	8	1532	Harris Publishing	2568.12	449.42	3017.54
	9		Harris Publishing Total			3017.54
	10	2134	Singh Developments	19.91	3.48	23.39
	11	2134	Singh Developments	658.00	115.15	773.15

FIGURE 8.10

(4) **Outlining a Database**. Three buttons, labelled 1, 2 and 3, are displayed at the top left of the screen. They provide different outlines – click each in turn:

Button **2** – the records are hidden and only the subtotals and grand total are displayed.

Button **1** – only the grand total is displayed.

Button **3** – the records, subtotals and grand totals are all displayed again.

(5) Experiment with the **MINUS** buttons on the left of the screen – you can hide individual groups of records so that only the subtotals are displayed. The button then changes to a '+' sign. Click it again to re-display them.

(6) **Removing Subtotals**. Open the **DATA** menu and select **SUBTOTALS**, then click the **REMOVE ALL** button in the dialog box. The database is now displayed without subtotals.

Searching using AutoFilter

The data form that we have used so far is limited to displaying one record at a time. We also cannot use 'or' conditions such as 'Webb Joinery or Wilson's Golf' in a data form. AutoFilter is more flexible in that it sets up the search criteria on the worksheet itself. You can then filter out or hide records that you do not wish to view.

(1) Make sure that the **Customer Invoices** worksheet is displayed and select one of the cells in the database.

(2) Open the **DATA** menu and select **FILTER**, then the **AUTOFILTER** options.

Arrow buttons are attached to each field name in row 1. Click each button in turn and you will see that they list all the values for that particular field.

③ **Searching by a Field Value**. Click the arrow button next to the **Customer Name** field.

Select Berger Products from the list offered – only the records for this customer are displayed – the rest are filtered out.

Click the arrow button on the **Customer Name** field again, this time selecting **ALL** – all the records are redisplayed.

Note: If you find that you cannot restore all the records then open the **DATA** menu and select **FILTER**, then the **SHOW ALL** option.

④ **Building a Custom Search**. Say that you wish to display all invoices dated 5th or 8th March. You can do this using your own custom search.

Click the down arrow on the **Invoice Date** field and select (**CUSTOM...**) from the list.

A dialog box appears. Complete the entries as follows, using Figure 8.11 as a guide.

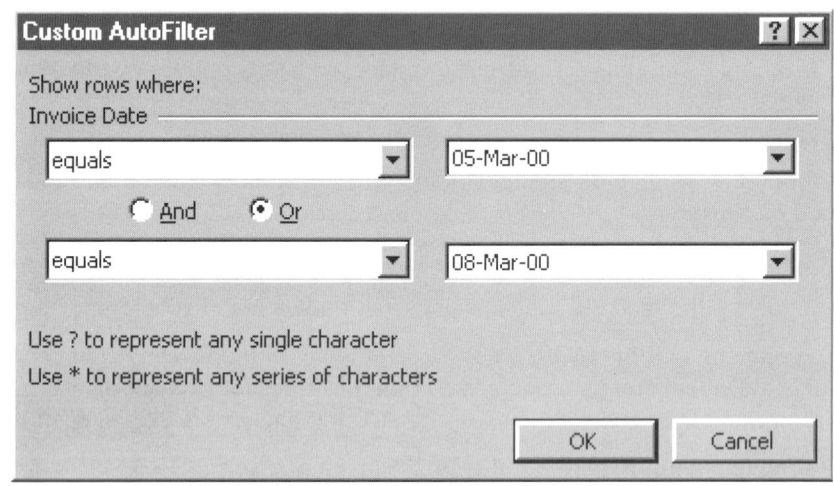

FIGURE 8.11

Custom AutoFilter

Show rows where:
Invoice Date

equals   05-Mar-00

○ And   ● Or

equals   08-Mar-00

Use ? to represent any single character
Use * to represent any series of characters

OK   Cancel

⑤ You have 4 list boxes to complete plus an 'And' or an 'Or' button to select as follows:

a. Leave the 'equals' in the top left box as it is.

b. Click the **DOWN** arrow on the top right box and select the date **5-Mar**.

c. Click the **OR** button.

d. Click the bottom left box and select **EQUALS**.

e. Click the bottom right arrow box and select the date **8-Mar**.

f. Finally click the **OK** button and the 2 records that meet the search criteria, 5th March or 8th March, are displayed – the rest are hidden.

⑥ Click the arrow button on the **Invoice Date** field heading again and select **ALL** and all the records are re-displayed.

(7) **Independent Task**. Use the arrow box on the **VAT** field to select invoices with VAT payable of between 100 and 200. You will need to search for VAT values greater than or equal to 100 and less than or equal to 200.

Refer to Appendix 6 for guidance on the dialog box entries if necessary; 4 records should be selected.

(8) **De-selecting AutoFilter**. Open the **DATA** menu and select the options **FILTER-AUTOFILTER** again to de-select AutoFilter. The database will revert to its normal appearance.

(9) Save and close the workbook.

Summary of commands and functions
Note:
Menu commands show the menu name first, followed by the command to choose from the menu, e.g. **EDIT-CLEAR** means open the Edit menu and select the Clear command.

Menu commands

Command	Description
DATA-FILTER-AUTOFILTER	Search database using AutoFilter
DATA-FORM	Use a data form
DATA-SORT	Sort selected cells
DATA-SUBTOTALS	Subtotal database/remove subtotals
EDIT-FILL-DOWN	Copy cell values to cells below
EDIT-FILL-SERIES	Create a data series
EDIT-UNDO SORT	Reverse a sort operation
FORMAT-CELLS	Format cells/cell contents
TOOL-OPTIONS-AUTOCOMPLETE	Turn AutoComplete on/off

TOPIC 9

Using linked worksheets

Introduction

This topic shows you how you can link worksheets together and share data between them. Having done this you can edit them as a group, so that changes made to one worksheet will update the others. As several worksheets can be displayed at once you can see the effects of linked changes straightaway.

Linking worksheets can be used, for example, in the departments or branches of a company; the same data is recorded for each, and they are combined into an overall summary.

In this topic we will create two simple worksheets summarising the costs for two branches and a third worksheet to summarise them.

This unit also covers organising files into folders and locating workbooks using Excel's Find feature.

Topic objectives

- To copy cells between different worksheets.
- To link cells in different worksheets.
- To display multiple worksheet windows.
- To create folders for workbooks.
- To search for workbooks using different search criteria.

Creating the worksheets

① We will first create a template or framework for the worksheet, which we can then copy and adapt for each branch.

Open a new workbook and enter the cell headings and labels shown in Figure 9.1.

	A	B	C	D	E	F
1			Cost Summary - Branch			
2						
3			1st Quarter	2nd Quarter	3rd Quarter	4th Quarter
4						
5	Raw Materials					
6	Machinery					
7	Salaries					
8	Heating and Power					
9	Maintenance					
10						
11	Total					

FIGURE 9.1

Topic 9 · Using linked worksheets

2 Change the name of the worksheet to **Branch 1**.

3 **Copying Between Worksheets**. Select cells **A1** to **F11**.

  a. Open the **EDIT** menu and select the **COPY** option.

  b. Select the sheet tab for **Sheet2**.

  c. Select cell **A1** in Sheet2 if necessary then open the **EDIT** menu and select the **PASTE** option.

  d. The cells are copied from one worksheet to the other. Change the sheet name from Sheet2 to **Branch 2** and adjust the column widths if necessary.

4 Now open **Sheet3** and paste the cells again into this worksheet (there is no need to select the Copy command again). We now have 3 worksheets containing the same framework.

Name the third worksheet **Summary 1**.

5 Now we need to enter the individual costs for branches 1 and 2.

Amend the sheet **Branch 1** as shown in Figure 9.2. Use a SUM formula to create the totals in row 11.

	A	B	C	D	E	F
1			Cost Summary - Branch 1			
2						
3			1st Quarter	2nd Quarter	3rd Quarter	4th Quarter
4						
5	Raw Materials		436	465	519	653
6	Machinery		692	398	793	487
7	Salaries		10687	8976	9775	1185
8	Heating and Power		2490	1986	1789	2654
9	Maintenance		769	678	956	882
10						
11	Total		15074	12503	13832	5861
12						

FIGURE 9.2

6 Similarly amend the sheet **Branch 2** as shown in Figure 9.3.

	A	B	C	D	E	F
1			Cost Summary - Branch 2			
2						
3			1st Quarter	2nd Quarter	3rd Quarter	4th Quarter
4						
5	Raw Materials		1376	1196	1745	945
6	Machinery		1244	856	513	967
7	Salaries		12657	11856	9456	10745
8	Heating and Power		2546	1987	1067	1756
9	Maintenance		758	523	849	689
10						
11	Total		18581	16418	13630	15102
12						

FIGURE 9.3

7 The Summary 1 worksheet will combine the two sets of branch totals. Let's display the 3 worksheets in separate windows first.

Topic 9 · Using linked worksheets

Displaying multiple worksheet windows

① **Opening Multiple Worksheets**. We have already used the Window-Arrange command to display more than worksheet window on screen – see Topic 5 page 61.

Make sure that the worksheet **Branch 1** is displayed first

Open the **WINDOW** menu and select the option **NEW WINDOW**. A second window appears, overlaying the first. Click the **Branch 2** sheet tab for this window.

② Open the **WINDOW** menu and select **NEW WINDOW** again.

Click the **SUMMARY 1** tab in this window. Three worksheets are now open, each in their own window.

③ **Displaying Multiple Worksheets**. Open the **WINDOW** menu and select **ARRANGE** – a dialog box appears. Click the **CASCADE** option then the OK button.

FIGURE 9.4

The overlapping edges of the 3 worksheets are now visible – see Figure 9.4. If only one worksheet is visible then try clicking the **RESTORE** button to reduce the window size.

④ Try selecting each worksheet window in turn as follows:

a. Click the edge of the worksheet or,

b. Open the **WINDOW** menu and select a worksheet from the bottom of the menu – this is useful if you cannot see the worksheet window. However, you will find that the menu refers to them by numbers, eg Branches:1, rather than by name which may not be helpful.

Note: If a workbook appears blank check that the you have not selected a blank worksheet or that you have not accidentally scrolled the top rows of cells out of view.

⑤ Open the **WINDOW** menu and select **ARRANGE** again. This time click the **TILED** option on the dialog box then **OK**. The workbooks are arranged side by side on the screen.

Click each workbook in turn and it becomes the active workbook (confirmed by the Title Bar in blue).

Linking worksheets with formulae

We will now use worksheet **Summary 1** to link the two other worksheets together by means of formulae that contain 'external references'. We need, for example, a formula that adds together the value for raw materials for the 2 branches and places the result in the summary worksheet.

① Select cell **C5** in the **Summary 1** worksheet; begin a formula in this cell by typing **=SUM(**

② In this situation it is easier to click the cells that you wish to include in the formula rather than type in their references.

   a. Click the worksheet **Branch 1** to activate it, then click cell **C5** in this worksheet.

   b. Now check the Formula Bar of the **Summary 1** worksheet; it should read **=SUM('Branch 1'!C5**

   c. Click the Formula Bar and type a ➕ sign on the end of this formula.

   d. Click the worksheet **Branch 2** to activate it, then click cell **C5** in this worksheet.

   e. Now check the Formula Bar; it should read:
   =SUM('Branch 1'!C5+'Branch 2'!C5

   f. Press the **ENTER** key to complete the formula. The two amounts for raw materials are added and placed in cell C5 of the summary worksheet (the total should be 1812).

   Note: If a cell that you wish to select is not visible then use the scroll bars or the Maximise button to enlarge the worksheet. Use the Restore button when you have finished.

③ **Explanation of the Formula**. The linking formula **SUM('Branch 1'!C5+'Branch 2'!C5)** uses external references to the 2 worksheets Branch 1 and Branch 2. An external reference has to include the full sheet name as well as the cell reference, both separated by an exclamation mark. If the formula is correct then Excel will add the final bracket to the formula.

④ **Copying Linking Formulae**. Now that we have one linking formula we can copy it using the Fill command in the usual way:

   a. Maximise the **Summary 1** worksheet.

   b. Select cells **C5** to **F5**, then use the **EDIT** menu and select the options **FILL-RIGHT**.

   The linking formula, with its external references, is copied to the other cells.

   c. Now select the cells **C5** to **F11** and select **EDIT-FILL-DOWN**.

   d. Next clear the contents of cells **C10** to **F10** using the **DELETE** key.

   e. The Summary 1 worksheet should now resemble Figure 9.5 – check the totals with yours.

⑤ Open the **WINDOW** menu and select **ARRANGE** to view the 3 workbooks in tiled display again if necessary.

   Now the worksheets are linked, changes made to either worksheet – Branch 1 or Branch 2 – will update the summary worksheet.

   a. At the moment the total costs for the first quarter for both branches is £33,655 – see Figure 9.5 – the target is to reduce costs to £32,000. Try the following:

FIGURE 9.5

	A	B	C	D	E	F
1			Cost Summary - Branches 1 and 2			
2						
3			1st Quarter	2nd Quarter	3rd Quarter	4th Quarter
4						
5	Raw Materials		1812	1661	2264	1598
6	Machinery		1936	1254	1306	1454
7	Salaries		23344	20832	19231	11930
8	Heating and Power		5036	3973	2856	4410
9	Maintenance		1527	1201	1805	1571
10						
11	Total		33655	28921	27462	20963
12						

b. Change the Heating and Power costs for the first quarter to 1500 for the **Branch 1** worksheet and 1600 for the **Branch 2** worksheet.

c. Now check cell **C11** in the **Summary 1** worksheet – the target is now achieved.

d. Undo these changes using **EDIT-UNDO**.

6 At the moment each of the three worksheets is open in its own window; close two of them – use the **CLOSE** button.

Maximise the remaining worksheet window. You can activate each worksheet in the normal way using the sheet tabs.

7 Carry straight on with the next task, which involves saving the workbook.

104

Organising folders

1 We will save the workbook as **Branches** and create a folder to store the workbook in (plus any other related files). The instructions that follow assume that you are saving your work to diskette, if not you will need to substitute the appropriate drive.

2 Open click the **FILE** menu and select the **SAVE AS** option. A dialog box is displayed, use Figure 9.6 as a guide to completing it.

3 Make sure that the diskette containing the Excel workbooks that you have created so far is in the diskette drive.

Click the down arrow on the **SAVE IN:** box and select the drive 3½ **FLOPPY (A:)**.

4 Move the mouse pointer onto the **CREATE NEW FOLDER** button – a screen tip box will open and identify it. Click the button and a new dialog box is displayed.

Name the new folder **Excel Files** and click the **OK** button – see Figure 9.7.

The new folder is now displayed in the **SAVE IN:** box. As it is a new folder it contains no files yet.

5 Select the **FILE NAME** box and enter the name **Branches** for the workbook.

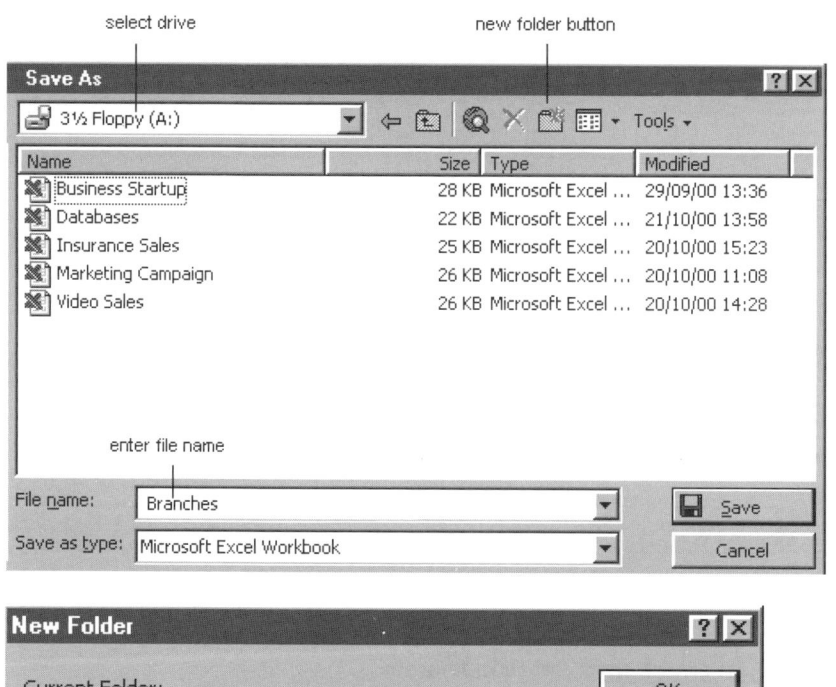

Topic 9 · Using linked worksheets

FIGURE 9.6

FIGURE 9.7

6 Finally click the **SAVE** button – the workbook **Branches** is saved in the **Excel Files** folder.

Locating workbooks on disk

In the previous task we saved a workbook in a new folder. If you save without specifying the folder or the drive then the workbook will be saved in whichever one is in use at the time. Often this is the default folder My Documents which will soon become very full if used indiscriminately; this means that workbooks become hard to find in a long list of other files. However well organised you are, the structure of folders and subfolders can also get quite complex. In this situation you can use Excel's search facility to locate workbook files.

Note: In the following instructions I assume that you have created your workbooks on diskette; if not then substitute the drive and folder where you have stored them.

1 Close any open workbooks but keep Excel open. Make sure that the diskette containing the Excel workbooks that you have created so far is in the diskette drive.

Open the **FILE** menu and select the **OPEN** option. The Open dialog box is displayed – see Figure 9.8.

Topic 9 · Using linked worksheets

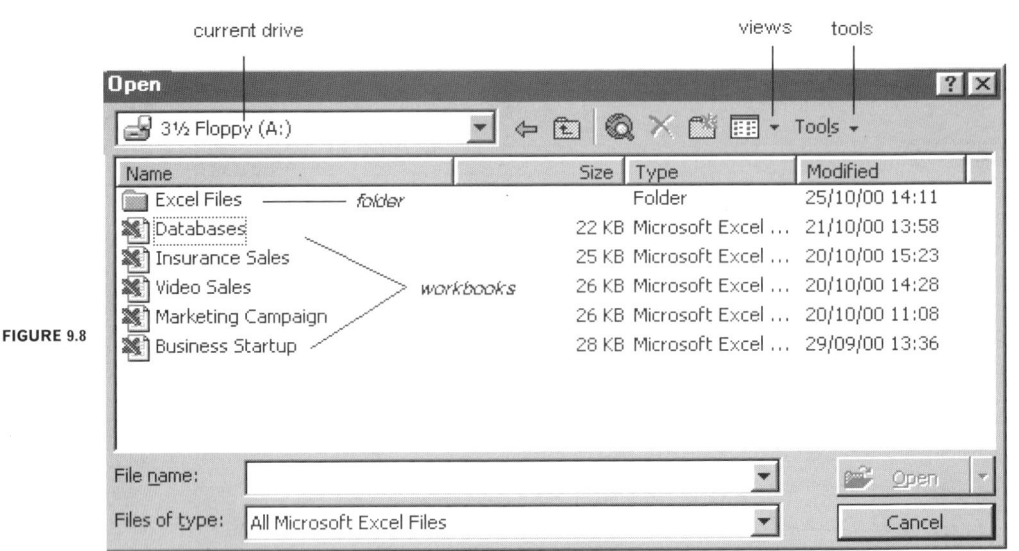

FIGURE 9.8

```
Open                                                                      ? X
   [3½ Floppy (A:)]          ← ↑  🔍 ✕ 📁  ▦ ▼  Tools ▼
   Name                            Size  Type              Modified
   📁 Excel Files  ——— folder           Folder            25/10/00 14:11
   ▣ Databases                      22 KB Microsoft Excel ... 21/10/00 13:58
   ▣ Insurance Sales                25 KB Microsoft Excel ... 20/10/00 15:23
   ▣ Video Sales    ⎱ workbooks     26 KB Microsoft Excel ... 20/10/00 14:28
   ▣ Marketing Campaign             26 KB Microsoft Excel ... 20/10/00 11:08
   ▣ Business Startup               28 KB Microsoft Excel ... 29/09/00 13:36

   File name:  [                                          ]▼   📂 Open  ▼
   Files of type: [All Microsoft Excel Files              ]▼     Cancel
```

(annotations: *current drive*, *views*, *tools*)

Change the current drive/folder to 3½ **FLOPPY [A:]** if necessary. The folders and/or workbook files on this drive are displayed. Note the buttons displayed on the right of the dialog box.

② More Details on a Workbook. Click the down arrow next to the **VIEWS** button – see Figure 9.8 above, and click **DETAILS**.

Fuller details of each workbook are given – size, type and date of creation or last modification.

Repeat this operation, this time selecting the **LIST** option, the workbook names only are displayed, allowing more workbooks to be displayed.

③ File Properties. Select one of the workbooks listed (do not open it).

Click the down arrow next to the **VIEWS** button and click **PROPERTIES** – more details of the workbook, including the name of its creator are also given.

Finally click **LIST** again.

④ Moving Between Folders. Double click on the **Excel Files** folder. It opens becoming the current folder – this is confirmed in the **LOOK IN** box on the dialog box. The workbook **Branches**, saved in the last task, is shown.

Click the down arrow on the **LOOK IN** box and re-select the diskette drive again – the **Branches** folder is closed and the files on the diskette drive are re-displayed.

⑤ Searching for a Workbook. Let's locate all the workbooks with the word 'sales' in the file name:

    a. Click the down arrow next to the **TOOLS** button and select the **FIND** option. A new dialog box is displayed.

    b. Enter *sales* in the **VALUE** box and press the **ENTER** key on the keyboard.

Click the **FIND NOW** button – if a dialog box opens click **YES**.

2 workbooks are displayed in the Open dialog box – **Insurance Sales** and

Topic 9 • Using linked worksheets

Video Sales. These workbooks could now be opened if you wished. Obviously this search will only work if these workbooks are located in the current folder and drive.

c. To return to the previous display and show all the other workbooks in the Open dialog box erase 'sales' from the File name box and click the **OPEN** button.

6   **Searching for a Workbook by its Contents**. If you can't remember the workbook name then you can search for it by its contents, eg a workbook that contains data about invoices:

a. Select the **FIND** option as before and when the Find dialog box is displayed click the down arrow next to the **PROPERTY** box – see Figure 9.9.

b. Select **CONTENTS**.

c. Check that the **CONDITION** box now reads **'Contains words'**.

d. Enter *Invoice* in the **VALUE** box and press the **ENTER** key on the keyboard. Click the **FIND NOW** button.

e. One workbook is located – **Databases**.

7   **Cancelling Search Conditions**. Select the **FIND** option as before and when the Find dialog box is displayed click the **NEW SEARCH** then the **FIND NOW** buttons to re-display the other workbooks.

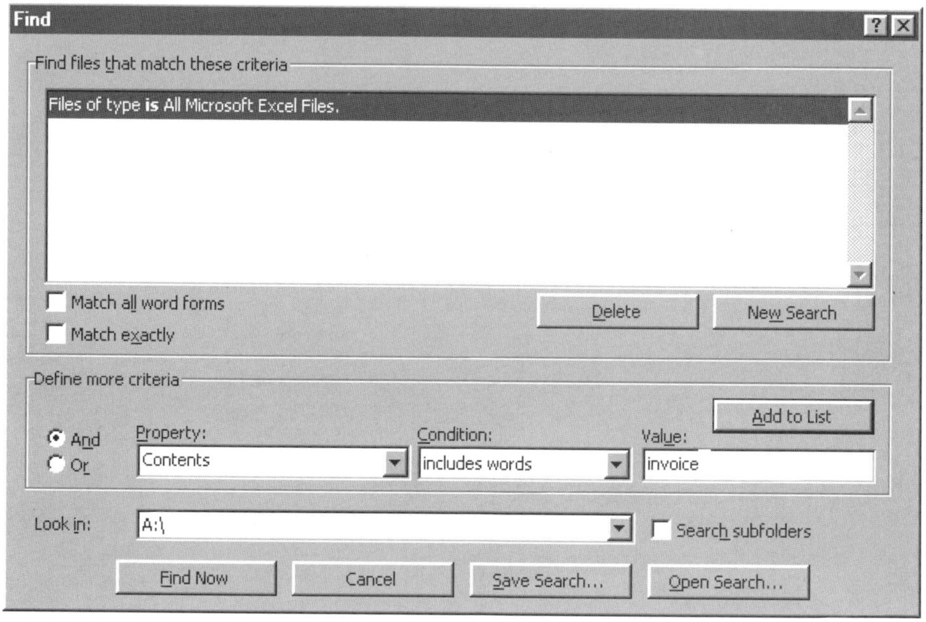

FIGURE 9.9

8   Cancel the Open dialog box. If you are not proceding to the next topic then exit Excel.

Summary of commands and functions

Note:
Menu commands show the menu name first, followed by the command to choose from the menu, e.g. **EDIT-CLEAR** means open the Edit menu and select the Clear command.

Menu commands

EDIT-COPY	Copy selected cell(s)
EDIT-PASTE	Insert cut or copied cells
EDIT-FILL-RIGHT	Copy selected cells to selected right hand columns
EDIT-FILL-DOWN	Copy selected cells into selected lower rows
FILE-CLOSE	Close current workbook
FILE-OPEN	Open an existing workbook
FILE-SAVE AS	Save a new workbook, or copy an existing workbook under a new name
WINDOW-ARRANGE	Arrange open windows
WINDOW-NEW WINDOW	Display workbook or worksheet in own window

TOPIC 10

Linking and copying workbooks

Introduction

In Topic 9 we linked together worksheets within a single workbook. In this topic we will link two separate workbooks. Linked workbooks may be more convenient than linked worksheets in some situations, for example where workbooks from separate sources need to be combined and linked.

Topic objectives

- To copy and modify a workbook.
- To link workbooks with formulae.
- To add comments to a workbook.
- To demonstrate links between workbooks.

Copying and modifying a workbook

1 Open the **Branches** workbook – it is in the **Excel Files** folder – see previous task if necessary:

  a. Open the **FILE** menu and select **SAVE AS** (not Save) – the Save as dialog box appears – see Figure 10.1 for guidance.

  b. The File Name box contains the current name **Branches**, enter the new name ***Materials and Machinery***.

  c. Check that the folder name **Excel Files** appears in the Save in box and click the Save button.

  d. The original workbook **Branches** is copied under the new name **Materials and Machinery** and then closed, leaving the Materials and Machinery workbook displayed – check this in the Title Bar.

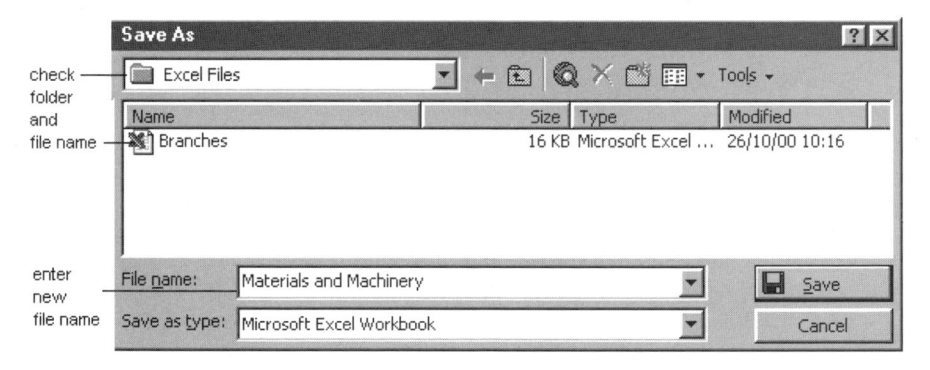

FIGURE 10.1

② Delete the worksheets **Branch 1** and **Branch 2** from the **Materials and Machinery** workbook, using the **EDIT-DELETE SHEET** command. The Summary 1 worksheet will now display errors, as the external formulae based on these two deleted worksheets will now be invalid.

③ Select rows **7** to **11** of the **Summary 1** worksheet and use the `DELETE` key to remove them.

Delete the contents of cell range **C5** to **F6**.

Rename the Summary 1 worksheet **Summary 2**.

Amend the worksheet title in row 1 and the worksheet will now consist of the framework shown in Figure 10.2.

	A	B	C	D	E	F
1			Cost Summary - Raw Materials and Machinery				
2						
3			1st Quarter	2nd Quarter	3rd Quarter	4th Quarter
4						
5	Raw Materials					
6	Machinery					
7						

FIGURE 10.2

Handling multiple workbooks

① Make sure that two workbooks **Branches** and **Materials and Machinery** are open. Use the **WINDOW** menu and the **ARRANGE – TILED** options to display the workbooks side by side – see Figure 10.3. It doesn't matter if your workbooks are in a different order to that shown.

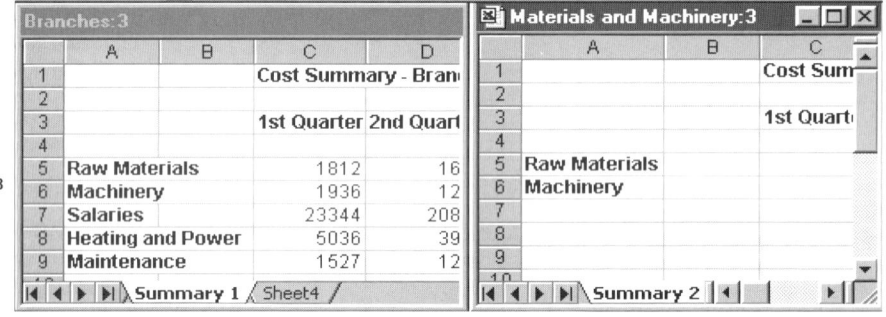

FIGURE 10.3

Branches:3

	A	B	C	D
1			Cost Summary - Branc	
2				
3			1st Quarter	2nd Quart
4				
5	Raw Materials		1812	16
6	Machinery		1936	12
7	Salaries		23344	208
8	Heating and Power		5036	39
9	Maintenance		1527	12

Summary 1 / Sheet4

Materials and Machinery:3

	A	B	C
1			Cost Sum
2			
3			1st Quart
4			
5	Raw Materials		
6	Machinery		
7			
8			
9			

Summary 2

② **Linking Workbooks With Formulae.** We now need to link the workbooks with formula:

a. Select the **Materials and Machinery** workbook and select cell **C5** of the Summary 2 worksheet – you may have to scroll it into view.

b. Enter an `=` sign in this cell to begin a formula.

c. Now select the **Branches** workbook and click cell **C5** in the **Summary 1** worksheet.

d. The cell is enclosed in a dotted rectangle and the following linking formula appears in cell C5 of the Summary 2 worksheet:
='[Branches.xls]Summary 1'!$C$5

Topic 10 · Linking and copying workbooks

Compare your workbook with Figure 10.4 to check this.

e. Press the **ENTER** key and the formula appears in the Formula Bar.

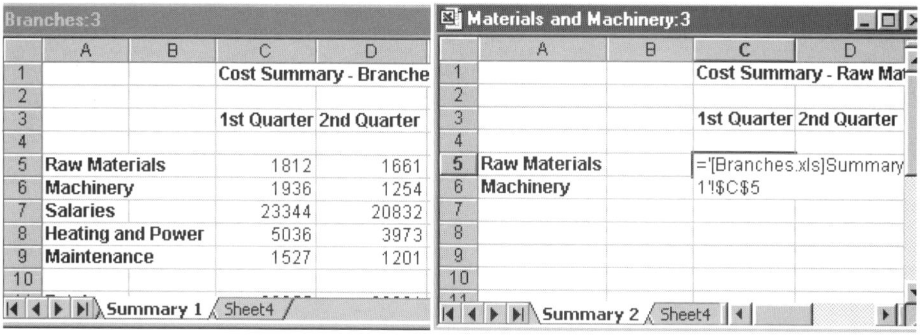

Branches:3			
	A	B	C	D
1			Cost Summary - Branche	
2				
3			1st Quarter	2nd Quarter
4				
5	Raw Materials		1812	1661
6	Machinery		1936	1254
7	Salaries		23344	20832
8	Heating and Power		5036	3973
9	Maintenance		1527	1201
10				

Summary 1 / Sheet4

Materials and Machinery:3			
	A	B	C	D
1			Cost Summary - Raw Ma	
2				
3			1st Quarter	2nd Quarter
4				
5	Raw Materials		='[Branches.xls]Summary	
6	Machinery		1'!$C$5	
7				
8				
9				
10				

Summary 2 / Sheet4

FIGURE 10.4

③ **Linking Formulae.** We have now linked the workbooks with an external reference. It consists of:

a. The name and extension (.xls) of the external workbook in square brackets, plus,

b. the worksheet name – both are enclosed in single quotes eg, **'[Branches.xls]Summary 1'!**.

c. The cell reference(s) is separated from the first part of the formula by an exclamation mark, eg **!$C$5**

d. The dollar signs in the cell reference indicate an *absolute* reference; ie when we copy the formula into another cell the cell reference C5 will *not* be adjusted to reflect its new location. We saw in Topic 4 that this can be useful but in this case we need a *relative* reference, so that the cell reference *will* be automatically adjusted when we copy it into other cells.

④ Select cell **C5** in the **Materials and Machinery** workbook if necessary and edit the formula using the Formula Bar.

Remove the two dollar signs so that the formula reads
='[Branches.xls]Summary 1'!C5

Press the **ENTER** key to execute the formula.

⑤ Maximise the **Materials and Machinery** workbook and copy the linking formula as follows:

a. Select cells **C5** to **C6**. Open the **EDIT** menu and select the **FILL-DOWN** options – the linking formula is copied to the next cell.

b. Select cells **C5** to **F6**. Open the **EDIT** menu and select the **FILL-RIGHT** options – the linking formula is copied to the cell range.

⑥ Calculate the totals in row 8, using a SUM formula or AutoSum.

The **Materials and Machinery** workbook now summarises the two cost categories 'Raw Materials' and 'Machinery' from the **Branches** workbook. Check it with Figure 10.5.

⑦ View the 2 workbooks in tiled display again if necessary. Changes made to the 'supporting worksheet' – **Branches** – will be reflected in the summary

FIGURE 10.5

	A	B	C	D	E	F
1			Cost Summary - Raw Materials and Machinery			
2						
3			1st Quarter	2nd Quarter	3rd Quarter	4th Quarter
4						
5	Raw Materials		1812	1661	2264	1598
6	Machinery		1936	1254	1306	1454
7						
8	Totals		3748	2915	3570	3052
9						
10						

or 'dependent' workbook **Materials and Machinery**. Try the following experiment:

a. Select the **Branches** workbook and select the worksheet **Branch 1**.

b. Amend cell **C6** to **700** and press **ENTER**. The value of the dependent cell **C6** in the **Summary 2** sheet of the workbook **Materials and Machinery** also changes – to 1944.

c. Use the **EDIT-UNDO** command to reverse the change.

8 Before starting the next task save and close both workbooks and exit Excel.

Links between workbooks

Once workbooks are linked Excel records details of the links. This means that even if the workbooks are opened and closed separately you will be prompted to update them.

1 Start Excel again and open the **Materials and Machinery** workbook (the dependent workbook). A dialog box will prompt you to update the links with any changes made to the supporting workbook. Click the **YES** button.

2 Open the **Branches** workbook next; this time you are *not* prompted to save any links as it is the supporting workbook and will not be affected by changes to the dependent workbook Materials and Machinery.

3 **Workbook Comments**. You can remind yourself and co-workers about the status and purpose of a workbook by adding comments:

a. Make **Materials and Machinery** the active workbook. Open the **FILE** menu and select the **PROPERTIES** option.

b. A dialog box appears; select the **SUMMARY** tab if necessary. Add a suitable title and brief summary to the workbook.

c. Select the **SAVE PREVIEW PICTURE** box at the bottom of the dialog box. You will now be able to preview the workbook before opening it using the **OPEN** dialog box – see previous Topic, page 106. This is useful for large workbooks that take a long time to open.

4 Save and close the two workbooks.

Summary of commands and functions

Note:

Menu commands show the menu name first, followed by the command to choose from the menu, e.g. **EDIT-CLEAR** means open the Edit menu and select the Clear command.

Menu commands

EDIT-DELETE	Delete selected worksheet element(s)
EDIT-DELETE SHEET	Delete selected worksheet
EDIT-FILL-RIGHT/DOWN	Copy selected cells to selected right hand/lower columns
FILE-PROPERTIES-SUMMARY	Add a comment to a workbook
FILE-OPEN	Open an existing workbook
FILE-SAVE AS	Save a new workbook, or copy an existing workbook under a new name
WINDOW-ARRANGE	Arrange windows on screen

TOPIC 11

Using tables and Goal Seek

Introduction

In previous topics we have tried out different values in a formula to see their effect on the final result. Once the range of values gets larger this can become time consuming and it is quicker to use a data table to hold the values. We will be creating two types of table:

Input Tables are generated from data based on variables and formulae. In Figure 11.1 below an input table of loan repayments is built up from a column of different interest rates.

Lookup Tables work in the opposite way to input tables; you use a function to look up values in a table that has already been created. In Figure 11.7 below the table is used to calculate sales commissions.

Goal Seek performs a similar function to tables, except that is is used to find a single value rather than a range of values.

Topic objectives

- To create a data series.
- To create one-input and two-input tables.
- To use the PMT function to calculate loan interest.
- To create a lookup table.
- To use Goal Seek to determine a target value.

Creating one-input tables

1 The simplest type of table is a one-input table which holds values for one variable; in our example below possible interest rates.

Create the worksheet shown in Figure 11.1, using a new workbook. Widen columns A and B and format it as shown.

Enter **6.00%** in cell **A9** – enter the percentage sign too.

2 We will use a data series to enter the percentages in column A, make sure that cell A9 is still selected:

a. Open the **EDIT** menu and select the options **FILL – SERIES**.

b. Enter the values in the dialog box, using Figure 11.2 as a guide.

c. The data series requires you to enter the **STEP VALUE** – the amount by which you want the series to increase (or decrease), and the **STOP VALUE**

Topic II · Using tables and Goal Seek

	A	B	C
1		Loan Repayment Table	
2			
3	Repayment term in months	72	
4	Interest Rate	8%	
5	Amount Borrowed	10000	
6			
7	Possible Interest Rates:	Monthly Repayment	
8			
9	6.00%		
10	6.25%		
11	6.50%		
12	6.75%		
13	7.00%		
14	7.25%		
15	7.50%		
16	7.75%		
17	8.00%		
18			

FIGURE 11.1

– the value at which you want the series to end. The series will occupy a **COLUMN** so click this option too.

d. Click the **OK** button and the range of possible interest rates shown in Figure 11.1 is created, if not use **EDIT – UNDO** and repeat, carefully checking the values that you have entered.

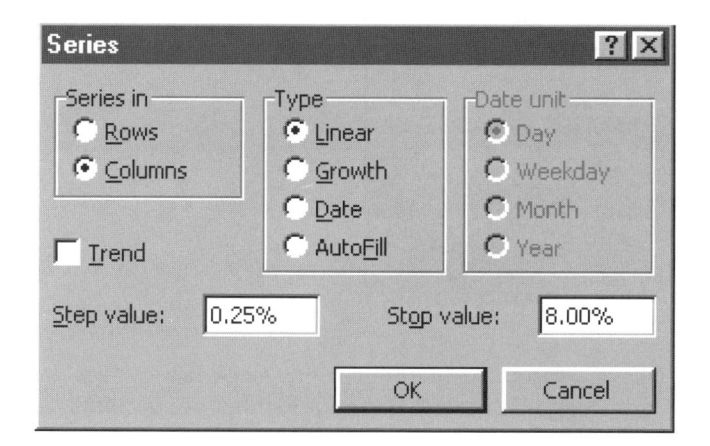

FIGURE 11.2

③ Enter the interest rate, repayment term and loan amount as shown in Figure 11.1.

Use **FORMAT – CELLS – BORDER** to outline cell **B8** where the result will appear.

④ Save the workbook as **Tables** and name the worksheet **One-input Table**.

⑤ **The PMT Function**. To calculate payments made at regular intervals at fixed interest rates, such as loans or mortgages, we can use the Excel PMT function. It is a little more complex than the previous functions that we have used, in that it requires you to enter three variables. The syntax of the function is, **=PMT(interest,term,principal)** where interest is the interest rate, term is the repayment term, and principal the amount borrowed.

a. Cell B4 holds the interest rate, B3 the repayment term and B5 the principal so enter the formula **=PMT(B4/12,B3,-B5)** in cell **B8**.

b. The monthly repayment of **175.33** is now displayed in cell B8, based on the values in cell range **B3** to **B5**.

Notes: Rate is divided by 12 to give the monthly repayment and the – sign converts the result to a positive rather than a negative number.

If your formula is not correct then check the cell data, names and the formula.

6 We can now create a table in cells **A9** to **B17**, based on the interest rates we have entered. This will let us see the effect on the monthly repayments of varying interest rates.

a. Select cell range **A8** to **B17**.

b. Open the **DATA** menu and select the **TABLE** option, a dialog box appears – see Figure 11.3.

c. The dialog box requires you to enter the cell reference for the column or row input cell box; as the table forms a vertical column enter the reference **B4** in the **COLUMN INPUT CELL** and click **OK**.

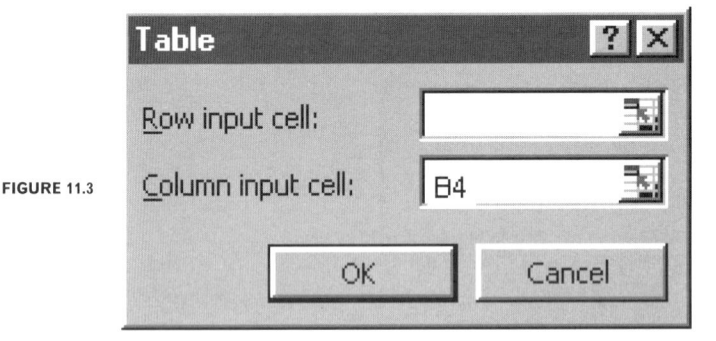

FIGURE 11.3

7 Cell range A8 to B17 now forms an input table and cell B4 is the cell where different interest rates can be entered. Different monthly repayments, based on different rates of interest, are now shown in cells **B9** to **B17**, and can be compared with the present repayment figure shown in cell B8.

a. At the moment the values in cells B9 to B17 are shown to a large number of decimal places. Open the the **FORMAT** menu and select the **CELLS** option. Make sure that the **NUMBER** tab is selected.

b. Choose the **NUMBER** category and format the cells to 2 decimal places. Your table should now look like Figure 11.4 below.

8 **Independent Tasks.**

a. Amend the interest rate to **6%**, the loan amount to **7000**, and the repayment term to **84**. The new loan repayment is shown in cell B8 – 102.26 per month. The other repayments in the input table cells are also re-calculated.

Topic II · Using tables and Goal Seek

	A	B	C
1		Loan Repayment Table	
2			
3	Repayment term in months	72	
4	Interest Rate	8%	
5	Amount Borrowed	10000	
6			
7	Possible Interest Rates:	Monthly Repayment	
8		£175.33	
9	6.00%	165.73	
10	6.25%	166.91	
11	6.50%	168.10	
12	6.75%	169.29	
13	7.00%	170.49	
14	7.25%	171.69	
15	7.50%	172.90	
16	7.75%	174.11	
17	8.00%	175.33	
18			

FIGURE 11.4

b. Try out a range of interest rates to find out at what loan amount would you start to pay more than £150 per month, given the same repayment term and interest rate as a. above. Compare your answer with Appendix 7.

Creating two-input tables

The one-input table we created was based around a single variable, the interest rate; a two-input table uses two variables. The table that we are going to create, shown in Figure 11.5, uses purchase amount and discount rate to calculate discount.

	A	B	C	D	E	F	G
1					Table of Discounts		
2							
3							
4							
5							
6				6%	7%	8%	9%	10%
7			1000				
8			1500				
9	Amount purchased		2000				
10			3000				
11			4000				
12							

FIGURE 11.5

① Enter the information shown in Figure 11.5, using a new worksheet in the **Tables** workbook. Format it as shown – use the Drawing Toolbar to draw the arrows – see page 41. Name the new worksheet **Two-input Table**.

② The discount given is the discount rate multiplied by the amount purchased. The formula must be entered where the row and column variables intersect – cell B6.

Enter the formula =*B3*B4* in cell **B6**. At the moment the result is a 0.

Note: Cells B3 and B4 have been chosen for the above formula but these cells will be left blank as the two-input table generates all the values we need. Unlike the one-input table we don't need to enter the second

Topic II · Using tables and Goal Seek

variable. As the table needs to use two cells when it calculates we chose B3 and B4, but any empty cells outside the table will do.

3 Now select cell range **B6** to **G11** – these are the cells that will hold the table:

a. Open the **DATA** menu and select the **TABLE** option – the same dialog box appears that we used for the one-input table.

b. Enter **B3** in the Row Input Cell box and **B4** in the Column Input Cell box. Click **OK**.

c. The discount table is created, showing 25 separate calculations – it should now look like Figure 11.6. The alternative would be to enter all them all as separate formulae, but this is obviously far quicker.

FIGURE 11.6

	A	B	C	D	E	F	G
1				Table of Discounts			
2							
3							
4							
5							
6			0	6%	7%	8%	9%	10%
7			1000	60	70	80	90	100
8			1500	90	105	120	135	150
9	Amount purchased		2000	120	140	160	180	200
10			3000	180	210	240	270	300
11			4000	240	280	320	360	400
12							

4 **Independent Task.** The present table represents the discount offered on goods purchased by customers in a one week period. We will adapt it to calculate discount for any number of weeks:

a. In cell **A13** enter the label **Enter no. of weeks**.

b. Change the formula in cell **B6** so that it also includes **B13** in the multiplication formula – at first all the table cells will be zeroed as B13 currently contains no numeric value.

c. Now enter **5** in cell **B13** – the table is recalculated, showing the discount for 5 weeks at various discount rates – compare your table with Appendix 8.

5 **Notes on input tables.**

a. To delete a table select the whole table and then use **EDIT – CUT** or **EDIT – CLEAR** or press the **DELETE** key.

b. To modify a table select the whole table and select **DATA – TABLE**.

c. To extend the range of a table first enter the extra values then modify it as above.

Using lookup tables

One and two-input tables are based on formula and one or more variables input by the user. Lookup tables use the opposite approach – the table values are already

Topic II · Using tables and Goal Seek

created and are looked up using variables entered in another part of the worksheet.

Look at the worksheet in Figure 11.7 below. In columns E to G is a table to look up commission, based on the sale value – from £0 to £8,000 – and the type of sale – cash or credit. If we were to look up the table manually then we could work out, eg:

- A credit sale of between £0 and £500 would attract no commission.
- A cash sale of £3000 would attract a commission of 10% as it falls in the 1 – 4000 range.

	A	B	C	D	E	F	G
1					Commission Lookup Table		
2							
3	Cash Sale						
4	Amount Sold						
5	Commission Due				Amount of Sale	Cash	Credit
6					0	5%	0%
7	Credit Sale				500	8%	5%
8	Amount Sold				1000	10%	8%
9	Commission Due				4000	15%	10%
10					8000	20%	15%
11							
12							

FIGURE 11.7

As the commission rates in the table do not follow a regular numeric sequence, we could not generate them by using a formula; however, Excel provides two lookup functions, HLOOKUP and VLOOKUP:

HLOOKUP is for values arranged horizontally in a row. The function is
=HLOOKUP(x,range,index)

VLOOKUP is for values arranged vertically in a column, as they are in Figure 11.7. This is the usual arrangement. The function is **=VLOOKUP(x,range,index)**

- **x** is the value that you want to look up in the table (text, number, or a cell reference)
- **range** is the cells making up the table
- **index** is the reference of the columns or rows to look in.

In the example shown in Figure 11.7:

- **x** is cell **B4** where the value of the sale is entered.
- **Range** is the lookup table, cell range **E6** to **G10**.
- **Index** are columns F and G holding the lookup values.

Note: The LOOKUP function will not work unless the first column of the lookup table (column E) holds entries that look up items in immediately adjacent columns (column F and G). Entries must be unique and in ascending order.

1. Enter the data shown in Figure 11.7 in a new worksheet in the **Tables** workbook. Enter **800** in cell B4.
2. Enter the formula **=VLOOKUP(B4,E6:G10,2)** in cell B5.
3. Notes:

   a. Enter the formula in lower case – if correctly entered Excel converts it to upper case.

   b. The formula means 'look up the value in cell B4, from the table in cell range E6 to G10, in the 2nd column of the table'.

c. The VLOOKUP function searches the first column of compare values – column E – until it reaches a number equal to or higher than 800 (in this case cell E8). It then goes back a row if it is higher (to cell E7), then goes to the second column (F) and looks up the commission of 8% (in cell F7). For this reason the values in the first column of the table – column E – must be in ascending order.

4 The commission is displayed in cell B5 as **0.08**.

Open the **FORMAT** menu and select the options **CELLS-NUMBER**. Select **PERCENTAGE** from the category list and **0** from the decimal places box. The commission is now displayed as 8%.

5 **Independent Task**. Repeat these operations to enter another VLOOKUP formula in cell **B9** calculating the commission on credit orders.

Note: You should modify the cell reference for the lookup value (B8) and the column number (3) where the lookup values are held.

a. Enter a credit order value of **7,000** in cell B8. Check that the commission is 10%.

If necessary check the formula that you have entered with Appendix 9.

6 Name the worksheet **Lookup Table.**

Goal Seeking in worksheets

Tables allow us to find the values for the range of values contained in the table, however, if you wanted to know the value a variable needs to be for a formula to equal one particular value then goal seeking can be more useful. Excel's Goal Seek keeps changing the value of a variable until a formula achieves the target value. We have already used Goal Seek in charts in Topic 7 – see page 82.

First open the **TOOLS** menu and check that you have **GOAL SEEK** listed as an option. If not then select the **ADD-INS** option on the **TOOLS** menu. If it is listed then you can open it now. If not then it will need to be installed, using the Excel or Office installation disk.

1 Open a new workbook and create the simple worksheet shown in Figure 11.8:

a. Format all the numbers to whole numbers, using the **FORMAT-CELLS-NUMBER** command.

b. Total columns B and D down, and multiply the values in rows 5 to 7 across to calculate the profit figures shown in column D.

c. Save the workbook as **Profits**.

2 Open the **TOOLS** menu and select **GOAL SEEK** – a dialog box appears.

If necessary move the dialog box so that you can see column C of the workbook, alternatively you can use the **COLLAPSE** button, located next to the data entry boxes on the dialog box, to reduce its size – see Figure 11.9. Click it again to restore the dialog box.

Topic II · Using tables and Goal Seek

	A	B	C	D	E
1					
2		No of	Profit	Total	
3		Units	per Unit	Profit	
4					
5	Product A	100	46	4600	
6	Product B	100	53	5300	
7	Product C	100	69	6900	
8					
9	Totals	300		16800	
10					

FIGURE 11.8

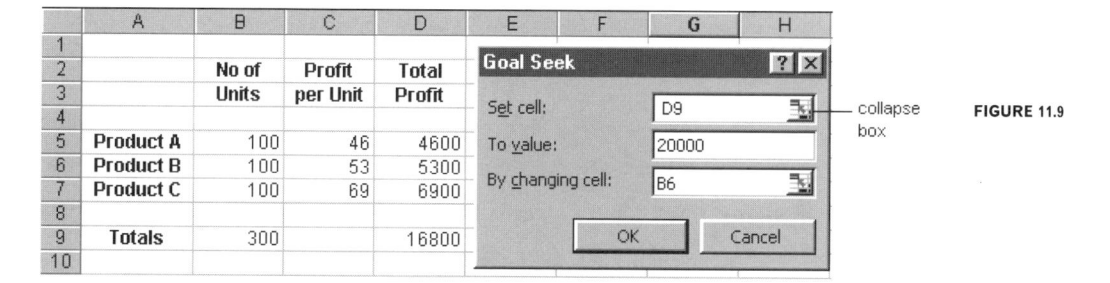

	A	B	C	D	E	F	G	H
1								
2		No of	Profit	Total	Goal Seek			?X
3		Units	per Unit	Profit				
4					Set cell:		D9	
5	Product A	100	46	4600	To value:		20000	
6	Product B	100	53	5300	By changing cell:		B6	
7	Product C	100	69	6900				
8								
9	Totals	300		16800		OK		Cancel
10								

— collapse box

FIGURE 11.9

3   We want to find out how many of product B we need to make to raise total profits from £16,800 to £20,000.

     a.   Complete the box as shown in Figure 11.9 above, ie:

        SET CELL   D9
        TO VALUE   20000
        BY CHANGING CELL   B6

     b.   Make a note of the present value of cell B6 and click **OK**.

     c.   A further Goal Seek Status dialog box appears, reporting the solution.

     d.   The value of cell B6 is changed to **160** – the number of product B needed to reach the £20,000 goal.

4   Click the **CANCEL** button now; this restores the previous value for cells D9 and B6. If you click OK by accident then select **UNDO** from the Edit menu.

5   Now try the following Goal Seek; what profit per unit for Product C (cell C7) would achieve a total profit of £18,000?

6   **Independent Task**. Open the workbook **Insurance Sales** created in Topic 4 and make **Sales Data** the active worksheet – see Figure 11.10.

     How many Business Insurance policies would you need to sell in June raise the overall total sales (cell E9) to 4000? Compare your **GOAL SEEK** dialog box with Appendix 9.

	A	B	C	D	E
3		Home	Business	Holiday	Total Sales
4	April	587	148	89	824
5	May	695	241	168	1104
6	June	734	198	207	1139
7					
8	Average Sales per Quarter	672	196	155	1022
9	Total Sales per Quarter	2016	587	464	3067
10	% of Total	65.73%	19.14%	15.13%	

FIGURE 11.10

121

7. ***Note***: Goal seeking will only work if these two conditions are met:

a. The cell whose value you set contains a value, not a formula.

b. The cell whose value you set must be related by a formula to the cell whose target value you are changing.

Summary of commands and functions

Note:
Menu commands show the menu name first, followed by the command to choose from the menu, e.g. **EDIT-CLEAR** means open the Edit menu and select the Clear command.

Menu commands

DATA-TABLE	Create a data table
EDIT-FILL-SERIES	Create a data series
FORMAT-CELLS-NUMBER	Format numeric values
FORMAT-CELLS-BORDER	Add borders to cells
TOOLS-GOAL SEEK	Change values of selected cell(s) so formula achieves a specified target value

Functions used

HLOOKUP(x,range,index)	Look up a value in a table where the values are displayed horizontally
PMT(interest,term,principal,[,fv,type])	Find the repayments required for a loan amount.

TOPIC 12

Using functions

Introduction

This topic cannot cover every Excel function; there are over 200 and many, such as financial and engineering functions, need specialised knowledge to use. We have already covered a number of the more common functions in earlier topics; these are reviewed at the end of this topic.

Topic objectives

- To review the range of Excel Functions.
- To perform date calculations.
- To use the logical function IF.
- To use statistical functions MAX, MIN, AVERAGE, STDEV, FORECAST and TREND.
- To use the financial functions Future Value and Straight Line Depreciation.
- To use Paste Function to enter function arguments.

Notes on using functions

- Functions are ready-made formulae that perform useful calculations.
- They produce their result in the cell in which they are entered.
- Functions are used in formulae so they must start with the = sign.
- Functions can be entered in lower or upper case. It is a good idea to type functions in lower case – if Excel converts it to upper case then you know that it is typed correctly.
- Normally a function contains no spaces.
- Functions can form part of a formula – or another function.
- Functions require you to supply information for their operations, called *arguments*, eg SUM(range) requires the cell range argument to be added.
- You can either type the function yourself or use Paste Function, which lets you choose the function from a list and paste it into a cell.

The range of Excel functions

1. **Function Types.** Open a new workbook. Open the **INSERT** menu and select the **FUNCTION** option (or use the **PASTE FUNCTION** button on the Standard Toolbar marked 'fx').

    a. The **PASTE FUNCTION** dialog box appears; 11 categories of functions are listed – see Figure 12.1. If the Office Assistant dialog box opens then read the note to section 3 below – it can be used as supplementary guidance in this task.

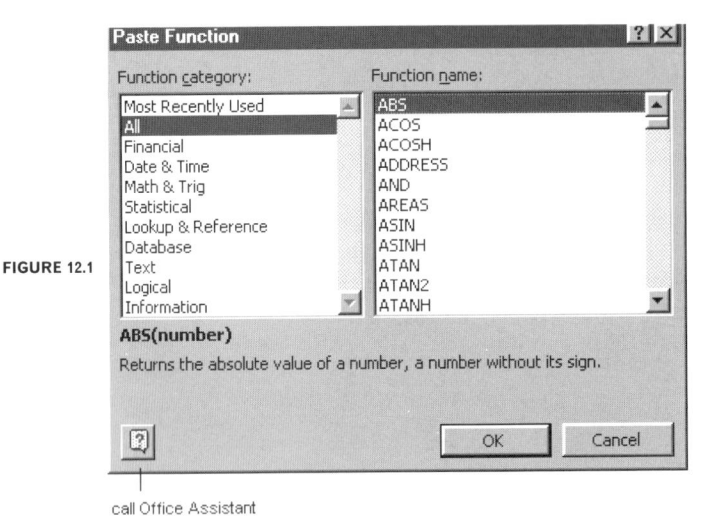

FIGURE 12.1

Paste Function dialog box showing Function category list (Most Recently Used, All, Financial, Date & Time, Math & Trig, Statistical, Lookup & Reference, Database, Text, Logical, Information) and Function name list (ABS, ACOS, ACOSH, ADDRESS, AND, AREAS, ASIN, ASINH, ATAN, ATAN2, ATANH). ABS(number) – Returns the absolute value of a number, a number without its sign.

call Office Assistant

b. Click the first Function Category – **MOST RECENTLY USED**. In the right hand box – **FUNCTION NAME** – are some of the functions you (or other users of Excel) have used recently.

c. Click each function in turn – the 'syntax' or structure of the function and a brief explanation are given at the bottom of the dialog box.

d. Click the second function category – **ALL**. All the functions are listed alphabetically in the Function Name box.

2 Now carry on reviewing the other Function Categories in the same way:

Financial functions are used to calculate depreciation, return on investments etc. We used the PMT function in the previous task.

Date and Time functions are used in this and later topics.

Mathematical and Trigonometric functions calculate square roots, cosines etc, as well as the simpler functions such as SUM.

Statistical functions include average, which we have already used, and standard deviation which we will use later in this topic.

Lookup and Reference functions are used to look up values in cells and tables. We used VLOOKUP in the previous topic.

Database functions carry out operations on database records only, eg summing or averaging selected records.

Text functions manipulate strings of text, eg finding the length of text or converting to upper case.

Logical functions test for the truth of certain conditions. An IF condition is used later in this topic.

Information functions test and report on cell references and contents, eg blanks or errors.

Topic 12 · Using functions

③ **Using the Office Assistant for Help on Functions.** When you start Paste Function the **OFFICE ASSISTANT** dialog box may be displayed too. If not click the Office Assistant button (marked with a '?') in the *bottom* left-hand corner of the Paste Function Dialog box – see Figure 12.1 above. If nothing happens then Office Assistant has not been installed – go to the next task.

a. Click the **FINANCIAL** function Category, then select **FV**.

Click the **OFFICE ASSISTANT** (animated paperclip) logo.

b. Take the 'Help with this feature' option in the Office Assistant dialog box.

A further dialog box appears, click the 'Help with this feature' then the 'Help on selected function' options.

c. Help text explaining the Future Value function is displayed. Close the **HELP** window – you are returned to the Paste Function dialog box.

d. Close the **OFFICE ASSISTANT** window – simply click the Office Assistant button in the Paste Function Dialog box.

e. If the Office Assistant logo is still displayed then right click it and select **HIDE** from the menu that appears.

Note: At stage b it is also possible to enter a brief description in ordinary English, eg 'find the minimum value in a database' and then click the **SEARCH** button. Office Assistant should select the functions best fitting your description. Such searches depend heavily on your skill in finding the appropriate search terms to narrow down the search to the function that you want. If for example you use word 'lowest' for 'minimum' in your description then Office Assistant may not find it

④ Click the **CANCEL** button on the Paste Function dialog box to return to the blank worksheet.

Some Excel functions

Now that we have reviewed the major categories of function we will try some of them out, bearing in mind that they only represent a small proportion of those available.

① The worksheet in Figure 12.2 monitors the performance of shares over a two week period (weekends excluded). Enter the data shown in a new workbook and save the workbook as **Share Performance**.

② **Displaying the Date.** Select cell **E1** and enter the formula =*NOW()*

A row of hash symbols (###) indicates that the column needs widening.

③ **Formatting the Date.** Format the date to a 4 digit year as shown in Figure 12.3 below. Use the **FORMAT** menu and select the option **CELLS**. Click the **NUMBER** tab and select the **DATE** category. Notice that Excel offers a variety of date formats.

④ Enter the rest of the worksheet data, formatting cell range **B5** to **B19** to 2 decimal places – see Figure 12.2.

⑤ Rows 16 to 18 are used to calculate the maximum, minimum and average

Topic 12 · Using functions

FIGURE 12.2

	A	B	C
1		Share Analysis	
2			
3	Date	Sutton	
4		Products	
5	1-Apr	27.44	
6	2-Apr	27.44	
7	3-Apr	32.65	
8	4-Apr	32.30	
9	5-Apr	31.25	
10	8-Apr	33.00	
11	9-Apr	33.35	
12	10-Apr	33.47	
13	11-Apr	32.83	
14	12-Apr	32.50	
15			
16	Hi Val		
17	Lo Val		
18	Av Val		
19	St Dev		

value of the shares. Row 19 shows the standard deviation – how much share values have varied from the average.

Enter the function =**MAX(B5:B14)** in cell **B16**.

Enter the function =**MIN(B5:B14)** in cell **B17**.

6. Now use the **AVERAGE** function in a formula in cell **B18** and the STDEV function in a formula in cell **B19**.

7. We will use the logical function **IF()** to monitor whether the shares have shown an overall increase or decrease. If share values have increased then a 'share increase' message is displayed, if not a 'share decrease' message is displayed.

   a. Select cell **E14** and enter the formula:

   =**IF(B14>B5,"share increase","share decrease")**

   b. If you have used the same share values as those shown then a 'share increase' message should be displayed.

   c. Test the function by amending the value of cell **B14** to **22.50**. The message in cell E14 is now 'share decrease' – the if condition is now false. Use **EDIT-UNDO** to restore the original value and the original messasge is re-displayed.

8. **Calculating with Dates**. Dates can used in calculations in a straightforward way, often without the need for a function. We will calculate the time in days between the opening date in cell A5 and the closing date in cell A14.

   a. In cell **E9** enter the label **No of Days**.

   b. Enter the formula =**A14-A5** in cell F9. The result in days is displayed. If necessary format the cell to a whole number – see section 3 above. Check your worksheet with Figure 12.3.

	A	B	C	D	E	F
1		Share Analysis			November 1, 2000	
2						
3	Date	Sutton				
4		Products				
5	1-Apr	27.44				
6	2-Apr	27.44				
7	3-Apr	32.65				
8	4-Apr	32.30				
9	5-Apr	31.25			No. of Days	11
10	8-Apr	33.00				
11	9-Apr	33.35				
12	10-Apr	33.47				
13	11-Apr	32.83				
14	12-Apr	32.50			share increase	
15						
16	Hi Val		33.47			
17	Lo Val		27.44			
18	Av Val		31.62			
19	St Dev		1.86			

FIGURE 12.3

Independent tasks

Open **Sheet2** of the **Share Performance** workbook and re-name it **Financial Functions**. Try the following:

1 **Future Value Function.** You are going to save £5000 every year for 8 years at 5% annual interest.

Enter the formula **=FV(5%,8,-5000)** in a blank cell.

The result is the value of your investment after 5 years – £47,745.54. A row of hash symbols (###) indicates that the column needs widening.

2 **Straight Line Depreciation Function.** You have bought a car for £7000 and estimate that in 3 years it will be worth £3000. Paste Function gives you help on entering functions:

a. Select a blank cell and open the **INSERT** menu and select the **FUNCTION** option.

b. The Paste Function dialog box appears; select **FINANCIAL** from the Function Category box and **SLN** from the Function name box.

c. Click the **OK** button – the second **PASTE FUNCTION** dialog box appears.

Try entering the 'arguments' or elements of the function yourself – as each box is selected Paste Function explains what to enter.

d. The annual depreciation is calculated at £1,333.33. If necessary check your Paste Function dialog box with Appendix 10.

3 Save and close the workbook.

Topic 12 · Using functions

Trend and forecast functions

Forecast and Trend are Excel statistical functions used to predict trends using existing data as a basis. Many types of trend can be predicted in this way, eg sales, commodity prices and goods in stock.

1 Open the workbook **Video Sales**. The worksheet **Sales Data** records video sales and revenue for June to October. We will use the Forecast function to predict November sales. However, as the function requires numeric data we must change the months in column A to numbers – see Figure 12.4.

Enter **11** in cell **A9**.

FIGURE 12.4

	A	B	C	D	E
1		Video Sales - Current Year			
2					
3	Month	No. Sold	Revenue	Advertising	Adv as % of Revenue
4	6	750	1915	280	15%
5	7	910	3054	401	13%
6	8	1075	3447	498	14%
7	9	1330	4450	733	16%
8	10	1618	5009	801	16%
9	11				
10					

enter month 11

2 Click cell **B9**.

a. Select **INSERT – FUNCTION** and select **STATISTICAL** from the Function Category box and **FORECAST** from the Function name box.

b. Click **OK** and enter the arguments as shown in Figure 12.5 in the second dialog box.

c. Click the **OK** button and the sales forecast for month 6 is shown as 1783. The Forecast function is displayed in the Formula Bar – =**FORECAST(A9,B4:B8,A4:A8)**. It assumes a linear trend, ie that sales will increase by the same proportion each year.

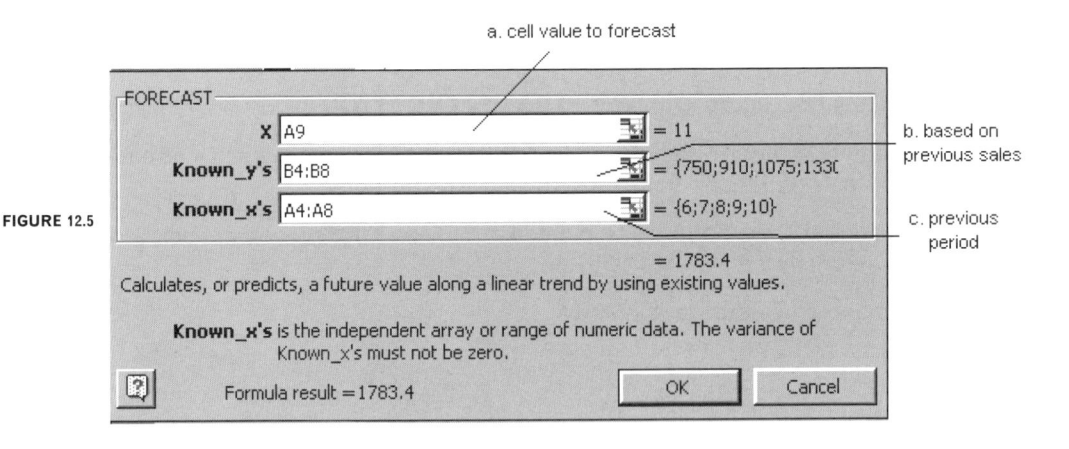

a. cell value to forecast

FORECAST

X A9   = 11   b. based on previous sales
Known_y's B4:B8   = {750;910;1075;1330}
Known_x's A4:A8   = {6;7;8;9;10}   c. previous period

= 1783.4

Calculates, or predicts, a future value along a linear trend by using existing values.

Known_x's is the independent array or range of numeric data. The variance of Known_x's must not be zero.

Formula result =1783.4   OK   Cancel

FIGURE 12.5

128

③ We will now use the Trend function to calculate how fast the cost of video advertising will continue to rise. We can use AutoFill to calculate it quickly rather than use Paste Function.

　a. Select cell range **D4** to **D8** and move the mouse pointer onto the AutoFill handle – this is the small square in the bottom right hand corner of the selected cell range.

　b. Use the *right* mouse button to drag down – see Figure 12.6 – the linear trend figures are shown for each cell 'dragged'.

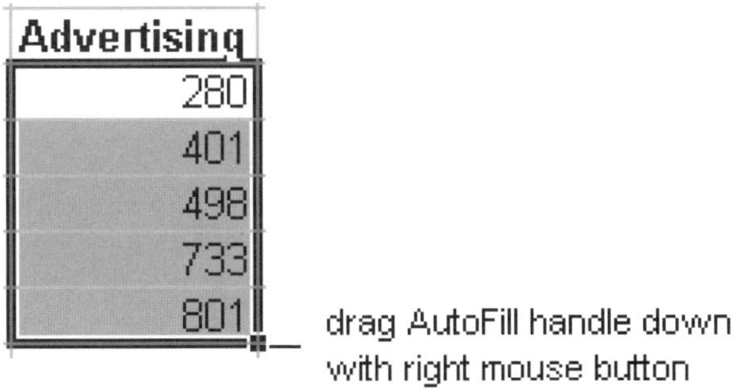

Advertising
280
401
498
733
801

drag AutoFill handle down with right mouse button

FIGURE 12.6

　c. Release the mouse button. Select either **LINEAR TREND** or **GROWTH TREND** from the popup menu. Use **EDIT-UNDO** to undo the trend calculation if necessary.

Note: You can also forecast by adding trendlines to charts – see Topic 4.

④ If you wish to save the changes to the **Video Sales** workbook then do so, otherwise exit without saving.

Summary of commands and functions

Note:
Menu commands show the menu name first, followed by the command to choose from the menu, e.g. **EDIT-CLEAR** means open the Edit menu and select the Clear command.

Menu commands

EDIT-UNDO	Undo an operation
FORMAT-CELLS-NUMBER	Format numeric data in cells
INSERT-FUNCTION	Use Paste Function

Review of functions

　a. Date and time functions display dates and times, or can calculate the time elapsed between two dates or times; eg the function **NOW()** used in this topic.

b. Financial functions calculate such things as investments, repayments and depreciation, eg:

   FV – calculates the future value function of an investment – see above.

   NPV – net present value of an investment.

   PMT calculates the repayments required on a loan – see above.

   SLN calculates depreciation using the straight-line method – see above.

c. Statistical Functions – we have already used some of these in this topic – **AVERAGE, MIN, MAX** and **STDEV**.

d. Logical Functions test for the truth of certain conditions and include **IF, AND** and **OR**. We have used IF in this topic.

e. The Lookup function **VLOOKUP** was used in Topic 11.

TOPIC 13

Introduction to macros

Introduction

A macro lets you record and save a series of keyboard strokes, menu choices and mouse movements and run them again when you need to. This has the advantage of saving time on a series of repetitve actions; you can also achieve greater consistency and accuracy as errors are reduced by simply 're-playing' a series of commands.

The advanced use of macros uses the programming language Visual Basic to build a whole series of programs or applications. In this introductory topic we will create some simple macros which automate routine tasks such as printing or adding the current date to a document.

Topic objectives

- To record a macro.
- To assign a macro to a shortcut key.
- To assign a macro to a button.
- To run and test macros.
- To appreciate problems caused by macro viruses.

More information on macros

You can use macros to control worksheets, charts and databases. Every macro is saved and run under a different name. You can run macros in several ways; the simplest is from a shortcut key where you press the **CTRL** key and a letter on the keyboard. You can also add the macro to a new or existing menu or run it from a button.

A simple date-stamp macro

1 Our first macro will record a few key strokes and menu choices to automate the task of adding the date and time to a worksheet. We will use the workbook Tables, but any worksheet will do.

   a. Open the worksheet **Lookup Tables** in the workbook **Tables**.

   b. Open the **TOOLS** menu and select the options **MACRO** then **RECORD NEW MACRO**. The Record Macro dialog box appears; use Figure 13.1. as a guide to completing it.

   c. Enter the name *Date_Time* in the name box.

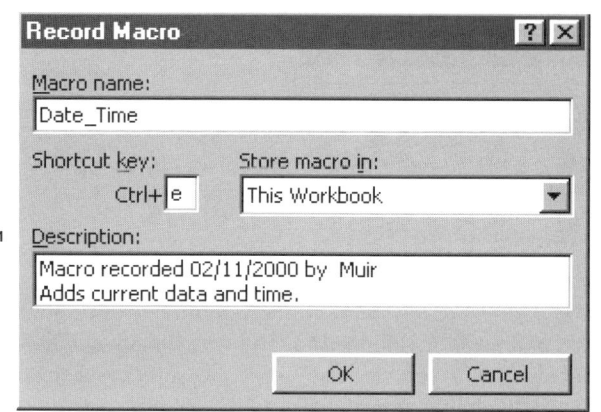

FIGURE 13.1

    d.   Enter the letter **e** in the Ctrl+ box (Ctrl plus letters a – d are already used as Excel shortcut keys).

    e.   Make sure that the option **THIS WORKBOOK** is selected in the **STORE MACRO IN:** box.

    f.   Select the **DESCRIPTION** box. It always contains the creation date plus the name of the author or organisation. Add the description **Adds Current Date & Time** to the box.

    g.   Click the **OK** button. The message 'Recording' is displayed in the Status Bar, bottom left of the window. A single **STOP RECORDING** button may also be displayed.

2   **Recording the Macro.** We are now ready to record the steps of the macro. All your actions will be recorded, right or wrong, so don't issue any unnecessary commands.

    a.   Select cell **A1**. Enter the function **=NOW()** in cell A1 then click the 'tick' button in the Formula Bar or press the **ENTER** key.

    b.   Making sure that cell A1 is still selected open the **FORMAT** menu and select the option **CELLS** then the **NUMBER** tab (even if already selected).

    c.   Select the **DATE** category, then a suitable date/time format. Click **OK**.

The date appears, correctly formatted, in cell A1 of the worksheet.

    d.   Open the **TOOLS** menu and select the options **MACRO-STOP RECORDING** (or click the **STOP RECORDING** button). You have now recorded your first macro, Date_Time, which automates entering the date and time.

3   *Note*: If you make a mistake while recording a simple macro then stop recording. Open the **TOOLS** menu and select the **MACRO** then the **MACROS** option.

Select the macro and click the **DELETE** button on the dialog box.

4   **Running the Macro.** Hold down the **CTRL** key on the keyboard and press the **E** key. The macro will run, updating the date and time in cell A1.

You can also run a macro from the menu – open the **TOOLS** menu and select the **MACRO** then the **MACROS** option. Select the macro and click the **RUN** button – the macro runs again.

Topic 13 · Introduction to macros

About macro viruses

1 Save and close the **Tables** workbook, then open it again. A dialog box will appear warning you of viruses and giving you 3 options. Click the **TELL ME MORE** button for Help text.

2 When you open any workbook containing macros, Excel will alert you to the danger of hidden viruses. A virus is a small, hidden program that will attach itself to various types of programs, including the operating system, and can cause considerable damage. Macro viruses have become one of the most common types of virus and are activated whenever an infected workbook is opened. A macro virus can also be spread if the workbook is opened via a network (including the Web). All that Excel does is to warn you of the possible presence of macros in a workbook that you are about to open. To find out whether any viruses are actually present you need to have antivirus software installed.

3 Close the Help text and return to the warning dialog box; the two other options are:

a. **Enable Macros**. This option will open the workbook and allow the macros to work normally. If the workbook comes from a known, reliable source then this is ok. Often a workbook will not work properly without the macros enabled so the temptation is to take this option; however, if the workbook is from an unfamiliar source, especially the Internet or the Web, and you did not expect it to contain macros, then it is safest either to use a virus checker first or to take the next option.

b. **Disable Macros**. This will open the workbook with the macros disabled – a safer option which will allow you to view and edit macros but not run them. Bear in mind, however, that the macro-driven features will not work.

Running a macro from a button

Our first macro **Date_Time** can be run in two ways – from a shortcut key or by running it from the Macro menu. In this task we will create a macro that prints a worksheet and then assign it to a button. Clicking the button will run the macro, without the need for key strokes or menu choices.

1 Open the workbook **Video Sales**. If you don't have this workbook then use any other workbook containing worksheet data, although you may need to adjust some of the cell references.

2 We will create a print macro that prints the video sales held in cells A1 to E8 of the **Sales Data** worksheet – make sure that this is the active sheet.

a. Open the **VIEW** menu and select **TOOLBARS**.

b. Select **FORMS** from the **TOOLBARS** list. The Forms toolbar is displayed, click the **CREATE BUTTON** tool – see Figure 13.2. The screen pointer changes to cross hairs.

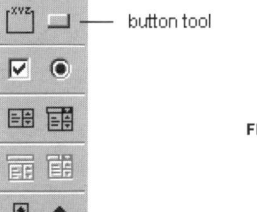

FIGURE 13.2

③ Drawing the Button. Drag the screen pointer to draw a button that covers cells **G2** and **G3**.

Let go the mouse button and the button is drawn with the default name '**Button1**'. We can reposition it later if necessary.

④ Linking the Button to a Macro. The **ASSIGN MACRO** dialog box opens automatically:

a. Close the **FORMS** toolbar. Click the **RECORD** button on the dialog box. The **RECORD MACRO** dialog box appears.

Using Figure 13.3 as a guide, complete the dialog box as follows:

b. Enter the macro name as ***Print_Sales***.

c. Leave the **SHORTCUT KEY** box blank as the macro will be run from a button.

d. Make sure that **THIS WORKBOOK** is selected in the **STORE MACRO IN** box.

e. Complete the Description box as shown in Figure 13.3.

f. Click **OK** – the macro is now assigned to the button and you are ready to start recording.

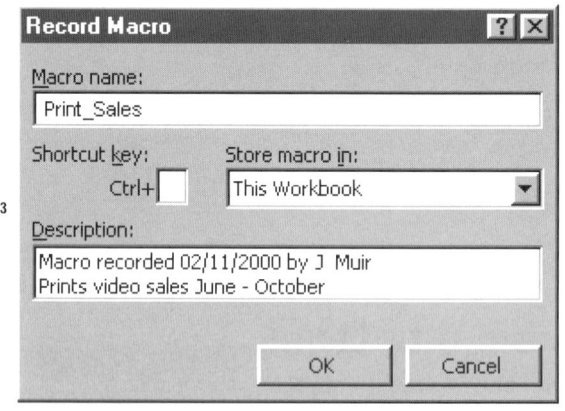

FIGURE 13.3

⑤ Macro Recording. Make sure that your printer is turned on and connected, then:

a. Open the **FILE** menu and select the option **PAGE SETUP**.

b. Click the **SHEET** tab on the dialog box.

c. Click the **PRINT AREA** box and enter the cell references **A1:E8**. Click **OK**.

d. Open the **FILE** menu again and select **PRINT**; choose 1 copy and whatever other settings you wish. Click **OK**.

e. Printing will now take place; when it is finished open the **TOOLS** menu and select the options **MACRO-STOP RECORDING** (or click the **STOP RECORDING** button).

You have now created a print macro.

⑥ Troubleshooting – see section 12 below.

Topic 13 · Introduction to macros

(7) Button Formatting – Font. We will change the size and colour of the button text:

a. First you must select select the button – hold down the **CTRL** key and click the button – selection handles appear round the button. If you forget to hold down the **CTRL** key the macro will run and print the sheet again.

b. First highlight the default name on the button and press the **DELETE** key to erase it.

c. Right click the button and select **FORMAT CONTROL** – a dialog box appears – see Figure 13.4.

d. Select **BOLD** from the **FONT STYLE** box and **8** from the **SIZE** box.

e. Click the down arrow button on the **COLOR** box and select a colour for the text. Click **OK**.

f. The button should be still selected; type the new label for the button **CLICK TO PRINT**.

Click elsewhere on the worksheet to de-select the button.

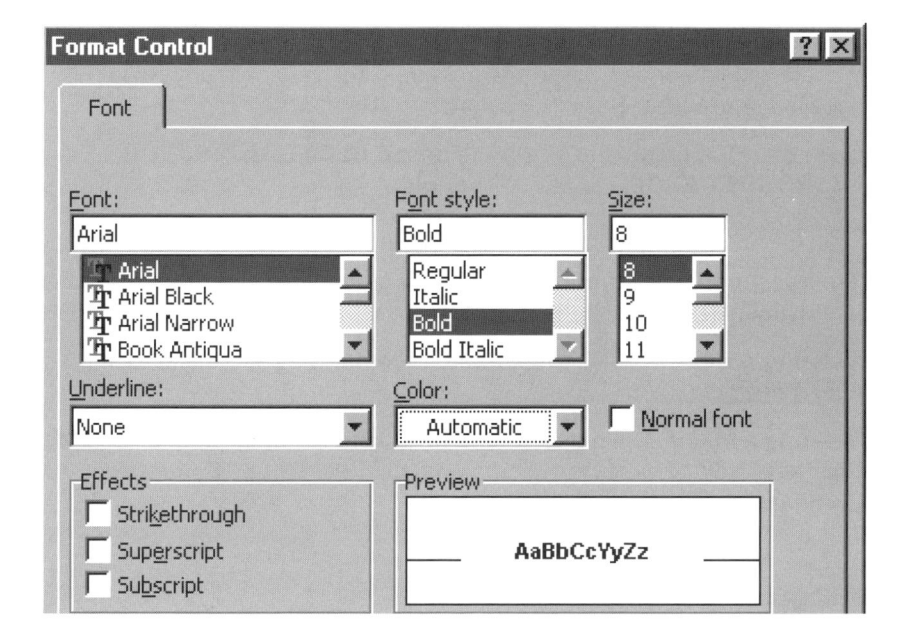

FIGURE 13.4

(8) Button Size and Position. Hold down the **CTRL** key and click the button again – selection handles appear.

a. To change the button *size* drag one of the selection handles – see Figure 13.5 – the screen pointer will change to a double-headed arrow.

b. To *move* the button place the screen pointer on the edge of the selected button – not on a selection handle – and drag. The button can now be moved. Don't move the button within the print area or the button outline will be printed along with the worksheet.

c. Finally press the **ESC** key to de-select the button and remove the selection handles.

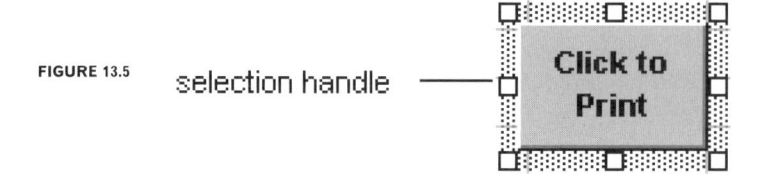

FIGURE 13.5 selection handle ⎯⎯⎯ [Click to Print button]

9. **Running the Macro.** If you are happy with the appearance of your button then try running it. Move the screen pointer on top of the button – the screen pointer becomes hand-shaped.

   Click once and the worksheet should print as before.

10. **Viewing the Macro.** The macro has been recorded as Visual Basic code in a module sheet in the **Video Sales** workbook. We will check this.

    a. Open the **TOOLS** menu and select the **MACRO** then the **MACROS** option. A dialog box appears; select the **PRINT_SALES** macro.

    b. Click the **EDIT** button and the Module1 sheet appears. Maximise it – it contains the macro in VB code. It is quite lengthy as all the standard page setup settings are listed.

       You are recommended not to try amending the code without some knowledge of Visual Basic

    c. Open the **FILE** menu and select the option **CLOSE AND RETURN TO MICROSOFT EXCEL**.

11. Save and close the **Video Sales** workbook.

12. **Troubleshooting – Information only.** If a simple macro doesn't work then it is usually best to delete it and re-record it.

    a. **Deleting a Button.** Select the button as before (**CTRL** – click) then press the **DELETE** key.

    b. **Deleting a Macro.** Open the **TOOLS** menu and select the options **MACRO** then **MACROS**. Select the macro name then the **DELETE** option from the dialog box.

Independent task

A print macro such as Print_Sales sets a print area that only applies to one worksheet and workbook. This task gives you more practice in creating a print macro for another workbook.

1. Open any other suitable workbook and create a new macro to print off a cell range.

2. Name the macro and assign it a shortcut key.

3. Create a print button and assign the macro to it.

4. Test both shortcut key and button.

Running a macro from a toolbar button

We now know three ways to run a macro – shortcut key, running it from the Macro menu and assigning it to a button on the worksheet. A fourth method is to attach a macro to a custom button on a toolbar. We will create a button that will format a worksheet. We will select the button, add it to the formatting toolbar, and record a macro to run from the button.

1 Open the workbook **Insurance Sales**. Select the worksheet containing the sales data and drag aside any embedded chart to show the data. If you don't have this workbook then use any other workbook, although you may need to adjust some of the cell references.

2 **Selecting the Custom button.**

   a. Open the **TOOLS** menu and select the **CUSTOMISE** option.

   b. A dialog box appears. Click the **COMMANDS** tab.

   c. Select **MACROS** from the **CATEGORIES** list – you may need to scroll down to see it.

   d. Drag the custom button *from* the dialog box *onto* the **FORMATTING** Toolbar next to the **BOLD** button – see Figure 13.6. Do *not* close the Customise dialog box.

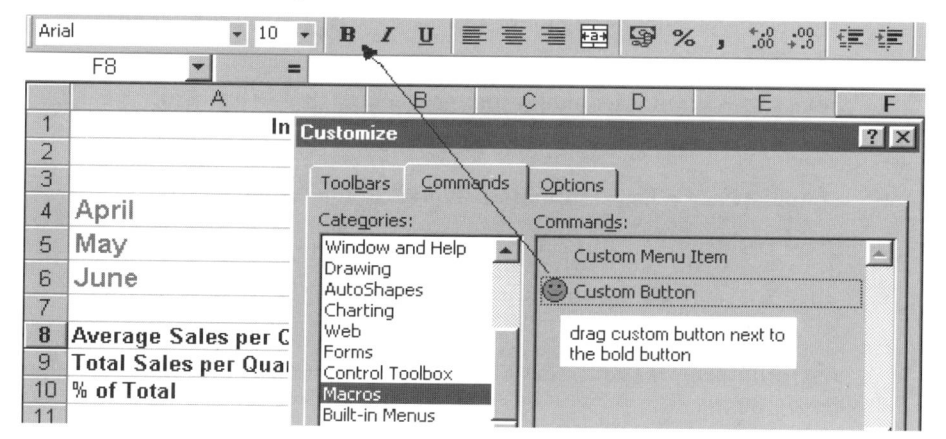

FIGURE 13.6

3 **Choosing the Custom Button Design.**

   a. With the Customise dialog box still open, right click the custom button *on the toolbar* (not in the dialog box).

   b. Select the option **CHANGE BUTTON IMAGE** option from the popup menu that appears.

   c. Select another button icon – the custom button on the toolbar changes.

   d. Close the Customise dialog box.

4 **Recording the Customise Macro.**

   a. Select the menu options **TOOLS – MACRO – RECORD NEW MACRO**.

   b. In the dialog box enter the macro name ***Formats_Worksheet***.

   c. Do not enter anything in the **SHORTCUT KEY** box as the macro will be run from the custom button.

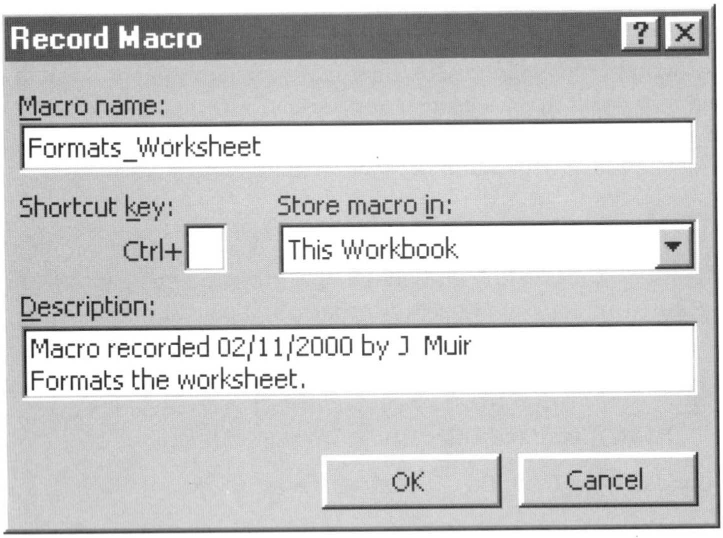

FIGURE 13.7

Record Macro dialog box:
- Macro name: Formats_Worksheet
- Shortcut key: Ctrl+
- Store macro in: This Workbook
- Description: Macro recorded 02/11/2000 by J Muir. Formats the worksheet.

    d. In the **STORE MACRO IN** box select the option **THIS WORKBOOK**.

    e. Enter a description of the macro in the Description box, eg, **Formats the worksheet**.

    f. Check your entries with Figure 13.7. Click **OK** – your next actions will be recorded.

5 Select the cell range holding the insurance data – **A1** to **E10**.

    a. Open the **FORMAT** menu and select the option **AUTOFORMAT**.

    b. Scroll down the list of formats and choose the format **COLORFUL 2**. Click **OK**.

    c. Open the **TOOLS** menu and select the options **MACRO-STOP RECORDING** (or click the **STOP RECORDING** button).

6 **Assigning the Macro.** Click the custom button on the toolbar – a dialog box appears.

Select the macro **FORMAT_WORKSHEET** and click **OK**.

7 **Testing the Macro.** First we will restore the worksheet to its normal format, open the **EDIT** menu and select the **UNDO AUTOFORMAT** option.

Now click the special custom button that you have created on the Formatting Toolbar – the macro reformats the worksheet to the AutoFormat previously recorded.

8 *Notes: Information only*

    a. If you cannot undo the format using the Edit menu then you can use the Format menu. First make sure that the cell range **A1** to **E10** is still selected, then open the **FORMAT** menu and select **AUTOFORMAT** again.

This time select the format **NONE** from the list box – you may have to scroll down to see it. Click **OK** and all formatting is removed (including the original formatting added in previous topics).

b. To delete a custom toolbar button open the **TOOLS** menu and select the **CUSTOMISE** option. A dialog box appears – drag the custom button from the toolbar back onto the dialog box. Close the dialog box.

c. **Deleting a Macro**. Open the **TOOLS** menu and select the options **MACRO** then **MACROS**. Select the macro name then the **DELETE** option from the dialog box.

9. Close the **Insurance Sales** workbook. If you don't wish to keep the formatting or the macro then don't save it.

Summary of commands

Note:
Menu commands show the menu name first, followed by the command to choose from the menu, e.g. **EDIT-CLEAR** means open the Edit menu and select the Clear command.

Menu commands

Command	Description
CTRL-[letter]	Run macro using shortcut key
CTRL-[select]	Select screen button
FILE-PAGE SETUP	Modify page settings
FORMAT-AUTOFORMAT	Select automatic worksheet format
FORMAT-CELLS-NUMBER	Format a date or number
FORMAT-CONTROL	Format a selected object, eg button
TOOLS-CUSTOMISE-COMMANDS	Add/remove custom toolbar button
TOOLS-MACRO-MACROS	Run, edit or delete a macro
TOOLS-MACRO-RECORD NEW MACRO	Record a new macro
TOOLS-MACRO-STOP RECORDING	Stop recording a macro
TOOLS OPTIONS-GENERAL	Display/hide virus warning messages
VIEW-TOOLBARS-FORMS	Display/hide forms toolbar

TOPIC 14

Excel on the Web

Introduction

Excel and other Microsoft Office components such as Access and Word all include Web-based features. In Excel you can create worksheets and charts and turn them into Web pages; they can then be viewed using a Web browser such as Netscape or Internet Explorer. You can make your Excel Web pages interactive so that other users can change the data, or non-interactive so that users can view the data but not change it.

Putting your Excel data on the Web has several advantages. It lets users access your worksheet data without needing to have Excel installed on their computers; all they need is a Web browser and access to the Web server where the pages are stored. You can also combine different types of data on a single Web page, from where they can be easily viewed or updated.

You can also use Excel to download or copy numeric and financial data from a Web site, provided that you have the Internet Explorer Web browser installed on your PC and access to the Web.

Topic objectives

- To create and run a Web query.
- To create and edit a Web page in Excel.
- To insert hyperlinks into a Web page and a workbook.

Running a Web query in Excel

1   **The Web Toolbar**. Open a new workbook and save it as **Web Query**.

Open the **VIEW** menu and select the **TOOLBARS** option then **WEB**. The Web toolbar is displayed; move the screen pointer over the various buttons and a screen tip labels them. The toolbar has similar buttons to a Web browser – Back, Forward, Stop etc. Clicking some of the buttons, eg 'Search the Web' or 'Home' simply calls up your Information Access Provider and/or starts your Web browser such as Internet Explorer.

Close the Web toolbar.

2   **Running a Static Query**. Excel Query allows you to create a query for a particular Web site and download the results into an Excel workbook, provided of course that the data is compatible with Excel. This is particularly useful for rapidly changing information such as financial data. Once the data is downloaded into a workbook it can be analysed using the

Topic 14 · Excel on the web

normal Excel features. We will try two of the sample sites and queries provided by Microsoft.

a. Make sure that the **Web Query** workbook is open and make sure that cell **A1** of Sheet1 is selected. Select the menu options **DATA – GET EXTERNAL DATA – RUN SAVED QUERY**. If the option is not available then you will need to install it from the Excel setup CD-ROM.

b. Microsoft has provided a number of Web-based queries for users to try; select any one and click the **GET DATA** button.

c. A dialog box asks you where you want to store the data, select **EXISTING WORKSHEET** and click **OK**. If you are prompted to connect to your Internet Access Provider then do so.

d. After a short delay the external data is downloaded into your workbook; if you wish you can disconnect from your Internet Access Provider now.

e. Check that the External Data toolbar is displayed, if not then open the **VIEW** menu and select the **TOOLBARS** then the **EXTERNAL DATA** options. Move the screen pointer over the various buttons and a screen tip labels them.

f. Click the **DATA RANGE PROPERTIES** button on the toolbar and a dialog box opens, offering various features, including how often you want the data refreshed or updated while you are connected to the Web site. Close the dialog box and toolbar and name the worksheet **Static Query**.

3. **Running a Dynamic Query**. The above query was a static query – it retrieves the same set of data each time it is run; to run a dynamic query you will need to specify the data.

a. Name the second worksheet in the **Web Query** workbook **Dynamic Query**.

b. Select cell **A1** in this worksheet and open the **DATA** menu. Select the options **GET EXTERNAL DATA – RUN SAVED QUERY** as before. When the dialog box opens select the query **MICROSOFT INVESTOR STOCK QUOTES** and click the **GET DATA** button.

c. When the dialog box appears asking you where you want to store the data select the default **EXISTING WORKSHEET** as before and click **OK**.

d. A second dialog box prompts you to enter a stock fund as a parameter value. Enter **MSFT** for Microsoft and click **OK**. If you are prompted to connect to your Internet Access Provider then do so.

e. A stock quote for Microsoft will be downloaded into your worksheet. If you wish you can disconnect from your Internet Access Provider now.

f. The way the financial data is formatted provides a good example of the use of colour, column and row layout. The blue text is hypertext; clicking on it will link you to a related Web site – try this, we will be creating hyperlinks later in this topic.

Creating an Excel web page

Designers who create Web pages professionally use a special purpose Web page editor which acts rather like a combination of word processor and desktop publishing application, allowing them to add text and graphics and design sophisticated page layouts. Excel is not intended to be a fully featured Web page editor in this sense and only offers limited features, it is much more effective to create the basic Web page in Excel and then use another application to improve layout, formatting etc. For example Microsoft Word offers superior page editing features and the special purpose application Microsoft FrontPage (or the simpler version FrontPage Express included in Windows) is even better. Another reason for using a Web page editor to enhance the basic Excel Web page is that some of the original Excel formats may be lost when it is saved as a Web page – refer to the appropriate Help text for a list of these.

① Viewing an Existing Workbook as a Web Page. Open the workbook **Marketing Campaign** or any other suitable workbook.

Open the **FILE** menu and select the option **WEB PAGE PREVIEW**. An Internet Explorer window opens; click the sheet tabs to see how your worksheets, charts etc will look as a Web Page. Bear in mind that Internet Explorer is a browser so you can view the worksheets but not change them; to edit them you would need to return to the Excel window.

Close Internet Explorer at this point and any open workbooks.

② Creating a Web Page in Excel. We will use the Workbook **Video Sales** as the basis for our Web page; make sure that the sheet containing the sales data is the active sheet.

a. Select cells **A3** to **D8**, containing the first 5 months data, including the row and column headings but excluding the title – see Figure 14.1.

	A	B	C	D	E
1		Video Sales - Current Year			
2					
3	Month	No. Sold	Revenue	Advertising	Adv as % of Revenue
4	June	750	1915	280	15%
5	July	910	3054	401	13%
6	August	1075	3447	498	14%
7	September	1330	4450	733	16%
8	October	1618	5009	801	16%
9					

FIGURE 14.1

b. Open the **FILE** menu and select the option **SAVE AS WEB PAGE**. When the dialog box appears alter the file name to ***Video Sales Web Page*** and click the **SELECTION** button to save only the selected cells – see Figure 14.2.

c. Click the **CHANGE TITLE** button and a dialog box appears; enter the title ***Video Sales – First 5 Months*** and click **OK**. Finally click the **PUBLISH** button.

d. On the next dialog box the various details are confirmed, check them and select the further option **OPEN PUBLISHED WEB PAGE IN BROWSER** if necessary.

e. Click the Publish button again and the worksheet cells are displayed as a Web page in the Internet Explorer browser. Close the browser.

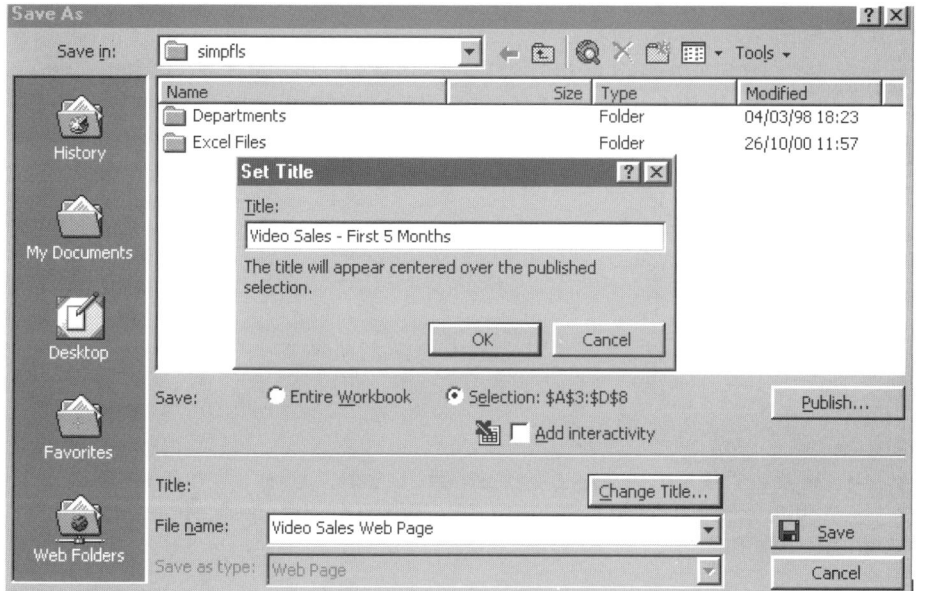

FIGURE 14.2

3. **Adding Data to an Excel-based Web Page**. We now have a Web page containing a number of worksheet cells. We will add one of the charts from the **Video Sales** workbook to it. Select one of the chart sheets in the workbook, eg a bar chart, and follow the following steps:

a. Select the menu options **FILE – SAVE AS WEB PAGE**.

b. On the **SAVE AS** dialog box click the **SELECTION** button to save only the chart; there is no need to add a title as the chart already has one.

c. Click the down arrow on the file name box and select **VIDEO SALES WEB PAGE** – this ensures that it will be saved on the same Web page as the cell data.

d. Click the **PUBLISH** button. On the next dialog box check the name of the Web page in the File name box; also check that the option **OPEN PUBLISHED WEB PAGE IN BROWSER** is selected.

e. Click the **PUBLISH** button again. A dialog box may appear, reminding you that the Web page file **BOOK SALES WEB PAGE** already exists and offering you the option of replacing it or adding to it. Take the option **ADD TO FILE**.

f. The Web page opens in the Internet Explorer browser; it now contains two elements, the worksheet cells and the chart. Close the browser.

Topic 14 · Excel on the web

Inserting hyperlinks

① A hyperlink is any part of a worksheet or Web page that you click in order to go to other Web pages or simply to another part of the same page. A hyperlink can be text, an icon or an image. First we will insert a hyperlink to take you from the bottom to the top of the Video Sales Web Page, then we will link to another workbook and the Web itself.

② **Inserting a Hyperlink**. Make sure that the Video Sales Web Page is displayed (not the workbook Video Sales).

  a. First click a suitable cell at the top of the page, eg cell G1.

  b. Open the **INSERT** menu and select **HYPERLINK** – a dialog box appears – see Figure 14.3.

  Click the option **PLACE IN THIS DOCUMENT**.

  c. In the **TEXT TO DISPLAY** box enter some suitable text to act as the hyperlink, eg **Bottom of Page**.

  d. In the **TYPE THE CELL REFERENCE BOX** insert a cell reference at the bottom of the Web page, eg D26. Click **OK** and you have created a hyperlink.

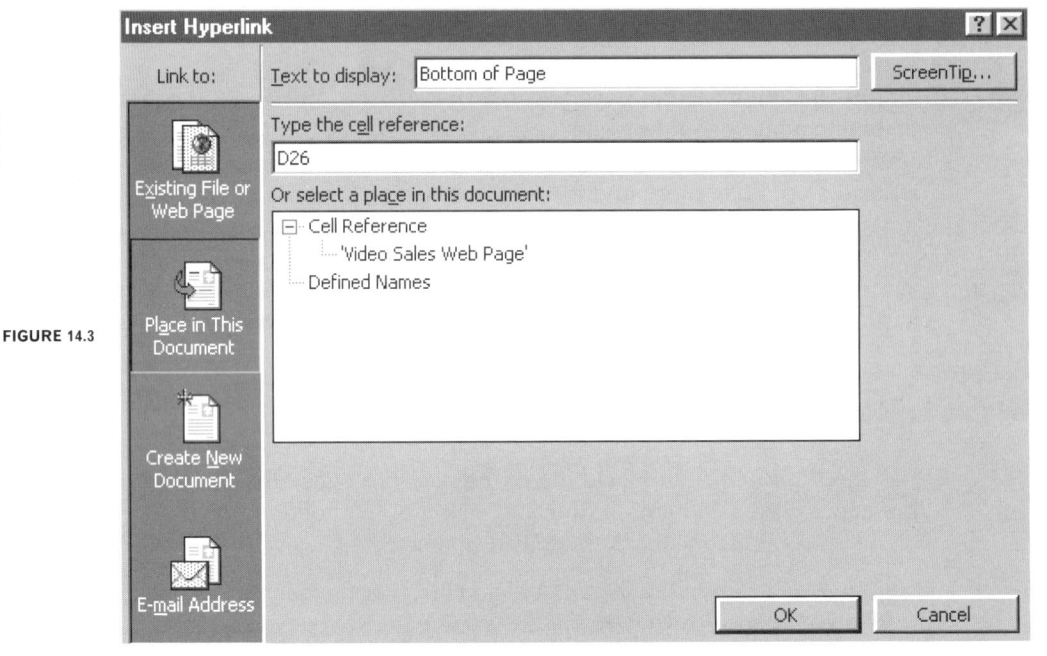

FIGURE 14.3

③ **Testing the Hyperlink**. The hyperlink text is displayed in blue at the top of the Web page, try the following:

  a. Move the screen pointer on top of the hyperlink – a screen tip opens, showing the path of the hyperlink – the drive, folder, workbook and cell it is linked to.

  b. Click the hyperlink and you are taken to the linked cell at the bottom of the page; this is useful once a Web page gets over a certain length.

    c. Scroll back to the top of the page; you will see that the hyperlink has now changed colour to maroon, indicating that the link has already been used. This feature becomes useful when the user has many hyperlinks to try out.

    Note: To delete or edit the hyperlink right click the text end select **HYPERLINK** from the popup menu.

4 Now we need to insert a hyperlink from the bottom of the page back to the top. Select a suitable cell at the bottom of the Web page, eg cell D26, then proceed as follows:

    a. Open the **INSERT** menu and select **HYPERLINK** – the dialog box is displayed again.

    Click the option **PLACE IN THIS DOCUMENT**.

    c. In the **TEXT TO DISPLAY** box enter the text *Back to top*.

    d. In the **TYPE THE CELL REFERENCE BOX** insert a cell reference at the top of the Web page, eg cell G1. Click **OK**.

    e. Test the hyperlinks – you should be able to go from the bottom to the top of the page and back again.

5 **Inserting a Hyperlink to a Workbook**. We will now establish a link from the Video Sales Web Page to its 'parent' workbook **Video Sales**; this will enable users to move easily between the two documents. Proceed as follows:

    a. Select a suitable cell at the top of the **Video Sales** Web Page for the hyperlink text, then open the **INSERT** menu and select **HYPERLINK**.

    b. When the dialog box appears click the section **EXISTING FILE OR WEB PAGE** – we are going to link to the **Video Sales** workbook which already exists.

    c. Next click the **FILE** button in the dialog box – the **LINK TO FILE** dialog box appears next.

    d. Use the **LOOK IN** box on this dialog box to locate the workbook **Video Sales**. Select it and click the **OK** button – you are returned to the Insert Hyperlink dialog box.

    e. In the **TEXT TO DISPLAY** box enter the text *Go to Video Sales Workbook* – see Figure 14.4. Click **OK**.

    f. Now try out this hyperlink, it will open the **Video Sales** workbook.

6 **Independent Task**. Create a hyperlink that will take you in the opposite direction, ie from the Video Sales workbook back to the Video Sales Web Page. It is best if you choose a worksheet rather than a chart for this.

7 **Linking to a Web Page**. It is possible to link from a workbook or one of your own Web pages to a page anywhere on the Web; we will create a link to the Yahoo Web site.

    a. Open the workbook **Web Query** and select a new blank worksheet.

    b. Open the **INSERT** menu and select **HYPERLINK**.

    c. When the dialog box appears click the section **EXISTING FILE OR WEB PAGE**.

Topic 14 • Excel on the web

FIGURE 14.4

insert hypertext here

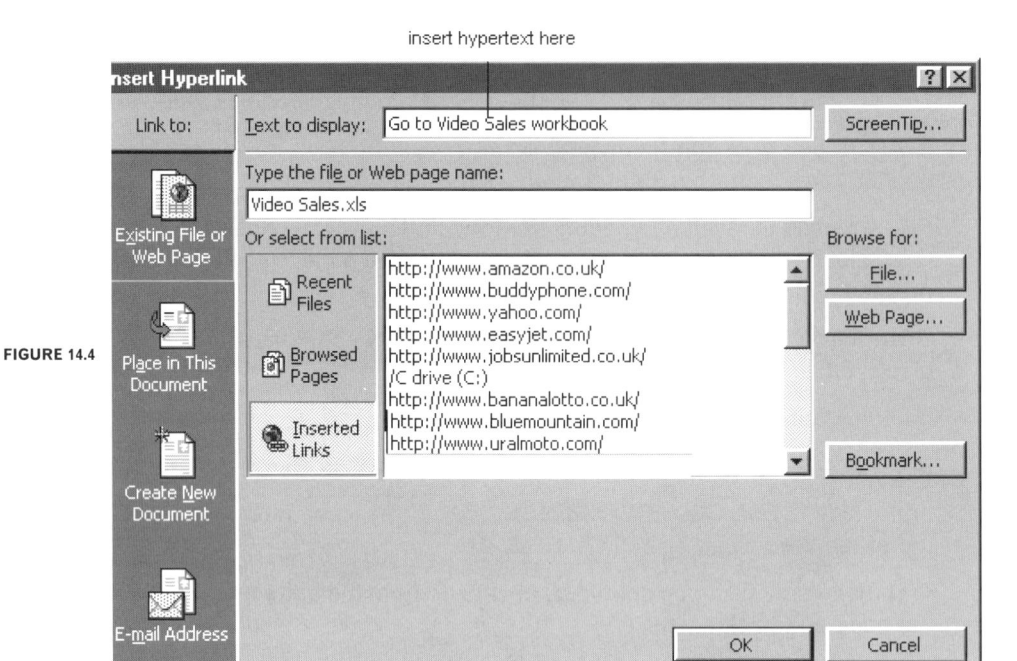

Insert Hyperlink dialog box with "Text to display: Go to Video Sales workbook", "Type the file or Web page name: Video Sales.xls", and a list of URLs including http://www.amazon.co.uk/, http://www.buddyphone.com/, http://www.yahoo.com/, http://www.easyjet.com/, http://www.jobsunlimited.co.uk/, /C drive (C:), http://www.bananalotto.co.uk/, http://www.bluemountain.com/, http://www.uralmoto.com/

In the **TEXT TO DISPLAY** box enter the text *Go to Yahoo*.

d. Enter the web site address *http:\\www.yahoo.com* in the section **TYPE THE FILE OR WEB PAGE NAME**.

e. Click **OK** and the hyperlink is inserted into the workbook – test it out.

Summary of commands

Note:
Menu commands show the menu name first, followed by the command to choose from the menu, e.g. **EDIT-CLEAR** means open the Edit menu and select the Clear command.

Menu commands

DATA-GET EXTERNAL DATA -RUN SAVED QUERY	Run a Web query
FILE-SAVE AS WEB PAGE	Save a workbook in Web page format
FILE-WEB PAGE PREVIEW	View a worksheet as a Web page
INSERT-HYPERLINK	Insert a hyperlink
VIEW-TOOLBARS-EXTERNAL DATA	View External Data Toolbar

APPENDICES

Appendix 1

	A	G	H	I	J	K
1						
2						
3		Week 6	Week 7	Week 8	Week 9	Week 10
4	INCOME					
5	Opening Balance	£ 3,090.00	£ 2,935.00	£ 2,780.00	£ 2,625.00	£ 2,470.00
6	Bank Loan					
7	Startup Grant					
8	Gardening Work	£ 180.00	£ 180.00	£ 180.00	£ 180.00	£ 180.00
9	Total Income	£ 3,270.00	£ 3,115.00	£ 2,960.00	£ 2,805.00	£ 2,650.00
10						
11	OUTGOINGS					
12	Food	£ 35.00	£ 35.00	£ 35.00	£ 35.00	£ 35.00
13	Accommodation	£ 80.00	£ 80.00	£ 80.00	£ 80.00	£ 80.00
14	Van Purchase	£ 60.00	£ 60.00	£ 60.00	£ 60.00	£ 60.00
15	Equipment	£ 100.00	£ 100.00	£ 100.00	£ 100.00	£ 100.00
16	Fuel and Travel	£ 60.00	£ 60.00	£ 60.00	£ 60.00	£ 60.00
17	Total Outgoings	£ 335.00	£ 335.00	£ 335.00	£ 335.00	£ 335.00
18						
19	CLOSING BALANCE	£ 2,935.00	£ 2,780.00	£ 2,625.00	£ 2,470.00	£ 2,315.00

Appendix 2

	A	G	H	I	J	K
1						
2						
3		Week 6	Week 7	Week 8	Week 9	Week 10
4	INCOME					
5	Opening Balance	£ 1,530.00	£ 1,385.00	£ 1,240.00	£ 1,095.00	£ 950.00
6	Bank Loan					
7	Startup Grant					
8	Gardening Work	£ 300.00	£ 300.00	£ 300.00	£ 300.00	£ 300.00
9	Total Income	£ 1,830.00	£ 1,685.00	£ 1,540.00	£ 1,395.00	£ 1,250.00
10						
11	OUTGOINGS					
12	Food	£ 35.00	£ 35.00	£ 35.00	£ 35.00	£ 35.00
13	Accommodation	£ 80.00	£ 80.00	£ 80.00	£ 80.00	£ 80.00
14	Van Purchase	£ 90.00	£ 90.00	£ 90.00	£ 90.00	£ 90.00
15	Equipment	£ 100.00	£ 100.00	£ 100.00	£ 100.00	£ 100.00
16	Fuel and Travel	£ 60.00	£ 60.00	£ 60.00	£ 60.00	£ 60.00
17	Part time wages	£ 80.00	£ 80.00	£ 80.00	£ 80.00	£ 80.00
18	Total Outgoings	£ 445.00	£ 445.00	£ 445.00	£ 445.00	£ 445.00
19						
20	CLOSING BALANCE	£ 1,385.00	£ 1,240.00	£ 1,095.00	£ 950.00	£ 805.00

Appendix 3

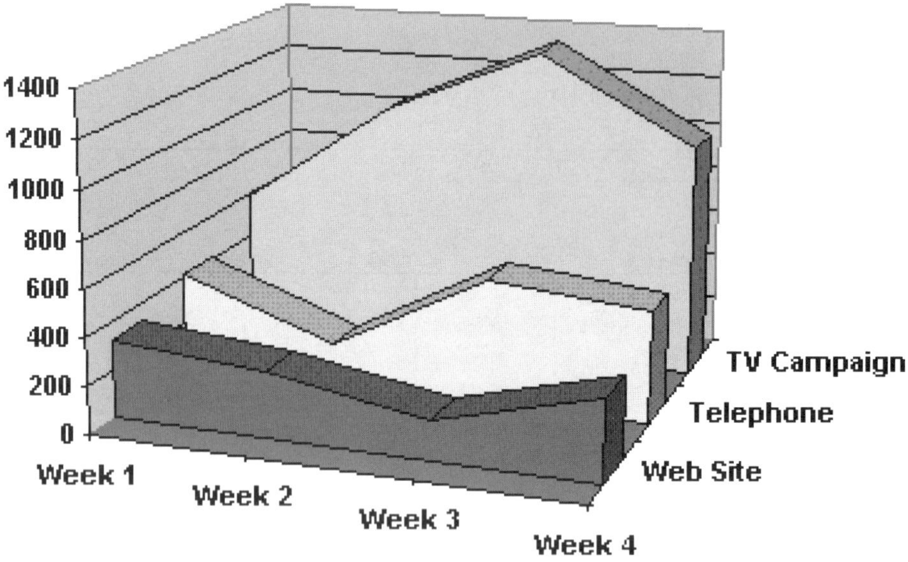
1400
1200
1000
800
600
400
200
0
Week 1
Week 2
Week 3
Week 4
TV Campaign
Telephone
Web Site

Appendix 4

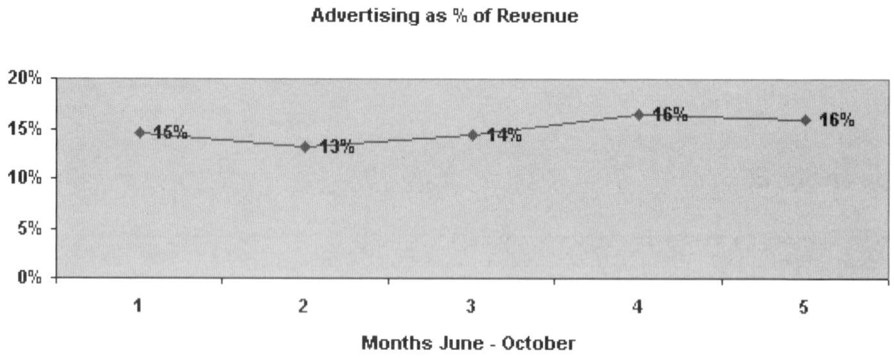
Advertising as % of Revenue
20%
15%
10%
5%
0%
15%
13%
14%
16%
16%
1
2
3
4
5
Months June - October

Appendix 5

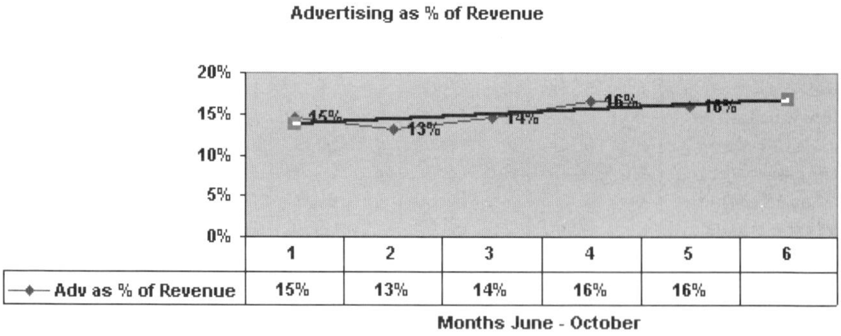
Advertising as % of Revenue
20%
15%
10%
5%
0%
15%
13%
14%
16%
16%
1 2 3 4 5 6
Adv as % of Revenue 15% 13% 14% 16% 16%
Months June - October

Appendix 6

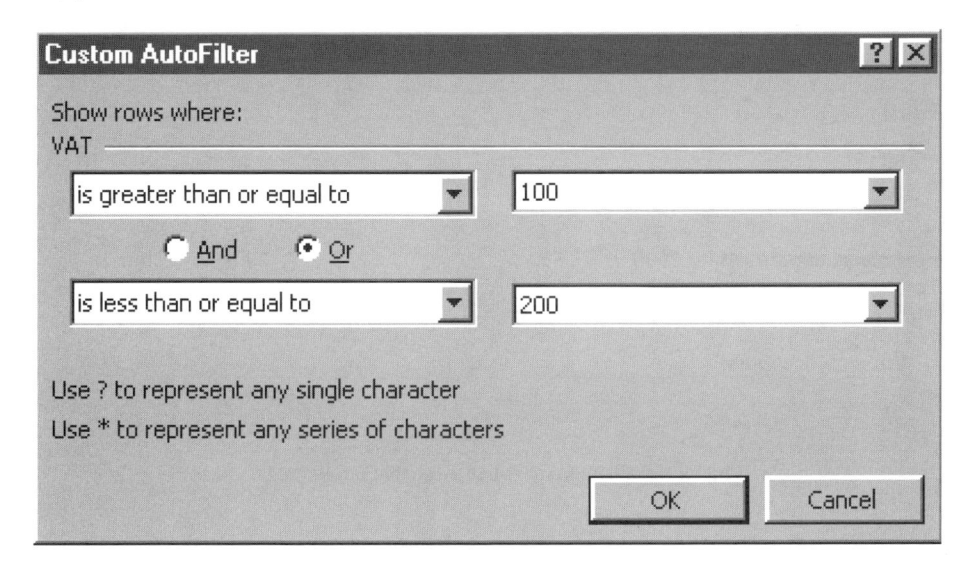

Custom AutoFilter

Show rows where:
VAT

is greater than or equal to — 100

○ And   ● Or

is less than or equal to — 200

Use ? to represent any single character
Use * to represent any series of characters

[OK]   [Cancel]

Appendix 7

	A	B	C
1		Loan Repayment Table	
2			
3	Repayment term in months	84	
4	Interest Rate	6%	
5	Amount Borrowed	10000	
6			
7	Possible Interest Rates:	Monthly Repayment	
8		£146.09	
9	6.00%	146.09	
10	6.25%	147.29	
11	6.50%	148.49	
12	6.75%	149.71	
13	7.00%	150.93	
14	7.25%	152.15	
15	7.50%	153.38	
16	7.75%	154.62	
17	8.00%	155.86	
18			

Appendix 10

	A	B	C	D	E	F	G
1				Table of Discounts			
2							
3							
4							
5							
6			0	6%	7%	8%	9%	10%
7		1000	300	350	400	450	500
8		1500	450	525	600	675	750
9	Amount purchased	2000	600	700	800	900	1000
10		3000	900	1050	1200	1350	1500
11		4000	1200	1400	1600	1800	2000
12							
13	Enter no. of weeks:	5					
14							

The lookup formula is: =VLOOKUP(B8,E6:G10,3)

Appendix 9

Goal Seek

Set cell: E9

To value: 4000

By changing cell: C6

OK   Cancel

Appendix 8

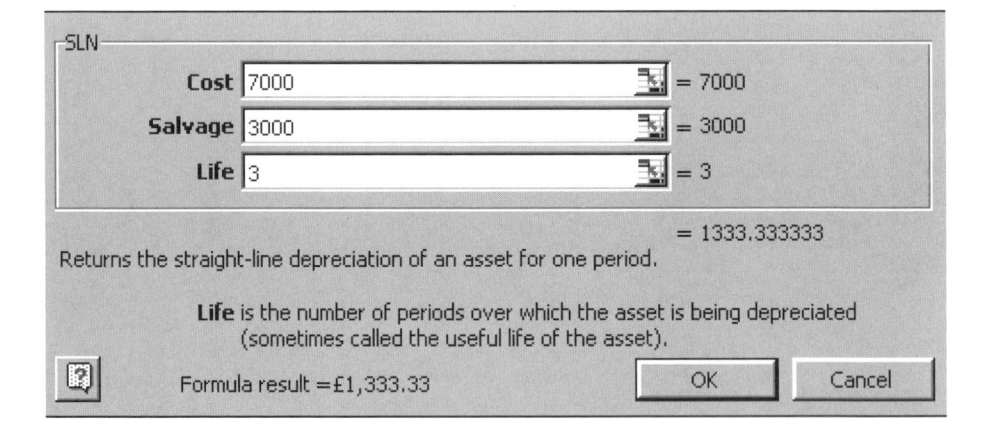

SLN

Cost 7000 = 7000

Salvage 3000 = 3000

Life 3 = 3

= 1333.333333

Returns the straight-line depreciation of an asset for one period.

Life is the number of periods over which the asset is being depreciated (sometimes called the useful life of the asset).

Formula result =£1,333.33   OK   Cancel

INDEX

(hash) sign, 23
Absolute references, 50
Active Cell, 5
Addition, 24-27
Aligning data, 52-53
Aligning text, 36
Alt Key, 6, 13
Answer Wizard, 16
Application window, 3
Area chart, 76-77
Arrow keys, 9-10
Arrow shape, adding, 40-41, 68
AutoCalculate, 26
AutoComplete, 89
AutoCorrect, 21
AutoFill, 34
AutoFilter, 97-99
Automatic formatting, 51-52
AutoSum, 26
Averages, 50

Backspace key, 21
Bar chart, 80-81
Bold text, 35-36
Borders, adding to cells, 38
  removing, 38
Button, adding to toolbar, 137-139
  creating, 133-139
  linking to macro, 134, 138

Calculated fields, 93-94
Cell, active, 10
  borders, 38
  gridlines, 39
Cells, merging, 37
  selecting, 10
Chart, adding values, 77-78
  altering size, 58-59
  and worksheet links, 62
  area, 76-77
  arrows, 68
  axes, 60
  bar, 80-81
  basic concepts, 60
  changing types, 60-61
  colours/patterns, 69-70
  column, 56-58, 82
  copying, 74
  custom types, 85
  deleting, 87
  doughnut, 85
  drag and drop, 86-87

editing components, 65-67
embedded, 86
font colour, 59-60
font size, 59-60, 67
formatting axis, 76
formatting text, 77
goal seeking, 82-84
gridlines, 79
legend, 57, 60, 66, 71
line, 70-73
naming, 73
non-adjacent cells, 72-73
opening, 62-63
pie, 60-61
printing, 68-69, 87
removing values, 77-78
reversing axes, 78-79
saving, 62-63
scale, 75
text boxes, 67
title, 57, 66, 71
toolbar, 59
trendlines, 82
ChartWizard, 56-58
Clipboard, 31
Close Button, 4
Closing a workbook, 28
Column chart, 56-58, 82
Column headings, printing, 42
Columns, adjusting width, 22-23
  deleting, 37
  inserting, 37
  selecting, 11
Conditional formatting, 53-54
Control menu, 4
Copying, data, 30-31
Ctrl key, 9-10
Currency symbol, 37
Custom chart, 85

Data, aligning, 52-53
  clearing, 31
  copying and pasting, 30-31
  cutting and pasting, 31
  deleting, 22
  editing, 22
  entering, 20-23
  form, 94-95
  indenting, 52-53
  rotating, 52-53

series, 90, 114-115
Database, AutoFilter, 97-99
  calculated fields, 93-94
  deleting records, 95-96
  editing, 95-96
  fields, 88
  outlining, 97
  records, 88
  rules, 88
  searching, 95-96, 97-99
  sorting, 91-93
  subtotalling, 96-97
Date, calculation, 126-127
  entering, 90
  formatting, 90-91, 125
  function, 125, 132
Deleting data, 22, 30-32
Depreciation function, 127
Desktop, 1
Dialog box, 11-12
Division sign, 50
Document window, 3
Doughnut chart, 85
Drag and drop, 86-87
Drawing Toolbar, 5, 40

Editing data, 22
Embedded chart, 86
Enter key, 20
Error messages, 26
Esc key, 65
Excel, exiting from, 17, 28
  starting, 1

Filenames, 27
Fill down command, 49
Fill right command, 31-32
Find command, 105-107
Folders, organising, 104-105
Font, changing, 36, 59-60
Footers, 43-44
FORECAST function, 128-129
Formatting, copying, 54
Formatting a worksheet, 35-41, 51-52
Formatting Toolbar, 4
Formula Bar, 5, 22
Formulae, editing, 25
  linking, 102-104, 110-111
  using, 24-27
Full screen, viewing, 41, 58-59
Functions, 123-130
Future value function, 125,

151

Index

127
FV function, 125, 127

Goal seek, 82-84, 120-122
Goto command, 11
Gridlines, hiding, 39
   printing, 42

Hash sign, 23
Headers, 43-44
Headings, freezing/
   unfreezing, 39
Help menu, exiting, 16
   using, 13
HLOOKUP function, 119
Horizontal Scroll Bar, 5
Hyperlink, inserting, 144-146

IF function, 126
Indenting data, 52-53
Italic text, 36

Keyboard shortcuts, 12

Landscape orientation, 43
Legend, chart, 57, 60, 66
Line chart, 70-73
Linking worksheets, 100-104
Lookup table, 118-120

Macro, defined, 131
   deleting, 136
   recording, 131-132
   running, 132
   running from button, 133-136
   shortcut key, 132
   viruses, 133
Macros, 131-139
MAX function, 126
Maximise Button, 4
Menu Bar, 4, 11
Menus, using pull-down, 11
Merge and centring, 37
MIN function, 126
Minimise Button, 4
Minimising a window, 5-6
Mouse, actions, 9
Moving a window, 8
Multiplication symbol, 93

NOW() function, 125, 132
Numbers, formatting, 37

Office Assistant, 16, 56, 125
One-input table, 117-118
Opening a workbook, 29
Oval shape, adding, 40-41
Overtyping, 22

Page, adding date, 44
   footer, 43-44
   header, 43-44
   numbering, 44
   orientation, 43
   setup, 42
Paste Function, 123-124
Percentages, 50-51
Pie chart, 60-61, 63-64
Pie chart, editing segments, 63, 66
PMT function, 115-116
Portrait orientation, 43
Print area, setting, 41-42, 45
Print preview, 44-45
Printing, worksheet, 41-45

Reference Area, 4
Relative references, 50
Re-sizing a window, 7
Restore Button, 5
Restoring a window, 5-6
Rotating data, 52-53
Row headings, printing, 42
Rows, adjusting height, 23
   deleting, 37
   inserting, 37
   selecting, 11

Saving a workbook, 27-28
Scroll Bars, 5, 9
Scrolling, 9-10, 13
Sheet Name, 5
Shortcut, using, 2
Shortcut keys, 12
SLN function, 127
Sorting, 91-93
Spelling, checking, 21
Standard Deviation function, 126
Standard Toolbar, 4
Start Button, 1-2
Start Menu, 2
Starting Excel, 1
Status Bar, 5
STDEV function, 126
Subtraction, 27
SUM function, 24-27

Tab key, 6
Table, lookup, 118-120
   one-input, 114-117
   two-input, 117-118
Taskbar, 1-2
Text, alignment, 20, 36
   centring, 37
   changing size, 36
Text box, 39-40, 67
Title Bar, 4
Tool Bars, 4-5
TREND function, 129

Underlining text, 36
Undo command, 31

Vertical Scroll Bar, 5, 9
VLOOKUP function, 119

Web, query, 140-141
   toolbar, 140
Web page, creating, 142-146
   linking to, 145
Window, displaying
   multiple, 61-62, 102, 110
   minimising, 5-6
   moving, 8
   re-sizing, 7
   restoring, 5-6
Windows, arranging, 61-62
Workbook, closing, 28
   copying, 109-110
   finding, 105-107
   linking, 109-112, 144-146
   naming, 27
   opening, 29
   previewing, 112
   properties, 106
   saving, 27-28
   vs. worksheet, 3
Worksheet, and chart links, 62
   copying, 46
   deleting, 49
   formatting, 35-41, 51-52
   goal seeking, 120-122
   linking, 100-104
   naming, 48-49
   printing, 41-45
   selecting, 11
   tab, 11, 48

Zoom button, 41, 44, 59